ACCLAIM FOR DR. ROBERT

The Autism B...

What Every Parent Needs to Know About Early Detection,
Treatment, Recovery, and Prevention

"Autism has many facets, from behavioral to educational to medical, and parents working for the best possible future for their children need a lot of options. Dr. Sears covers the territory broadly, fairly, clearly, with suitable cautions, and in very useful detail." —Martha Herbert, MD, PhD, Pediatric Neurologist, Massachusetts General Hospital, Harvard Medical School

"*The Autism Book* presents a clear, concise plan for the treatment of autism. Dr. Sears has covered a very complex topic and has done the groundwork for concerned parents and practitioners. He thoroughly discusses a myriad of topics, including the basics on vaccines, information on the diagnosis of autism, and therapies from routine medical and behavioral to the more complex biomedical. This is a *must-read* for anyone interested in the care of the child on the autism spectrum."
—Stephanie F. Cave, MD, author of *What Your Doctor May Not Tell You About Children's Vaccinations*

"Dr. Bob Sears has written a gem of a book geared toward parents, but extremely useful for professionals as well. In parent-friendly language, he provides a road map for parents of a child with autism, as well as those who may be questioning whether their child is developing typically. The biomedical chapters are incredibly informative, and, together with the educational-therapeutic intervention chapter, they lead you down a path of empowerment through knowledge. As a neurodevelopmental pediatrician, I know I will be referring to the biomedical section often and encouraging every one of my families with a child with an autism spectrum diagnosis to buy this book!"

—Marilyn C. Agin, MD, FAAP, neurodevelopmental pediatrician and coauthor of *The Late Talker: What to Do If Your Child Isn't Talking Yet*

"Dr. Sears has made another valuable addition to the Sears Parenting Library. *The Autism Book* is an easy-to-read, comprehensive, information-filled resource for parents of children with autism spectrum disorders."

—Kenneth A. Bock, MD, coauthor of *Healing the New Childhood Epidemics: Autism, ADHD, Asthma, and Allergies*

"Dr. Bob has done it again! *The Autism Book* is an important resource for both new and experienced parents of children with autism. Dr. Bob's balanced, integrative approach is a much needed fresh take on how we should confront the most troubling health epidemic of our times."

—Lawrence D. Rosen, MD, FAAP, founder of The Whole Child Center, Oradell, NJ

"This is a solid, accessible book by a wise pediatrician and teacher and, most important, a doctor who really practices the art of listening to his patients."

—Sidney M. Baker, MD, coauthor of *Autism: Effective Biomedical Treatments* and cofounder of Defeat Autism Now!

The
Autism
Book

The
Autism
Book

*What Every Parent Needs to Know
About Early Detection, Treatment, Recovery,
and Prevention*

Robert W. Sears, MD, FAAP

Little, Brown and Company
New York   Boston   London

Little, Brown and Company
Hachette Book Group
237 Park Avenue, New York, NY 10017
www.hachettebookgroup.com

First Edition: April 2010

Little, Brown and Company is a division of Hachette Book Group, Inc.
The Little, Brown name and logo are trademarks of Hachette Book Group, Inc.

Library of Congress Cataloging-in-Publication Data
Sears, Robert, MD
    The autism book : what every parent needs to know about early detection, treatment, recovery, and prevention / by Robert W. Sears—1st ed.
        p. cm.
    Includes index.
    ISBN 978-0-316-04280-2
    1. Autism in children—Popular works.   I. Title.
    RJ506.A9.S425 2010
    618.92'85882—dc22   2009034451

10 9 8 7 6 5 4 3 2 1

RRD-IN

Printed in the United States of America

For my dear wife,
Cheryl,
and our children,
Andrew
Alex
Joshua

Contents

VISIT DR. BOB ON THE WEB

For autism updates, links to resources, new research, new treatment ideas, conference announcements, and more, visit www.TheAutismBook.com.

For vaccine-related information and questions, visit www.TheVaccineBook.com.

An Encouraging Word
from Dr. Bob

Autism has become one of the most widespread childhood epidemics in recorded history. Except for some infectious disease epidemics of the past, no other serious condition has ever affected so many of our children. The latest research in *Pediatrics* reveals that autism affects a staggering 1 in 91 children (1 in 58 boys), with 673,000 currently affected. The CDC's latest study shows a rate of 1 in 110 kids (1 in 70 boys; see Resources, page 361). As five million babies are born every year, 50,000 new diagnoses will be made yearly. What makes it so devastating for parents is that autism can strike unexpectedly, seemingly out of nowhere; a healthy and neurologically normal infant can suddenly regress into autism between ages one and two. Some toddlers don't regress; they simply stop progressing through normal social and language milestones. Some infants appear to be born with autism, displaying some characteristics right from the start that eventually lead to a diagnosis.

We don't yet know what causes autism. There are many theories, but despite all the research currently under way, we are still far from answering this question. We do, however, know a great deal about how to treat autism and how to help children recover. That is what *The Autism Book* is all about.

If you are the parent of a child newly diagnosed with autism or if you have a child with borderline development who you worry may be at risk for autism, I will show you how you can best help your child minimize future developmental challenges. If you are a new parent with a healthy baby, I will show you what factors may possibly increase a baby's risk of developing autism and tell you how you can best minimize these risks.

Early recognition and intervention are perhaps the most important aspects of successful autism treatment. Noticing some developmental delays but postponing treatment until a definitive diagnosis of autism is made does that child, and his family, a great disservice. In chapter 1, I explain all the signs and symptoms of autism so you can suspect a diagnosis at the earliest possible age and begin early intervention.

Many developmental and behavioral therapy approaches have been proven effective in the majority of children with autism. These include speech and language therapy, occupational and sensory integration therapy, applied behavioral analysis therapy, social developmental therapy, and several others. I discuss these treatments in detail in chapter 6 and show you how to access them so you can begin your child's recovery. I also discuss certain psychiatric and behavioral medications that have been shown to decrease some symptoms of autism and improve behavior and learning.

A number of medical, nutritional, and vitamin-based treatments have been shown to not only improve symptoms but also address some of the possible underlying medical and biological causes of autism. Together, these treatments are called the *biomedical approach*. Although some physicians believe the biomedical treatments are unproven or alternative, they are based on solid scientific principles, as I will demonstrate to you. In the Resources, pages 351–380, I list numerous studies that provide scientific and medical validity for my recommendations. Any physician who doubts that the biomedical approach can help children with autism hasn't taken a recent look at available research. Many of the treatment steps in the biomedical approach can be done without a doctor's prescription, and in part 3 I show you how to start your child safely on these treatments with support from educated parents in your area. I also explain how to find a biomedical doctor and how to approach your own pediatrician or family doctor, so you can try some of the prescription treatments. The studies I provide in the Resources should help open your doctor's mind.

Underlying all of these treatment options remains the question of causation. There are two main schools of thought. The most common theory within the mainstream medical community holds that autism is caused by a combination of genetic susceptibility and environmental toxic exposure. The biomedical community believes this as well but suspects that there is more to the picture. They believe that there are a number of medical, nutritional, allergic, and infectious conditions that can also contribute to autism. In chapter 5, I explain how you can have your child medically tested to look for a variety of possible causes, and in the Resources I provide a plethora of scientific research that supports these theories.

I have been learning about biomedical treatments for autism since 2000. I have helped more than five hundred families begin this approach and have personally witnessed fantastic results. But these ideas are not yet accepted by some in the general medical community as legitimate treatments for autism. There is already some good research that supports the biomedical protocols, but many more years of study are needed before they become part of mainstream medicine and get taught in medical schools. The biomedical treatment approach does not help every child. I have seen children recover to the point where they are virtually "normal." I have also seen children improve to such an extent that most people do not notice anything unusual about them; to some observers there might be some minor "quirks" still apparent. Some children who follow these treatments show only minor improvement. And I have had a few patients show no improvement at all. Every year we learn more and more about the biomedical approach. New treatments are discovered, current ones are refined, and older treatments are proven. Some treatment ideas don't pan out and are discarded.

Because most biomedical treatments are not FDA-approved for the treatment of autism, many parents naturally worry about their safety. In my opinion, all of the treatment options that I discuss in this book that do not require a prescription are safe. They involve nutritional supplements, dietary changes, and natural treatments that anyone can do without a doctor's involvement. On the other hand, some prescription treatments in this approach do have an element of risk (just like all prescription treatments in any area of medicine). These can—and should—be done only under the careful guidance of a physician.

Even though mainstream medicine does not yet endorse the biomedical approach, the powers that be have taken notice and expressed some interest. The American Academy of Pediatrics has met with the leaders of the organization Defeat Autism Now!, as well as with other biomedical groups, to discuss the protocol. The AAP also sends representatives to biomedical conferences to listen to the information. As a longtime member of both the AAP and Defeat Autism Now!, I hope to see this relationship blossom into a partnership someday soon.

Because the biomedical approach targets treatable causes of autism, this raises the question of autism *prevention*. If we know (or suspect) what is causing autism, theoretically, we should be able to lower the risk of autism by limiting and avoiding the causes. This is useful information for every new baby, and it is even more critical for any baby who has an older sibling with autism and therefore already has the genetic cards stacked against him. In chapter 16, I explain how to limit the possible causative factors during pregnancy, infancy, and young childhood as much as possible and lower your child's risk of autism.

Autism leaves families feeling isolated and overwhelmed. You can't do this alone. You must have support from other parents who are also going through this. My favorite parent support organization is TACA (Talk About Curing Autism), at www.TACAnow.org. Throughout this book I suggest ways in which your local TACA group can help you navigate through the various aspects of your child's treatment. Many parents have gone through what you are going through right now. They can help you get started. And you, in turn, can help parents in the future.

I've seen biomedical treatments work over and over again. In my ten years of treating autism as a pediatrician and biomedical practitioner, I've never personally seen any child harmed by the treatments in this book. The clock is ticking for every child with autism. Children need these treatments now. Science has already validated many of these treatments, and ongoing research will continue to prove or disprove each treatment theory. In the meantime, you can rest assured that you've done everything you can to help your child recover. I wish you and your child all the best as you start on your journey.

Author's Note

This book is intended to provide general information for the treatment of autism. It is not intended to provide specific medical advice. The treatments presented here are for educational purposes only. If any of the information in this book conflicts with the advice you receive from your own physician, you should follow your physician's instructions. Any medical treatment, whether natural, over-the-counter, or prescription, has the potential to cause harmful side effects. You should seek the advice of your child's primary care physician before beginning any type of treatment for your child.

PART I

Diagnosing Autism

1

Symptoms and Early Detection

Autism. It's a word every new parent fears. You probably have a neighbor, friend, or relative who has a child with autism, and you see the challenges they face. You've always been slightly shielded from that world. You've been able to go home and be thankful you aren't faced with the same thing in your own home. But now that might be about to change.

People will pick up this book and begin reading for many different reasons. Some of you might not have children and might simply want to learn more about autism. Some of you might have just had your first baby and want to know if there are ways to prevent autism. You might have autism in your extended family and want to understand more about the condition before having your own children. All of you will find this book an invaluable source of information.

But I know that most of you are reading this book because a doctor, a friend, a teacher, or a relative has expressed concerns about your child. Or perhaps you yourself have noticed some unusual behaviors and lack of language development in your toddler. Or maybe you are further along in the process and your child has already received a diagnosis of autism, early autism, or at risk for autism. Or perhaps you have an older child who has autism and you are looking to understand more about the latest treatment options.

I'm going to start at the beginning for those of you who have just started the journey. I'm going to introduce you to the most important aspects of autism: what it is, why we think it happens, and what your very first steps should be to start your child on the path toward treatment and recovery.

Did I say *recovery?* Yes. While we don't yet know exactly what is causing autism, we do know a lot about how to treat it. And some children do recover completely. Many others improve to an amazing degree. That's what this book is all about. But before we jump into all the details about treatment, I want to answer a few questions you may have and give you an introductory understanding of autism.

Autism is a unique medical condition in that it is a spectrum disorder, which means it ranges from very mild to extremely severe. It can also worsen or improve over time, and the myriad of symptoms vary from child to child. There is no blood test, brain scan, or single physical finding that a doctor can use to make or exclude the diagnosis; it is diagnosed by observation and evaluation of behavior and development. Sometimes the clues are very obvious, but often they are subtle and easily missed in the beginning stages. Confirming a suspicion at the youngest possible age is critical because the earlier treatment begins, the better the outcome. I will even be so bold as to say that autism is preventable in some kids, so acting on the earliest possible signs of developmental delay may prevent a child from declining into autism.

Ten years ago, before doctors realized autism was treatable, the medical community didn't feel there was any rush to diagnose a child. If an eighteen-month-old toddler wasn't talking or showing normal social development, we used to take the wait-and-see approach because we thought that it didn't matter when treatment began; it didn't matter if a child was diagnosed and began therapy at age two or four. Autism was autism, and that was that, and the outcome would be the same no matter what we did. Many children were left untreated for too long because of this misunderstanding. Now we know better.

Yet I still see some doctors and parents delaying the diagnosis and treatment until a child has full-blown autism. Doctors will sit on a diagnosis of *at risk for autism* or *showing early signs of autism* and maybe only recommend some limited early therapy and another visit in six months for a recheck. Well, those are six long months of lost therapy potential. In my view, any child with noticeable features of early autism should be taken seriously and treated as if he were diagnosed with autism. The reason I'm so adamant about this is that in my practice I've seen countless at-risk babies and toddlers receive extensive early therapy and never go on to develop enough criteria for a diagnosis of autism. Many of them recover to such a degree that no one would ever believe anything was ever suspected.

The bottom line is this: Early detection and action is paramount. I wish I were sitting with you right now so I could give your hand a squeeze or even give you a big hug. Parents of a child with autism need a lot of support: intellectually, emotionally, and financially. I can't give you all of that, but I do promise that I will help you learn everything you need to know for your family and your child so that you can start him on the path to recovery. Let's get started.

WHAT IS AUTISM?

Autism is a neurological and medical disorder in which the parts of the brain that control communication, behavior, social interaction, learning, sensation, and motor coordination aren't functioning properly. Each person with autism is affected in different ways and to varying degrees. Some will show only a few autistic characteristics; others will display many or all. A variety of genetic, medical, environmental, nutritional, and infectious factors may contribute to this neurological dysfunction.

Different Types of Autism

It's important to understand the different types of autism and how they present. Many parents have the misconception that a baby is born with autism and will show signs during the first few months of life. This is generally not the case. There are four different kinds of autism:

Early onset. Some babies seem to be born with autism and don't develop the typical eye contact and social interaction that should begin during the first few months of life. They don't start babbling by nine months and don't go on to develop language during the second year of life. These babies are usually diagnosed early on, once it becomes obvious that they are in their own world, usually by twelve to eighteen months of age. In my experience, this is the least common type, accounting for less than 10 percent of the children I've seen.

Regressive. Many children who are diagnosed with autism have a normal developmental history during the first year of life. They are playful, happy, and interactive infants. Then, after age one, they begin to lose their milestones. They stop using the few words they knew. They lose eye contact and social interaction. Regressive autism is usually diagnosed by age two. In my experience, it is the most common type.

Halted progression. Sometimes a normally developing baby doesn't regress, but he stops progressing after age one. Because everything seemed normal for a while, and these kids don't actually lose developmental milestones, they are harder to spot. They aren't usually diagnosed until age two or three, when it becomes more obvious that their language and social interaction aren't age appropriate.

Asperger's syndrome. Also known as high-functioning autism, this type is the most challenging to detect early on because kids with Asperger's develop in a near normal manner, including their language, and often display advanced intellectual skills. But there's just something a little quirky about their behavior. It usually isn't until the child enters preschool that the teacher and/or parents notice enough social and behavioral differences in the child to seek further evaluation. Some children aren't diagnosed until mid–elementary school age, when social dynamics become more complex and the child's lack of understanding in this area becomes apparent.

PDD-NOS. Many toddlers with early signs of autism are given the diagnosis of PDD-NOS, which stands for Pervasive Developmental Disorder—Not Otherwise Specified. This means that there are enough autistic symptoms and developmental delays to warrant an evaluation and some early therapy, but things aren't bad enough to actually diagnose autism yet. A toddler with PDD-NOS could go on to develop any of the four types of autism described above. In some cases it is a pre-autism diagnosis. It's the "I'm concerned something is wrong but I'm not ready to call it autism yet" explanation given by a neurologist or developmental pediatrician. If left untreated, PDD-NOS can become autism within six to twelve months. So, in my mind, it should be viewed and treated the same way as autism. It's on the same spectrum.

To be diagnosed with autism, a child has to meet (or *not* meet) certain criteria, which I present on page 10, and he usually won't meet enough of these criteria until age two or three. However, the developmental problems will have started one to two years prior to the eventual diagnosis of autism. So, even though a child may not actually meet the criteria for full autism until age two or three, I believe it is more correct to say that the age at which the genetic, metabolic, environmental, or medical factors first initiated the developmental decline or delay actually mark the age when the autism first began.

THE CHANGING FACE OF AUTISM: IT ISN'T JUST RAIN MAN ANYMORE

We all remember the classic Tom Cruise/Dustin Hoffman movie that introduced us to the world of adult autism. Well, Rain Man was severely affected because the treatments that we have now weren't available when he was a child. Today, young children with autism receive so much intervention that most improve to a degree far beyond what we saw in that movie. Some children even recover fully. Unfortunately, until a precise cure is found, severe cases of autism may continue to show significant social and behavioral impairment throughout adulthood.

CLASSIC SIGNS OF AUTISM

Unless there is early intervention, most children with autism eventually develop many of the obvious and classic signs. Here is a list of the signs in layperson's terms so that you can get an overall picture of what autism looks like:

Speech delay.

- little or no language, inappropriate use of language, or repetitive speech
- echolalia (talks by echoing back what is said to him)

- video talk (speaks by using familiar phrases from movies or commercials)
- easily memorizes things like ABCs and counting to ten but can't make a simple request for something he wants

Social delay.

- doesn't understand typical social boundaries or how to behave and interact in normal social situations
- decreased imaginary and pretend play
- noticeably hyperactive or underactive and sedentary
- tantrums that are more extreme than usual
- plays alone in own world, tunes others out
- doesn't notice when someone enters the room
- often won't return a happy smile when a caregiver engages with a smile
- doesn't play with toys in the manner the toy is intended, or prefers to play with objects that aren't toys
- poor eye contact or may peer at objects sideways
- difficulty with transitions from one activity to another (will have tantrum)
- no fear or understanding of dangerous situations

Unusual obsessions or movements.

- self-stimulating behaviors, such as hand flapping, repetitive movements, or lining up of objects
- toe-walking much of the time
- obsessed with routines and "sameness"
- restricted to certain foods and is unusually reluctant to try unfamiliar ones
- obsession with spinning objects, such as wheels or fans
- overly aggressive or self-injurious

Abnormal responses to sensory input.

- unusually high or low pain tolerance
- bothered by large crowds, noises, and chaos
- may not crave and may even be averse to cuddling, hugging, and other close contact, or may be the opposite: have an abnormal desire for deep-pressure massages, squeezing, and hugging—called *sensory seeking*
- bothered by certain sensations, such as from clothing tags or shoes that don't feel right, the feel of grass or sand on the feet, or smells

CRITERIA FOR THE DIAGNOSIS

Specific and detailed criteria, called the *DSM-IV-R* criteria, have been established to make a diagnosis of Autism Spectrum Disorder. While the above discussion is a description of the signs a parent or other layperson may notice, the *DSM-IV-R* criteria are what a doctor uses.

Autism

In order to be diagnosed with autism, a child needs to have problems in all three of the following areas. A child who shows difficulties in only one or two areas does not receive an actual diagnosis of autism. But he can still benefit from many of the same treatments for the challenges that he does have. Here is an abbreviated summary of the diagnostic criteria for autism:

1. He has social impairment in nonverbal language (eye contact, facial expressions, posture, and gestures), peer relationships, interaction with others, and reciprocating emotions.

2. There is a communication impairment in speech, or in the case of those who do speak, a failure to initiate or sustain conversations, the use of repetitive or out-of-context phrases, or a lack of interest in pretend and imaginative play.

3. He engages in repetitive, obsessive, compulsive, or stereotyped behaviors, such as fixations on patterns or routines, abnormal body movements, or intense preoccupation with a narrow range of interests.

Asperger's Syndrome

Asperger's has a slightly different set of *DSM-IV-R* criteria, since the symptoms and the timing of their onset can be very different. The first and third points above are the same, but a child with Asperger's does not have a clinically significant delay in language development during the first few years of life. He will develop single words on time and progress into three-word phrases by age three. There is no delay in cognitive development, self-help skills, ability to adapt to changes (other than social), or childlike curiosity.

However, the following unusual features of communication are apparent:

- intense focus on topics of interest (often out of context; see page 18)
- deficits in social language (how to engage, maintain, or finish a conversation while reading the cues of the other person)
- unusual tone, rhythm, and pitch to their voice, often sounding too formal or precocious
- problems understanding humor, lies, or irony
- may be an early reader and develop an unusually advanced vocabulary but may lack comprehension

Some other features of Asperger's may include:

- poor organization and coping skills
- clumsiness
- some sensory sensitivity
- related disorders—Attention Deficit Hyperactivity Disorder (ADHD), Obsessive-Compulsive Disorder (OCD), learning disabilities

---

IS AUTISM REALLY ON THE RISE, OR ARE WE JUST DIAGNOSING IT MORE OFTEN THESE DAYS?

Years ago the medical community was in denial: Autism couldn't be increasing so dramatically; we must be simply diagnosing it earlier and more thoroughly. Very few professionals in the medical community believe that anymore. The Centers for Disease Control and Prevention has made it perfectly clear: Autism has risen dramatically in the past fifteen years. Studies have shown that a small percentage of the rise in autism may be due to better diagnosis, but most of the increase is in the number of cases.

EARLY AND SUBTLE SIGNS OF AUTISM

As you were reading through the classic descriptions of autism and the diagnostic criteria, you might have been nodding as you recognized many familiar signs in your child. Or you might have been saying to yourself, "My child doesn't have most of those signs!" It's possible that your child has only subtle and early signs that are difficult to notice. I want to walk you through the early signs of autism that I have seen over the years. If you are reading this to learn about prevention or early detection for your healthy baby, or if you have seen a few minor quirks and are try-ing to decide if they are anything to worry about, this section is for you.

Lack of eye contact. This may sound like an obvious sign, and sometimes it is. But it can be subtle and intermittent at first. A normally developing baby typically seeks eye contact with care-givers, especially when engaged by the caregiver. A baby might be looking at a toy or his hands, but when Mom or Dad walks up and starts talking to the baby, his eyes should move right to the face and engage. A baby's attention might linger on the toy for several seconds before moving on to Mom. Or a baby can occa-sionally be so focused on something interesting that you can't get his attention away. Those situations are fine as long as most of the time you can engage his eye contact. But if your baby doesn't usually turn and engage your face and eyes when you approach and stares for prolonged periods at other objects, this might be a sign of early-onset autism. Toddlers with regressive autism show a gradual decline in the frequency and intensity of their eye con-tact with you. You shouldn't have to engage a toddler to get eye contact. It should be his idea to engage you on and off through-out the day. Some parents miss this early sign because they feel they can successfully get their toddler to look them in the eye, but that's not enough.

Side glancing. A baby might show some early side-glancing behavior, in which he studies objects up close by looking at them sideways, out of the corner of his eye. This might be because the brain can't register visual pictures from the central part of the field of vision.

Focus on spinning objects. Fans and wheels can be fascinat-ing to a child with delays. He may stare at the ceiling fan. He may spin wheels on toy cars and stare at them up close. He may push a toy truck back and forth but stare only at the rotating wheels.

Lack of babbling. Babies should develop a vocal laugh by three months, be cooing and gooing at five months, start babbling with consonants by seven months, and begin spouting baby jibberish by nine months. These are all the stages a baby goes through in preparation for those first words by twelve or fifteen months of age. I have seen some quiet babies miss these milestones but then go on to develop just fine, so having a nonbabbling baby isn't necessarily cause for alarm. But if this and other subtle signs are noticeable, bring them to your doctor's attention.

No words by eighteen months. Normal language development goes like this: two words around twelve months, six words by fifteen months, ten words by eighteen months, and numerous words with two-word phrases beginning by age two. And the child should be using these words without prompting—simply repeating words doesn't count.

A story I hear from parents over and over again is this: "Our toddler had no words at eighteen months. At age two we got a language evaluation, and the speech therapist said our child might have autism. At that point, all the signs were obvious." What I prefer to hear from parents instead is this: "By eighteen months our baby had not yet said a single word, so we started speech therapy right away." Another recurring tale that parents share with me is that their former pediatrician told them not to worry at eighteen months: "Boys just talk late. We'll see how he's doing at two." I used to say those same words to parents. Now, it *is* true that some boys and even some girls will be a little slow to say Mama, and some toddlers will be a few months behind on the above timetable, and many of these kids will have a language explosion between eighteen months and two years. But some kids won't. I believe it's better to err on the side of caution by starting speech therapy and infant stimulation classes early (and perhaps unnecessarily) than to wait until your child is two and then realize his words haven't started flowing freely. If you wait, you've missed a developmental window of opportunity.

If this describes your baby, and you want to start therapy *now,* go to chapters 3 and 6 for advice.

Solo play. Some toddlers love to play alone, and that's okay. It's fun to watch a child's imagination develop. But toddlers should also crave and seek out play with their parents and siblings as well. A child who likes to play alone most of the time may not be blossoming in his social development.

Parallel play. Some kids will appear to play happily with other kids when they are actually playing alone right next to them. A child may even be mimicking other kids' play rather than engaging in play *with* them. For example, three kids are playing with cars, "vrooming" them around on the floor. Two kids make their cars crash together and race each other, but one is just vrooming around alone.

Lack of engagement with a new person. Whenever a new person walks into a room, a neurotypical (the term we use to describe children with normal development) infant or toddler typically looks at that person, checks her out, catches her vibe, determines that the person is okay (or not), and then either goes back to what he was doing, engages that person, or curls up on Mama's lap for protection. An at-risk child will usually show one of two reactions: Either he will have an unusual degree of fear and anxiety or he won't acknowledge the new arrival at all.

Obsession with certain toys. Trains, trains, and more trains. What is it with trains? At-risk toddlers tend to become obsessed with certain toys. It is often trains, but it can be any toy, usually one with wheels. I'm not saying that every child hooked on a certain toy is a concern, but this may be one piece of the puzzle.

Plays inappropriately with toys. Toddlers should learn that cars go vroom, dolls are fed and cared for, action figures move and act out imaginary scenes, and balls bounce and roll. A child with delays may not play in this manner. He may line up the cars and stare at them from different angles. She may drag her doll around by the foot as if it's not a "person." He may just hold and look at a ball but not bounce it or roll it.

Obsessive repetitive movements. Children who perform certain actions over and over again (turning lights on and off, opening and closing drawers or doors, rewinding movie scenes to watch again and again—the list goes on) are said to be *perseverating* or *stimming*. It can also involve body movements, such as arm flapping, shoulder shrugging, or hand gestures.

Unusual sleep patterns or night waking. We've all known that baby who goes through night waking phases every hour or two. Neurotypical babies, however, can usually be parented back to sleep. While many infants with autism sleep just fine, some babies or toddlers with autism (or at risk for autism) wake up at night and do not go back to sleep for hours. They'll want to stay up and play by themselves, or they'll fuss on and off but not accept consolation from the parent. An at-risk child may also have trouble settling down to sleep in the evening; he might stay active playing by himself and not crash to sleep until midnight or later.

Sensory problems. I devote a whole section to sensory problems in chapter 3, but they deserve a mention here because they can be a predictor of more significant developmental issues to come. Sensory Processing Disorder (SPD), otherwise known as Sensory Integration Disorder (SID), is a recently labeled condition in which a baby or child doesn't react to sensations such as touch and sound in a usual manner. One of the earliest signs, for example, is a baby who doesn't like to be snuggled and cradled and will fuss and squirm to get out of such positions and be more open, free, and held upright. Some older babies with SPD get extremely upset when their hands or face are dirty and sticky. Toddlers with SPD tendencies may refuse to walk barefoot in grass or sand or won't like it when their socks or shoes aren't put on just right. Clothing tags may annoy, itch, and irritate a baby. Some kids may be overwhelmed by sounds, such as at a party or in a play area where there are lots of loud kids. Some kids will show the opposite reaction to certain sensations. For example, some crave deep pressure. They love to be hugged and squeezed. They enjoy deep pressure on their tummy or head. They may enjoy pushing their head or abdomen into a couch pillow or up against Mom or Dad.

All of the above signs might seem like obvious problems when read in this context, but they can be subtle, and often parents don't notice them until they look back after a diagnosis of autism is made. Many neurotypical kids show one or two of these signs early on but then mature past them without any therapeutic intervention. It isn't easy to know which infants need help and which ones don't. If any of these signs describe your child, inform your pediatrician at the next checkup (or make an earlier appointment if the next routine check is a few months away). Your doctor will need to consider your observations within the entire developmental context. By understanding and acting on these early indicators of an at-risk infant or toddler, your doctor can begin intervention at a younger age.

ONLINE VIDEO LIBRARY OF SYMPTOMS OF AUTISM

Autism Speaks (a nonprofit organization), First Signs (an early-intervention organization), and Florida State University's First Words Project created an online database of more than 150 video clips of children with autism displaying the most common symptoms, along with corresponding neurotypical behaviors. If you are curious or wondering about any of your child's behaviors, visit www.AutismSpeaks.org, www.FirstSigns.org, or www.FirstWords.FSU.edu to view these videos free of charge.

SUBTLE SIGNS IN AN OLDER CHILD

Sometimes a diagnosis of mild autism or Asperger's syndrome is not made until a child is five years or older because there weren't many obvious clues early on. These kids often develop language in a somewhat normal manner, so autism isn't suspected, but as they get older, more social and developmental quirks begin to show. Realize that any child might have *one* of the following characteristics, so don't be overly worried if one of them is familiar to you. But if your child displays many of the following, there may be cause for concern:

Out-of-context language. A child's answers to questions or her own spontaneous statements are a little out of context. For example, when I'm evaluating a child in my office, I might ask, "What is the name of one of your friends at school?" The child might answer, "We played with a dog at school today." Then the mom chimes in, "No, dear, what is your best friend's name?" The child might then answer correctly. Or when I'm talking with a mom and child in my office, a child might be walking around the room saying random things like "I like Elmo" or "My daddy flies airplanes."

Unusually advanced language skills. This is common in Asperger's syndrome. A child will be able to say his ABCs and 123s, sing songs, or recite nursery rhymes long before his peers. Such a child may also talk incessantly about only one or two topics of interest. A clue that this is a concern is that the child won't converse on more general topics that a child should be interested in. This can be confusing to parents and doctors, because it's hard to imagine that a child who is so smart could have autism. I have seen parents in my office rave about how smart their three-year-old is (and they are right!), have him demonstrate his spelling and math abilities, and describe how he can name every make and model of every car they pass on the road. When I notice other signs of autism, it can be difficult to convince the parents that there may be an underlying social developmental disorder.

Answering a question with a question. It can be hard to realize that this is happening, but once it's pointed out to a parent, it becomes obvious. In the office I might ask a child, "What did you do at school today?" She might answer, "I did at school today....Played with trains!" Or I might ask, "What is your favorite color?" The child might answer, "What is your favorite color?...Green."

Being constantly busy without "checking in." I don't normally like to label a child hyperactive. My own first child was "one of those" boys who was pretty hyped up most of the time. He matured and slowed down when he turned five years old. But I do see some kids in my office who bounce around the room getting into things, banging on walls, opening cabinets, and exploring everything they see. It's not done in a crazy sort of way, just in a very busy manner. Now, there isn't anything wrong with this in and of itself. But in some of these kids, I'll notice a subtle lack of interest in or involvement with what is going on between the parent and me. Most kids cooped up in an exam room will get antsy, but they should also be clueing in to what's going on around them socially and involving themselves in it. They should be checking in, so to speak. Some kids will just do their own thing without engaging the people around them unless someone engages them first.

Missing social cues. A child on the autism spectrum does not pick up on social cues such as sarcasm, humor, teasing, or lying. He may understand and respond to what is said around him, but he won't clue in to any underlying nuances that the speaker is communicating through body language or tone of voice.

Lack of awareness of personal space. Because an older child with autism or Asperger's doesn't understand all social nuances, he may tend to invade another's personal space (or he may be the complete opposite: unwilling to go near a stranger). In my office I might have a four-year-old snuggle right up to me. Now, this is great if he is just comfortable and happy to see me. But if this is a recurring theme for your child, and there are other quirky characteristics, it could be a warning sign. You may also see your child hug other kids or stand too close to them.

Obsessive-compulsive tendencies. These can occur during the young toddler years or they might not become apparent until later. Here are some of the typical OCD behaviors I hear about from parents:

- repetitive opening and closing of doors or demanding that all doors remain either open or closed
- keeping food items separate on a plate and getting upset if foods get mixed
- obsessing over how items are arranged on a desk or table
- wearing only certain clothes

- obsessively touching or lining up certain objects through-out a room

The best thing you can do if you suspect your infant or child has a delay in development is to see your pediatrician right away. She can observe your child and advise you on whether or not to seek further evaluation.

CAN THE BRAIN BE HEALED?

As I introduce you to how autism is diagnosed and discuss what we know about causes, I want to reassure you that there is hope in the chapters that follow. We know so much about how to heal the body and the mind, and the biomedical treatment program that I will guide you through is based on that solid scientific foundation.

We know that good nutrition is one of the keys to improving many conditions. We know that numerous vitamins and minerals are essential for normal body functions. We know that making sure the intestinal system (often referred to as our *second brain*) is healthy is a prerequisite to healing the brain. We know that ensuring a strong immune system is critical. We know that supporting the brain with essential nutrients improves neurological function. We know that minimizing chemicals and toxins is important. We know that maintaining high antioxidant activity helps the entire body work better. We know that reducing inflammation within the body prevents numerous health problems.

These basic medical principles can be applied to every disease state. What I am going to show you in this book, besides mainstream therapy, is how these simple, straightforward principles apply to autism. And in the Resources, I back it up with science. I believe the benefits that these treatments have on the gut, the immune system, and the brain can potentially heal a child with autism.

2

Pediatrician Screening

Early detection of developmental delays is a responsibility shared by both pediatrician and parents. It's the doctor's job to detect problems with a child's social and language development by observing a toddler's behavior and interaction during each checkup. Parents should also be knowledgeable about normal social and language milestones at each age and disclose any worries to the doctor. Since a doctor's office isn't always going to bring out the best behavior and display of social and language skills in a child, the parents need to be open and accurate about what a child does at home. In a perfect world, this combination of doctor observation and parent reporting should detect every potential problem at the earliest possible age, right?

Wrong. In many cases, neither party is necessarily objective when it comes to detecting early signs of autism. From a parent's standpoint, this is completely understandable. Many parents don't want to admit that something might be wrong. Some might have concerns but not raise them if the pediatrician doesn't seem to notice anything. A few might be in denial even in the midst of some obvious signs.

And we doctors aren't always objective either. I will be honest.

One of the most difficult parts of my job as a pediatrician is telling parents when I think something might be wrong with their child. When the parents raise their own concerns about development, it's very easy for me to have an open and honest discussion about the possibility of autism and to say that we'd better act now. The challenge comes when I see some early signs that the parents haven't noticed (or haven't mentioned). I don't yet know for certain that anything is wrong with the child but I have a suspicion. I wonder if maybe the child is just shy or extra hyperactive because he's here in my office. So, what do I say to the parents, "I'm worried your child may have autism"? That would come as quite a blow. Then, depending on whether the baby's development progresses or regresses over the coming months, I would be either the hero for detecting problems early or the villain for bringing up the "A" word with regard to a toddler who went on to be just fine. Knowing how important early detection and intervention is, I'd rather be the bad guy on occasion in the interest of doing what's best for most kids. But this is a difficult and uncomfortable position for pediatricians to be in.

A recent conversation I had with a parent points out how hard it is to break this news. After observing and interacting with a two-and-a-half-year-old girl for about thirty minutes, I concluded she probably had autism. Her mother had brought up various concerns, like toe walking, hand flapping, and some speech immaturity, but she had not shared with me any worries about a major developmental problem. After discussing numerous behavioral and developmental concerns, I told her, "I know this is going to be difficult to hear, but I believe your child has autism." Her eyebrows went up, her mouth dropped, and her head literally recoiled in momentary shock. But then it all seemed to sink in and make sense to her. No matter how hard it is for a doctor to share this information, it's nothing compared with how hard it is for a parent to hear it.

A pediatrician's failure to point out (or even notice) some early problems and a parent's failure to bring to the doctor's attention any suspicious behaviors or subtle developmental delays means that early intervention is delayed. There has to be an approach to early detection that is more objective.

There are two ways that the American Academy of Pediatrics is attempting to make early detection more objective and thorough. First, they are making a concerted effort to educate parents about normal social and language development and the red flags for possible autism. Awareness campaigns and educational materials and posters at doctors' offices encourage parents to bring any concerns to their doctor's attention. Second, they are providing pediatricians with better screening tools to use at toddler checkups, which provide a more objective evaluation of a child's social and language skills. When open and honest parental reporting is combined with thorough and accurate physician observation, early detection of autism is a realistic goal that we can achieve together.

AUTISM SCREENING TESTS IN THE DOCTOR'S OFFICE

Autism screening is a new practice in pediatrics. We used to simply try to notice when something was wrong with a child's development, but now we have several screening tests that, if used properly, can provide a somewhat objective assessment of a toddler's social and language development. These tests aren't used for diagnosis. They are used only to screen children and identify those who should undergo further testing. In chapter 3 I will discuss how further testing is performed.

The parent either fills out a developmental questionnaire (without knowing it is designed to screen for autism) or is asked the questions directly. Then the pediatrician goes through a checklist of various social and language skills during the checkup, again without mentioning autism. The results of both assessments are scored by the pediatrician, and the number score reveals whether or not the child may be at risk. Several tests have been developed so far:

- CHAT (Checklist for Autism in Toddlers: 9 parent questions, 5 doctor observations)

- M-CHAT (Modified Checklist for Autism in Toddlers: 23 parent questions)

- CHAT-23 (Checklist for Autism in Toddlers: 23 parent questions, 5 doctor observations)

- PDDST-II PCS (Pervasive Developmental Disorders Screening Test—Primary Care Screener: 22 parent questions)

- CAST (Childhood Asperger Syndrome Test: 39 parent questions; for ages four to eleven)

You will notice that some of these tests are parent questionnaires only and some include specific observations made by the doctor. I prefer the latter, as it prompts me to test the child myself in several ways. I like to use the simple CHAT. I may also use the CHAT-23 if I have a suspicion of autism. Here is an example of the CHAT test, to give you an idea of what these tests involve (adapted from CHAT, Baron-Cohen et al., *Journal of Developmental and Learning Disorders,* 2000). Ask your doctor to perform a screening test for your child at the eighteen-month and two-year checkups.

Part I—Pediatrician asks the parent the following questions, or the parent fills out the questionnaire prior to the doctor coming in

- Does your child enjoy swinging or being bounced on your knee?

- Does your child show interest in other kids?

- Does your child like climbing on things, such as stairs?

- Does your child enjoy peekaboo, hide-and-seek, or other social games?

- Does your child play pretend games, such as having a tea party, feeding a doll, cooking?

- Does your child use the index finger to point to ask for something?

- Does your child use the index finger to indicate interest in something?

- Does your child play with toys the way they are intended (cars, blocks, dolls) instead of simply mouthing, fiddling with, or throwing them?

- Does your child bring you objects to show you?

Your doctor won't just take your word for it. He will be making some specific observations about how your toddler interacts during the appointment.

Part II—Pediatrician's observations

- Does the child make sustained eye contact with the doctor?

- Does the child show interest when the doctor points to something and says, "Look at that _____!"?

• Does the child play with a toy appropriately, such as when given a cup and doll, she gives the doll a drink?

• Does the child point at something with the index finger, such as the light, when the doctor says, "Where's the light?"?

• Can the child stack some blocks?

I won't provide you with details on how to score this or other tests, since you shouldn't be testing your own child. A pass/fail or low-risk, medium-risk, or high-risk determination is made by the doctor.

CHECKLIST FOR SOCIAL AND LANGUAGE DEVELOPMENT

Many pediatricians evaluate the development of every infant and toddler at each checkup. But some might not be as thorough as they should be. The ten or fifteen minutes you have for a checkup might not be long enough for a pediatrician to notice a developmental delay. It's up to you, the parent, to bring any delays to your doctor's attention. Here is a list of social and language developmental milestones published by the Centers for Disease Control and Prevention and the American Academy of Pediatrics (adapted from www.cdc.gov/actearly).

At 12 months, a baby should...

- look at something when you point to it and say, "Look"
- wave bye-bye or make other hand gestures
- babble with various consonant sounds and inflections, as if speaking a different language
- say two words, such as Mama, Dada, dog, ball, or other simple words

(continued)

- turn her head most of the time to look at you when her name is called
- look for a toy when you hide it under a blanket
- point to something he wants that is out of reach

Note: I do see a lot of infants who don't have that first word by one year but have reached all the other milestones. This generally isn't a concern as long as those words come out by eighteen months.

At 18 months, a toddler should...

- point to something when asked, such as a body part, person, or object in the room
- point out an interesting object to you
- use ten or more words (not just repeating when prompted, but spontaneously)
- play pretend with you, for example, hold and feed a doll or stuffed animal
- follow a simple request, such as "Show me the toy" without your making a gesture

Note: I have a very strict "no words by eighteen months" policy by which I send a toddler for a more detailed developmental assessment.

At 2 years, a toddler should...

- point to numerous body parts, pictures, or objects in the room when asked
- be able to do a simple puzzle, such as placing three shapes correctly
- understand about fifty words, and use them routinely
- put two or more words together when speaking, such as, "Want doll"

- follow two-step commands
- show interest in other children and play next to them

At 3 years, a child should...

- use four-word sentences
- play a matching game with shapes or colors
- correctly use most pronouns, like *I* and *you,* and plurals
- engage other children in play and imitate them
- play pretend games with dolls or figures and talk for them

At 4 years, a child should...

- use five-word (or longer) sentences that are understandable to a stranger
- follow a three-step command
- name a friend when asked
- show interest in a wide range of activities
- answer who, what, and where questions

At 5 years, a child should...

- state her own name and where she lives
- be able to count ten or more objects
- answer questions that ask why
- be understanding toward others' thoughts and feelings

While this checklist isn't designed to be a formal test or screening tool, it does provide guidelines that children should meet. Tell your doctor about any delays at your next checkup (or sooner). Missing one of the above milestones at any age might not be a worry, but any child who isn't meeting two or more should be more closely examined by the pediatrician.

DON'T WAIT FOR A DIAGNOSIS: ACT NOW!

It is critical that every child begin the appropriate therapies as soon as possible. Taking the "Let's wait six months and see how he does" approach before beginning any intervention isn't right. And spending six months consulting with various specialists to determine exactly what the problem is, without beginning developmental therapies, does your child a disservice. In almost all states, you don't need to wait for an actual diagnosis before your child qualifies for any state-funded services; most states will allow treatment to begin as soon as a developmental delay is noted, before the child even sees a neurologist. I saw a fifteen-month-old girl in my office who was showing clear signs of early autism and had an appointment with a neurologist in about six weeks. I asked the parents if they'd started any therapies and was pleasantly surprised to hear that the Regional Center (or Early Start Center, as they are called in many states) had already begun Applied Behavioral Analysis and occupational therapies (see pages 136 and 144) two weeks earlier, right after their first evaluation there.

If you believe your child has autism, then you are probably already in full action mode as far as seeking therapy. But if your child is showing only mild problems and the diagnosis is questionable, don't wait. Between ages one and two, children can decline very quickly into autism. You may not see many problems now, but I've seen some toddlers go from borderline to full autism in just a few months. If your child has enough early and subtle signs that you are reading this book, to my mind that's enough to begin therapy right away. In the next chapter I'll show you where to start.

Another good reason to get a developmental assessment early is that your child may qualify for more services during the early years. Policies vary from state to state, but in California, where I practice, a child under two might qualify for state-funded therapy if he shows more than a 33 percent delay in only one area of development. However, once a child turns two, he has to have a 50 percent delay in one area, or a 33 percent delay in two areas, in order to qualify for state-funded therapy. This clearly highlights the importance of getting a state assessment as early as possible.

You can also begin the biomedical approach. As you will read in part 3, the biomedical treatment plan identifies and corrects any medical, nutritional, and infectious factors that might be contributing to the developmental problems. The sooner you act to correct these, the better. You don't need to wait to find a doctor to help you. There are steps you can take at home right away. You will eventually need to get in touch with a doctor, but waiting until you can see a doctor is no excuse. Act now!

3

Referral to Specialists for Full Assessment and Diagnosis

You will take two initial steps to obtain a full assessment and diagnosis. The first is a developmental evaluation by a developmental therapist. It's very important to get started on speech, occupational, and behavioral therapy right away, so you want to take your child directly to the people who will be providing that therapy. The second step is an evaluation by a medical professional who will determine if a diagnosis of autism spectrum disorder is warranted.

STATE-FUNDED OR PRIVATE THERAPY CENTER: WHERE TO START

Parents can choose between having their child evaluated by a state-funded therapy program or getting a private-pay evaluation (which might or might not be covered by insurance), or both.

State-Funded Therapy Center

Virtually all states have county-based therapy centers to help provide developmental care for children with disabilities under three years of age (once a child turns three, his developmental therapy may be managed by the public school system; see page 36). In years past, these centers primarily took care of kids who were born with birth injuries or mental retardation from genetic disorders. But now these Early Start Centers, as they are called in many states, or Regional Centers (the term used in California and several other states) are inundated with children with autism. Some state services have risen to the occasion and are providing excellent care. Some have more limited resources and are struggling. Your local state-funded center may be the best place for you to start, however. Many do a very thorough job of evaluating a child and offering the right developmental and behavioral therapies, and at no cost to you.

Any parent can call their state program and ask for an evaluation without a doctor's prescription. It may help to have a note from your doctor indicating your child's delays, but this isn't mandatory in most states. After you answer some screening questions over the phone, you and your child will meet with a case manager. That person will determine if your child qualifies for a more thorough developmental evaluation. If so, a developmental specialist (usually not an MD) will give your child a complete evaluation to pinpoint what your child's delays are. In chapter 6, I will go into more detail about the actual therapies that and Early Start Center may set you and your child up with (such as speech, occupational, or social stimulation therapy, or more advanced behavioral therapies, such as ABA).

Infants and toddlers with only minor delays might not qualify for any state-funded developmental services. You may need to seek private therapy and fight with your insurance company to obtain needed services.

In past years, the state programs would begin therapies right away, free of charge, for those infants who qualified. However, during the writing of this book, some states began changing their policies and stopped paying for some services. In California, where I practice, the state program will do the developmental evaluation and identify the need for therapy but will then send your child back to the pediatrician to write a prescription for these therapies. You will then need to obtain insurance approval and begin therapy through a private therapy center. If your insurance refuses to pay for therapy, you can take their denial back to the state program, at which point the state will provide your child with therapy.

This whole system is currently in flux. Some states are continuing to provide services right away without requiring a child to go through medical insurance. Others are following California's example and shifting the responsibility over to private medical insurance. Even though laws are being passed in many states that will require insurance companies to begin paying for developmental therapies, the initial developmental assessments might not be covered and might remain the responsibility of the state-funded programs. Because every state's policy will vary, I can't provide you will specifics for your own state. Your pediatrician or local parent support group (such as TACA, see page 55) can help guide you.

At this stage of the process, I am mainly discussing how to get a thorough developmental evaluation so therapy can begin. In chapter 6, I will explain the developmental and behavioral therapies that your child will (or should) be receiving, and who will be paying for them.

As for making an actual diagnosis of autism through a state-funded program, some programs have neurologists or psychologists who come in and evaluate kids to make a formal diagnosis. Other programs may refer your child to an outside specialist (who may then be covered by the state) for an evaluation. This, too, may be changing state by state. Some may shift this diagnostic responsibility over to private medical insurance.

Some parents hesitate to go to a state-funded center because they worry that the evaluation won't be as thorough as at a private center. The comprehensiveness of the evaluation varies from state to state, but in my experience, the state programs do an adequate job in their assessment of a child's development. You might have to wait a month or two for your child's appointment, but it won't cost you a dime.

The main drawback to the state-funded centers is that they tend to underdiagnose during the toddler years when a child's signs are mild and subtle. They are very accommodating when it comes to offering early speech therapy for any child with language delay and occupational therapy for a child with motor-skill problems. But as for finally diagnosing a child with autism and approving the full spectrum of services, they might not reach this point until the problems are more obvious. Nobody wants to be too quick to diagnose autism, but under this system some children fall behind in starting the more advanced treatments, such as ABA and Sensory Integration OT (see pages 136 and 145).

Here is a typical story of what some of my own patients go through. The child gets referred to the Regional Center for speech delay at eighteen months. Two months later, the child has his screening evaluation and is approved for a more complete evaluation. In another two months, this is done, and the speech delay is confirmed. Two months after this, the child starts speech therapy (after waiting for a spot to open up in a private center or in the state-funded program). A few months of speech therapy go by and the therapist notices some additional unusual behaviors. The child, who is now over two years old, gets another full developmental evaluation, and more problems are detected. The child is approved for more therapy, such as more hours of speech therapy and some limited hours of OT and ABA. Two months later, after the insurance company approves the recommendations or denies coverage and sends the child back to the state program, these therapies begin. The child is also referred to a neurologist or psychologist. After waiting two more months for that appointment, the child is diagnosed with Pervasive Developmental Disorder—Not Otherwise Specified (if mild) or autism (if moderate to severe). The neurologist writes a note requesting more hours of therapy, which the parents take back to the insurance company or the state center. Now the child is two and a half to three years old and is just beginning the full range of needed therapy.

Please don't get the impression that I'm criticizing the state Early Start programs. They do everything they can based on their resources. The Early Start system does so much good, but its hands are tied by a larger system.

One final note on state programs: Many provide evaluations and therapy only until age three, and then they turn the child over to the public school system, at which point the child enters a preschool-based therapy program with all new therapists. Some state centers will continue select services beyond age three, especially if the school district doesn't provide a needed therapy, and the insurance denies coverage. But the public school system will become the primary case manager for the child. School districts are also limited by their funding, however, and public school services vary dramatically from one district to another. Where I practice, one district has a very good reputation for providing quality care and another one doesn't. Regional Centers seem to provide more thorough and consistent therapy. This points again to the importance of early diagnosis and therapy well before age three so that a child can benefit from this therapy before moving on to the public school system.

Private Developmental Evaluation

Parents who don't want to wait for their appointment at the state Regional Center (which can delay the start of therapy for a few months) can have their child evaluated by a private developmental therapist. Such evaluators are usually part of an autism treatment facility that provides all modes of therapy. The advantage of such centers is that you can usually get an assessment in a very timely manner and begin therapy right away. There are three main drawbacks, however:

1. The centers with the most experienced therapists often fill up quickly (word gets around), and sometimes they have waiting lists longer than the Regional Center's.

2. Going directly to a private center might not be covered by insurance. Under the new system, state laws are mandating that insurance cover needed therapies. However, I don't know if insurances will cover only therapies that are recommended by a state evaluation, or if they will equally cover recommendations made by a private therapist. You will need to investigate this issue in your own state before you decide to go directly to a private center for your child's initial evaluation and therapy.

3. The cost is considerable. Not only is the initial evaluation fairly expensive; the thirty hours a week of speech, OT, and ABA therapy can run between $5,000 and $10,000 per month. Two to three years of such therapy really adds up if it ends up not being covered by insurance.

One more point: You want an objective evaluation. A private center might have some financial incentive to diagnose your child with autism and prescribe numerous hours of therapy. If your child does have autism, then these hours are needed. But it wouldn't be unreasonable for a parent to wonder how objective such an evaluation really is. On the other hand, a state-funded program doesn't have enough resources, so it might lose some objectivity in the other direction, perhaps denying some therapy that really is needed. There is a potential conflict of interest in both types of centers, but that is unavoidable. Parents should do whatever they feel is best for their child.

Public School System

Children whose developmental delays are overlooked in the early years usually need to go through the public school system for a state-funded evaluation once they are three years old (some Early Start Centers provide this service beyond age three). Because there are far more school systems in our country than there are county Regional Centers, the quality of special-education evaluations and services varies dramatically. If your child has been managed by a Regional Center already, when he turns three, he may be turned over to a case manager at the public school that is in your district. If you haven't yet had an evaluation by a state-funded program and your child is three or older, call the public school that your child would be going to when he enters kindergarten (even if you weren't planning to enroll him there). You can also call the state-funded center to ask if they have an age cut-off. Tell them your pediatrician wants your child to have a neurodevelopmental evaluation and describe what the suspected problems are. Within the next month or two, the school will conduct this testing. A pediatric psychologist or a neurologist who works with the school district will usually play a role in the evaluation and make a determination of whether a child is on the autism spectrum. If it is deemed necessary, your child will enter a preschool program that provides developmental services. I will discuss this in further detail in chapter 6.

MEDICAL SPECIALISTS FOR EVALUATION AND DIAGNOSIS

Once you have determined that your child may have a delay in development that could lead to autism, and you have begun the process of looking into developmental therapy, the next step is to get a more detailed evaluation by a specialist to determine the precise degree of delay and whether or not your child may have, or may be at risk of declining into, autism. Your pediatrician should help you decide which type of specialist to see, as your decision can lead you in many different directions. Here are the available options from which to choose.

Pediatric Neurologist

Pediatric neurologists are primarily trained to care for children with seizure disorders, neurological injuries, and neuromuscular disorders. As the incidence of autism has dramatically increased over the past fifteen years, both the evaluation and the treatment have been learning processes for parents and neurologists alike. As this pediatric subspecialty has become the primary first stop for children with autism, many neurologists have had to go back to school, so to speak, to learn what to do for autism. Younger neurologists have likely received significant training in autism already. Some neurologists have joined forces to form centers for the evaluation and treatment of autism. It may be better to go to such a center, where neurologists are specializing in autism, rather than to an independent neurologist who cares for all types of neurological disorders and does autism "on the side." However, there are solo neurologists who specialize in autism because they have a particular interest in this area. Here is what a pediatric neurologist can do for you:

• Provide more in-depth developmental evaluation than your pediatrician can offer (called a Level 2 screening test—see below)

• Provide a good baseline determination of overall development to use as a comparison for future evaluations

- Perform a neurological physical examination to determine if there is an underlying neurological disorder that is leading to symptoms of autism (in my experience, this is rarely found to be the case)

- Determine if testing to rule out seizures is needed (see EEG testing, page 124)

- Determine if an MRI of the brain is needed to rule out any physical problem with the brain (in my experience, this test is almost always normal)

- Order detailed blood and urine tests that look for genetic and metabolic problems that might be causing or contributing to autism

- Provide a definitive diagnosis of autism so that your child can qualify for more developmental and behavioral treatments either through insurance or through state-funded programs

- Provide a "medical home" to give parents guidance on how to find the best developmental therapy services in their area and provide letters of referral as needed

- Incorporate your child into ongoing research programs that may benefit not only your child but other kids as well

- Provide early observation and screening for any subsequent children (some university neurology centers are very involved in studying these siblings to try to learn how to prevent autism)

Parents may have unrealistic expectations of what a neurologist can do. Many go primarily hoping that the doctor will be able to find a cause for their child's autism and then offer some medical treatment to improve or cure the autism. After all, this is what specialists do, isn't it? Almost all of my patients come back to me after seeing a neurologist and report, with a shrug of the shoulders, "Well, he didn't find anything (except the autism), all the tests he did were inconclusive, he didn't offer any medical treatment, he gave us a bunch of things to do, and he said come back in six months and we'll see how things are going." Because the neurologist isn't providing any active and ongoing medical therapy, many parents eventually stop going, and may not even return a second time. In my experience, a neurologist is almost never able to determine the cause of the autism, and he can't offer medical treatment for the child yet, apart from medications. But what a neurologist does provide is very helpful.

It is important to have ongoing evaluations with a neurologist. He might be able to direct you to some new services or find a new and better behavioral therapy program. You might be able to participate in some ongoing observational research that may benefit other kids down the road. If (or when) your child shows some significant improvement, you can tell your neurologist what you've been doing to achieve those gains so that the doctor can compare this information with what he hears from other parents and best learn how to help all patients. There is so much we don't know, and we can all learn and gain from shared experiences.

Developmental Pediatrician

This pediatric subspecialist can also offer a complete developmental evaluation and diagnosis of autism using the Level 2 tests. This type of doctor will likely be more skilled at the developmental aspects of the evaluation (compared with a neurologist) and will often spend more time observing and testing the child. However, he may not be as experienced in the detection of underlying neurological disorders or deciding when an MRI or EEG is necessary, areas in which a neurologist has more experience. Of course, doctors and programs vary. One particular developmental pediatrician could be outstanding and a nearby neurologist may be only mediocre. In general, though, I usually have my patients start with a neurologist. I might send a patient to a developmental pediatrician instead if the child has only very subtle delays in several areas and does not seem to have autism, and I want a thorough developmental assessment to establish what the delays are.

Child Psychologist

This type of specialist is also trained and equipped to diagnose autism. A psychologist might have more experience recognizing

---

LEVEL 2 SCREENING TESTS

Specialists administer the following Level 2 screening tests. The evaluator will decide which test to do.

Level 2 tests for autism for younger children:
- ABC (Autism Behavior Checklist, for ages 18 months and older). This behavioral checklist of fifty-seven items is administered by a trained professional.
- CARS (Childhood Autism Rating Scale, for ages 2 years and older). This checklist of fifteen items is administered by a trained professional.
- ADOS (Autism Diagnostic Observation Schedule, suitable for any age). The professional spends forty-five minutes interacting with and observing the child, then scores the results.
- ADI-R (Autism Diagnostic Interview-Revised, for mental age of 2 years and older). In this test, the professional asks the parent a series of questions.

the behavioral abnormalities of autism than other specialists do, but it depends greatly on the professional's experience. I might choose to refer a patient to a psychologist if the child's main problems are behavioral as opposed to developmental or neurological.

Speech Therapist

Because the most obvious first sign of autism is speech delay, a speech therapist (*speech and language pathologist* is the proper term) is often the first one to evaluate a delayed child, even before autism is suspected. As a pediatrician, I used to find myself sending a lot of speech-delayed children (who otherwise seemed to be developing normally) to speech therapists for evaluation and

---

Level 2 tests for autism and Asperger's syndrome for older children:

- ASDS (Asperger Syndrome Diagnostic Scale, for ages 5 and up). This fifty-item questionnaire is completed by a professional, parent, or teacher.
- ASSQ (Autism Spectrum Screening Questionnaire, for ages 6 and up). This is a twenty-seven-item parent questionnaire.
- GADS (Gilliam Asperger's Disorder Scale, for ages 3 and up). This thirty-two-item questionnaire is completed by a professional, parent, or teacher.

Not all specialists follow formal testing procedures, however. Some prefer to spend time interacting with the child more directly to get a better impression of his abilities and behavior while taking note of any problems that meet the criteria for autism. I believe this approach is just as valid in the hands of an experienced evaluator.

treatment. But over the years I learned that this might not be enough.

Here is a common story. A toddler isn't talking and the parents raise their concerns with their pediatrician at the eighteen-month checkup. The pediatrician sends them to a speech therapist, who begins language therapy. After six months, the child hasn't made much progress, and at the two-year checkup, more developmental concerns are noticed. Only then does the doctor send the child for a more thorough evaluation. Looking back, most parents feel that other early signs of autism were probably there at eighteen months but were missed. Because a speech therapist cannot provide a full developmental evaluation for autism, any suspicions should be brought to the attention of the pediatrician so that further evaluation can be done by a qualified specialist.

I think it does a child a great disservice to provide only speech therapy if there are other developmental delays. Some might consider it overkill, but I think it's better for any child who has delayed speech to get a full developmental assessment right away in addition to starting language therapy.

A HEARING TEST IS A MUST

Any child with speech delay should have his hearing tested by an audiologist. This can often be done at the same place where a speech evaluation is given. Ask your pediatrician to include a prescription for a hearing test and show it to your speech therapist. If she doesn't provide that service, ask for an audiology center nearby. Virtually all children with autism and speech delay end up having normal hearing, but it's worth ruling this out because hearing loss is treated *very* differently.

TYPICAL TIMELIME OF DIAGNOSIS

A major challenge in diagnosing autism is that symptoms and behaviors often don't peak until around two and a half years of age. The following is an average timeline for symptoms, screening, further evaluation, and diagnosis. It may help you understand where your child is right now, where he might be headed, and, most important, how you can speed up the process of starting the necessary therapies in order to slow down, halt, or begin to reverse the progression of symptoms. Since autism varies from mild to severe, it's hard to fit all children into one timeline. But this should give you a general idea of how the average child goes through this period of diagnosis:

Twelve to eighteen months of age. This is often when you first begin to realize that your child isn't saying any words yet and perhaps hasn't been much of a babbler either. A toddler may have developed a few words that then faded away. The child might be an easygoing low-key toddler who likes to play alone, or he might be on the other end of the spectrum, displaying tantrums that wake the neighbors. Most friends, family members, and doctors reassure you that this is just a phase. He'll mature past it. Others, including you, may notice some issues, and you may seek an early evaluation.

Eighteen months to two years of age. Junior still hasn't said his first word (or maybe he has a few but he isn't showing any signs of that language explosion you've been expecting). Your doctor finally refers him to a speech therapist for a language evaluation. Two months later you get in to see one, and your child begins weekly language therapy sessions. Other symptoms may have appeared by now that prompt further therapy, but often these are missed.

Two and a half years of age. The speech therapy has helped some, but not as much as you expected. Your doctor refers you to a neurologist, or you seek a developmental evaluation from the Regional Center. They notice more unusual behaviors that seem obvious now that someone has pointed them out to you. The first diagnosis you receive is PDD-NOS (see page 7), since the specialist doesn't see enough wrong to be diagnosed as autism.

Three years. Your child has not progressed socially, his language is still delayed, more symptoms of autism have appeared, and now your child receives the diagnosis. More extensive behavioral therapies are started in order to address all of your child's challenges.

Four or five years: mild autism/Asperger's syndrome. These kids follow a different timeline. There usually aren't enough delays early on to notice—besides a very slight quirkiness that no one can put their finger on. The child enters preschool or kindergarten, and the social awkwardness gradually becomes apparent. The child sees a developmental specialist, who gives the diagnosis.

DOES A FORMAL DIAGNOSIS OF AUTISM HELP OR HURT YOUR CHILD?

I have talked to numerous parents who have been afraid to allow their child to receive a diagnosis of autism. They worry that this stigma will follow him for the rest of his life and that he may be denied opportunities because of it. They don't want it to find its way onto any public school or medical insurance records. While I can understand this viewpoint, I believe this approach, in most cases, isn't in the best interests of the child. The state-funded therapy center and the public school system will provide a child who has not been diagnosed with autism with only limited therapy, usually a few hours of speech and occupational therapy each week. They may offer some ABA time as well during the toddler years, but if a child doesn't go on to be diagnosed with autism, that will likely be taken away (to make room for those children with an actual diagnosis). Such parents will then have to come up with as much as $10,000 per month for full-time private therapy. Some parents will actually keep their child out of the public program altogether and pay for private therapy from the start. In the end, as long as a child is receiving full-time ABA, speech therapy, OT, and social skills therapy, I suppose it doesn't really matter whether the child has an actual labeled diagnosis. But most (if not virtually all) families don't have an extra $120,000 lying around to pay for therapy every year for several years. I believe that if a child has autism, it is best to obtain a formal diagnosis so that he can receive the full array of therapies without financial barriers. Any child who improves to the point where he no longer fits the criteria for autism can have his diagnosis removed.

A related issue is that a child who shows signs of mild autism as a toddler but never actually gets diagnosed sometimes responds so well to early intervention that he never qualifies for a formal diagnosis of autism. Note that I call this an issue rather than a problem because it is always a wonderful thing when a child improves so quickly. I raise this point because state-funded services can be taken away from such a child once he turns three years old, if not sooner. Without enough ongoing therapy, the child may worsen again. But with another year or two of intensive treatment, that child's mild problems may resolve completely and permanently. Parents in this situation either have to fight hard for continued state services or turn to the private sector for continued therapy. Contrast this with a similar child who receives an actual diagnosis of autism at an early age; this child will likely receive more hours of therapy for more years, all provided by the state. The end result can be the same for both children, the eventual removal of the diagnosis. But one family will have to take out a second mortgage and the other won't.

Here's the take-home point: If it's possible that your child fits the criteria for a diagnosis of autism as a toddler, he might be better off receiving the formal diagnosis before he begins to improve. I'm not saying you should purposely try to prevent him from improving until you get a diagnosis. And you shouldn't try to get him falsely diagnosed. Just try to get an evaluation as quickly as possible. If your child truly doesn't qualify for a diagnosis, then you and he are blessed. Whether or not to obtain a formal diagnosis is a personal and individual decision that concerns just you and your doctor.

The same may hold true for a child who is diagnosed with high-functioning autism instead of autism. He may not get as many weekly hours, and as many years, of state-funded therapy. While this diagnosis may be appropriate in many cases, parents should discuss this issue with the developmental specialist who is making the diagnosis. In some cases, a specialist will tack on the high-functioning label to make the parents feel better. If you tell the doctor that you have fully accepted your child's diagnosis, he may leave off the "high-functioning" part of the diagnosis so that your child can benefit from the most hours of therapy possible.

Tragically, the other end of the spectrum also has its challenges. A child with severe autism may sometimes be given the additional diagnosis of mental retardation. We know that the intellect of most children with autism is completely intact, and that the label of mental retardation is almost never appropriate. Moreover, if such a diagnosis is given, some state programs will deny services, taking the position that the child's condition is too severe to treat. In my opinion, everybody should be given the same opportunities to improve. Allowing a child to go untreated is only asking for his condition to worsen. If a doctor tries to label your child with mental retardation, ask him to consider keeping the diagnosis limited to autism. In fact, a child can't be labeled with mental retardation unless he actually fails a formal IQ test. Most children with autism can't even take a standard IQ test because they won't answer the questions. Modified IQ testing has been developed to assess intelligence despite autistic deficits, but it might be better to steer clear of this. Most children will pass such tests with flying colors, but those who don't may find themselves denied much-needed therapy.

RELATED DISORDERS: ALL PART OF THE AUTISM SPECTRUM?

I have come to believe that any social, developmental, or learning disorder that falls outside the realm of normal may share some of the same underlying causes. We don't know exactly what those causes are, but some of the baseline treatments may be the same. There are many different developmental and behavioral disorders, virtually all of which are also seen in autism. For example, almost all children with autism have some elements of Sensory Processing Disorder, Obsessive-Compulsive Disorder, Language Processing Disorder, ADHD, and so on. On the other hand, a child can have SPD or OCD and not have autism. But when we discover what the underlying causes of all these problems are, we'll probably find them to be the same.

What's my point? Any child with one of the developmental disorders listed below should receive a full evaluation to make sure autism isn't going along with it. The biomedical therapies I cover in part 3 can help the following related disorders.

Sensory Processing Disorder (aka Sensory Integration Disorder)

It's important for you to recognize this disorder, and begin therapy for it, if your child has sensory problems. A baby or child with SPD (or SID) doesn't process sensations correctly. Hearing, touch, and balance are the three senses most affected (if we might consider balance a sense). When a child detects a sensation, the brain doesn't process that input correctly and in turn doesn't know how to create a natural response to it. Here are some examples:

• The scratchy feel of a clothing tag can usually be ignored by a neurotypical child as the local sensory nerves in that area of the skin stop registering the scratchiness. A child with SPD, however, will keep feeling the tag, and the sensory impulses will increase to the point that the brain can't handle them and the child demands to have the shirt removed.

• When a neurotypical child enters a loud, chaotic room with lots of children, the ears turn down the volume so the child's hearing center in the brain isn't overloaded. In the case of SPD, the brain keeps hearing all of the noise and chaos, and the child gets overwhelmed.

These and other situations overload the sensory systems. This can, in turn, prevent other areas of the brain (namely the ones that control social behavior, language, and learning) from developing correctly, eventually affecting the child's ability to cope with and interact with the world around him. But I'm getting ahead of myself. Let me go back to the beginning and describe how the symptoms of SPD may occur during the various ages so that you can recognize and treat it early.

Symptoms during early infancy may include:

• colic (hypersensitivity to life in general during the first few months; see page 342)
• abnormally frequent night waking (from irritating clothing and bedding)
• aversion to snuggling or rocking (balance and position sensitivities)

- demand to be held in only certain positions
- need for constant motion

Symptoms during later infancy (six to twelve months) include:

- refusal to try foods by nine months (oral aversions)
- uncomfortable with messiness (sticky hands, face) or wet clothes

Symptoms in toddlers include:

- refusal to wear certain clothes (that just don't feel right)
- refusal to wear socks or shoes unless they are put on just right (little bumps in the socks or inside the shoe are irritating)
- refusal to walk barefoot in grass or sand
- bothered by chaos and loud noises

Symptoms in preschoolers include:

- many of the above
- hyperactivity or constant moving, fidgeting
- social awkwardness (the years of sensory overload in the brain have spilled over into other parts of the brain)

In chapter 6, I will share how SPD is diagnosed and treated by an occupational therapist who specializes in Sensory Integration Therapy. This approach exposes children to the offending sensations gradually to allow their nervous system to learn how to handle them. If the therapy is done early on (in the first few years of life), it is likely that other parts of the brain won't be affected and the child will be less prone to develop social or learning challenges. Visit www.SPDfoundation.net for more information.

Language Processing Disorders

There are two ways a child's brain might not process language correctly. In *receptive delay,* a child can hear words, but the hearing center in the child's brain jumbles the words, so the child doesn't quite get the message. In *expressive delay,* a child receives and understands verbal input just fine, but anything the child tries to put together to say himself may come out slightly confused. A child may also have both processing challenges. LPDs cause abnormal speech patterns, such as the ones described for autism on pages 18 and 19 (speaking slightly out of context and answering a question with a question). Another common manifestation is misusing pronouns. For example, if you ask a child, "Do you want some candy," he may answer, "You want some candy" instead of "I want some candy."

Virtually every child with autism has language processing problems. But some kids may be completely normal in every other way and only have an LPD. So, having a problem processing language doesn't necessarily mean a child has autism, but any child who sees a speech therapist for LPD problems should also get a full developmental evaluation. LPD is treated through speech therapy (see page 142).

Central Auditory Processing Disorder

This disorder sounds similar to receptive LPD, but there is a difference. In both disorders, hearing is normal. The child with Central Auditory Processing Disorder (CAPD), however, has difficulty filtering out background noise (other conversations, loud noises), hearing all sound pitches (such as very high or low), ignoring distractions, and discriminating similar word sounds. For example, he might not be able to detect the difference between "How are you?" and "How old are you?" The language center in the brain doesn't receive the verbal input as accurately as it does in a child with receptive LPD. The resulting confusion and inaccuracy in how the child verbally responds begin to interfere with a child's social development. Diagnosis is made through an audiologist who has specific training in CAPD. See page 287 for treatment.

Childhood Apraxia of Speech

With this condition, the child has difficulty forming intelligible words. He will try to speak, even in full sentences, but the sounds his mouth forms are difficult to understand. The problem is thought to originate within the part of the brain that controls the muscles of the mouth, rather than to be an actual weakness of these muscles themselves. It is somewhat similar to expressive LPD. Although various terms have been used to describe this disorder, such as *apraxia* or *verbal dyspraxia*, the preferred professional term is Childhood Apraxia of Speech, or CAS. The word *praxis* literally means "practice of an art, science, or skill." So, the neurological dysfunction is thought to be in the area of the brain that controls the practice of moving the muscles of the mouth to form words. Diagnosis and therapy are provided by speech therapists.

Nonverbal Learning Disabilities (NVLDs)

This diagnosis describes a child who doesn't understand many aspects of nonverbal language and social cues but does not have typical behavioral and neurological features of autism. He also suffers from some fine- and gross-motor incoordination because the brain has difficulty integrating spatial awareness. This varies from Asperger's in that a child with an NVLD knows and cares that he doesn't pick up on nonverbal cues. He knows he's different, and it bothers him. Kids with autism don't know they are different (unless they recover), and children with Asperger's know but may not care (unless they recover). This diagnosis is not yet well understood, and it has significant overlap with SPD and LPD. It might not even be a separate disorder. Treatment involves many of the same behavioral therapies as autism (see chapter 6).

Obsessive-Compulsive Disorder

Most children with autism have OCD tendencies, but some neurotypical children display OCD characteristics, too. Common signs include:

- obsession with sameness, such as wanting the plate, cup, and silverware arranged in a certain way
- unusual demands, such as needing different food items to be separated on the plate or always wanting all doors they see to be closed
- obsession with a small number of certain toys, such as trains

If you notice these signs in your child, a full developmental evaluation is in order to rule out autism. As far as treatment goes, some of the potential biomedical causes of autism (discussed in chapter 4) can trigger OCD in neurotypical kids, so it's important to look into the same causes and treatments.

ADD/ADHD

This is generally believed to be a separate condition from autism, but I wonder if it really should be placed at the very beginning of the autism spectrum. With these kids, something in the mind that determines focus and attention isn't working correctly. In children with hyperactivity as well, the part of the mind that handles social boundaries and behavior is a little off. This is true of autism as well, just to a greater degree. I have had some success with biomedical treatments in children with ADD/ADHD. It doesn't help everybody, but it's worth a try. On page 294, I offer several specific natural treatment suggestions.

TACA: A RESOURCE FOR PARENT SUPPORT AND EDUCATION

Numerous groups have been established across the country to offer help to families with autism. Some focus on education and diagnosis, some provide lists of autism medical providers and behavioral/developmental therapists, some offer financial assistance to needy families to help cover therapy, and some focus on political action. Some provide only mainstream information and others incorporate biomedical interventions. I have interacted with a number of these groups and have been thrilled with how much help they can provide families. In the Resources, page 356, I provide a list of such organizations so you can seek assistance as needed.

My favorite group is Talk About Curing Autism (www .TACAnow.org). TACA covers pretty much everything about autism, and they have physical chapters in seventeen states so far (and they continue to grow every year). They can also help families living in states that don't yet have an outreach chapter. TACA provides families with hands-on assistance (both in group meetings and one-on-one) to help parents understand everything they can do for their child. They provide biomedical diet and supplement education, resource lists of behavioral and developmental therapists, lists of doctors who specialize in autism (both mainstream and biomedical approaches), social functions for families affected by or involved with autism, marriage counseling for parents, financial support for families in need, and online support from educated and experienced parents to answer questions directly. They also have resources in Spanish. And best of all, they have an autism mentor program that will match any newly diagnosed family with a family that has had experience with autism for several years and knows how to help them get the most out of the resources in their area.

PART II

Causes of Autism

4

What Causes Autism? Mainstream and Biomedical Theories

One of the first things parents want to know when their child is diagnosed with autism is why. What caused it? With most serious conditions, knowing the cause brings some comfort to many parents; at least they know why it happened and can move past that question and concentrate on treatment. Parents who are left to wonder why autism affected their child find it very unsettling. I sincerely apologize that I can't offer a definitive answer to this question right now. In this chapter, I share with you everything that doctors and researchers are working on as far as finding a cause or causes, and in subsequent chapters I will share with you how numerous biomedical treatments will address these causes. There is a significant time lag in bringing these promising treatments into the mainstream. Here is why.

The mainstream medical approach is slow and steady. It carefully and meticulously examines possible theories, sets up large studies in areas that look promising, studies them some more, ponders the results, repeats the research again to prove the findings, demonstrates to the world that the findings are practical, and then (maybe twenty years later) incorporates the findings into modern medical treatments. Causes are firmly proven before treatments are even tried. And those treatment trials are just as cumbersome as the original causation research. In the meantime, any such theories (whether causes or treatments) are kept restricted and not made available to the public. There's nothing wrong with this approach. It has served us well so far in general medicine. However, except for the behavioral and developmental therapies in chapter 6 and the psychiatric medications in chapter 7, it offers little hope for those children affected by autism right now or for those babies who are going to develop autism.

That was my frustration when I first began to see children with autism in my office twelve years ago. When I turned to my medical books, journals, and online resources, I couldn't find any information on what to do for these kids, other than to refer them for developmental therapy and ship them off to a psychiatrist for meds. I sent them to local neurologists, hoping they could help. They would confirm the diagnosis, but when parents asked what could be done to fix the problem, they were met with a shrug. These parents kept returning to me with empty hands and aching hearts. I decided I should do something.

As a science-based pediatrician, I have always approached medicine in a mainstream way. But I have also incorporated natural treatments into my practice for various problems that regular medicine hasn't yet learned how to fix. When I explored what research had to say about possible causes of autism, and what to do about it, I was shocked. There was a whole world of diagnostic and treatment possibilities. Although skeptical at first, I soon realized that these theories were based on solid scientific principles. Encouraged, I decided I would help parents try to figure out what was medically wrong with their children.

The world of biomedical treatments for autism functions in a manner I wasn't used to. It focuses more on active trial and error. It theorizes about the causes and jumps right into treatment. It starts with small test groups, then expands when something shows promise. Because it almost always involves natural treatments, the error part of this trial-and-error approach is simply that the treatment doesn't work, not that it causes any harm. The proof that something works is achieved more by consensus and not by the traditional scientific method, although the majority of the biomedical theories have now been validated in the traditional medical literature (see Resources, pages 351–380). The benefit is that it offers children hope now. The drawback is that time and money may be spent on something that ultimately doesn't help some kids. My experience helping my first few patients with autism met with considerable success, and since that time, I have never looked back. I, and my colleagues in the biomedical world, keep looking forward.

I believe that parents shouldn't wait around for the mainstream scientific world to tell them what to do for their child. Yes, science will give us the answer someday, but that day will come way too late for most of you reading this. I absolutely hope and pray that I am wrong, and that we'll find an answer tomorrow or next year. Realistically, I don't think that it will happen that quickly. The biomedical world offers some logical and reasonable answers right now that I believe are worth looking into. And as you will see, the approach is built on very solid science. There's nothing alternative about it.

MAINSTREAM MEDICAL THEORIES

Mainstream medicine's search for factors involved in the cause (or causes of) autism has yielded some significant results. As we learn more and more in the next few years, this knowledge should continue to translate into more options for treatment and prevention. But finding one all-encompassing answer to what is causing this autism epidemic, and exactly how we can make it stop, continues to elude researchers. This is especially challenging because we don't know if we are looking for one answer or several. Whatever the answer turns out to be, I believe we are on the right track in that we are studying numerous possibilities. Here are the various mainstream theories on what may be causing or contributing to autism.

Toxic Chemical Exposure

Numerous medical universities and scientists are currently studying this theory. In our modern-day society, we are exposed to many dangerous chemicals: pollution in the air and water; heavy metals through toys, food, and water; toxic chemicals added to household products and furniture; and chemicals and pesticides in food. We know that metals such as lead and mercury can damage brain tissue. We know that numerous chemicals can cause mutations that impair body function. Various body organs can be damaged by chemicals, creating metabolic and hormonal imbalances. The immune system can also be affected, leaving the body more open to various degenerative conditions. Is it possible that all these exposures add up and that some infants simply can't handle this load that begins in the womb and continues throughout childhood?

The Environmental Working Group studied the umbilical cord blood of ten randomly selected new mothers in 2004 and found a shocking number of chemicals and pollutants. Tests detected 287 different toxic chemicals, including mercury, flame retardants, pesticides, perfluorinated chemicals (PFCs), and polychlorinated biphenyls (PCBs), just to name a few. (You can find this study by searching "Body Burden: The Pollution in Newborns" on their website, www.EWG.org.) Most of the chemicals found are known to cause cancer, mutations, and birth defects. So, it's not a question of whether our babies are being exposed to toxins. Rather, it is what effects are those toxins having on our children?

An infant's developing nervous system (from conception through three years of age) is especially susceptible to damage from such exposures. When one brain cell is damaged, so are the dozens of nerve pathways that cell was supposed to connect with down the road. What happens if one thousand nerve cells in one part of the brain (say, the area that controls language development) are damaged? Could several areas of an infant's brain be affected in ways that eventually come out as autism? In the Resources, page 362, you can find various studies that demonstrate a possible link between environmental toxins and autism.

We don't yet know for sure which, if any, environmental toxins contribute to autism, and many more years of study are needed before we will know. This knowledge will be critical for autism prevention because we can then work to remove these from our society and limit infant exposure. From a treatment standpoint, we can learn how best to remove chemicals from our children who show signs of being affected. That's if this theory is even correct.

The chemical exposure theory doesn't answer the question of why autism occurs in some children but not in others. There has to be much more to the puzzle. But it could help explain why autism is a spectrum disorder, in which children are affected to varying degrees and display various symptoms.

While science is exploring the role chemicals and metals may play in autism, affected children need treatment *now*. There isn't any definitive way to test a child for such toxins, but in chapter 12, I will suggest some natural ways you can safely detoxify your child from these chemicals and explain the more advanced prescription detox treatments available from biomedical doctors and other alternative health care providers. As of now, metal detoxification is not an approved therapy for autism in mainstream medicine.

AUTISM AND MERCURY: DID VACCINES PLAY A ROLE?

Between the late 1980s and the year 2002, infants received numerous mercury-containing vaccines throughout infancy and childhood. While the amount of mercury in only one shot may have been tolerable, infants were routinely given several mercury-containing shots all at once at their two-, four-, and six-month checkups. Each of these episodes delivered a quantity of mercury that was as much as eighty times above the daily limit allowable by the FDA and EPA. This fact was discovered in 1998, and the government acted (slowly) to remove mercury from vaccines.

By 2002, the only vaccines that still contained large doses of mercury were most brands of the flu shot. Today, children can get the entire schedule of vaccines 100 percent mercury-free (as long as their parents know which brands of the flu shot are mercury-free; see www.TheVaccineBook.com for more information), so mercury is no longer an issue for families deciding about vaccines. But for those families who believe their children were affected, there is still a legal and moral issue of holding someone accountable and a medical issue of trying to eliminate mercury from the body. The mainstream scientific viewpoint is that there is not enough proof to implicate vaccine mercury in the autism epidemic. Some scientists, many alternatively minded physicians, and hundreds of thousands of parents believe otherwise.

Genetic Problems

Many researchers feel that the primary cause of autism is probably genetic. They are trying to find common genetic abnormalities among children with autism to explain the root cause. There are several known genetic syndromes that can have a profound effect on a child's development, yet most kids with autism *don't* have these major genetic abnormalities. There is so much we still don't understand about the genetics of autism, but the standard of care is to give each child an evaluation to look for a known genetic cause. Here is a brief explanation of the genetic/neurological conditions that we know about so far that may result in symptoms of autism:

Fragile X syndrome. This is the most common known genetic cause of developmental delay (although it is still very rare in our population as a whole). It occurs because a specific gene, called FMR1, on the X chromosome is defective. Boys have only one X chromosome, so if their X has defects, they are likely to develop Fragile X. Girls, on the other hand, have a second X chromosome, which, if normal, will fill in for the malfunctioning X genes and prevent many or all symptoms from showing up.

The symptoms of Fragile X are fairly indistinguishable from autism, although kids with Fragile X are more likely to be hyperactive and anxious. Unfortunately, Fragile X usually causes mental impairment, so these children have more challenges in the years ahead (most children with autism have normal mental function). Fortunately, the vast majority of children with autism have a normal X chromosome. Fragile X is passed down by the mother, so a family history of autism or mental impairment on the mother's side would make this diagnosis more likely.

Rett syndrome. A defect on the X chromosome is also responsible for this genetic disorder. However, it affects only girls, because male fetuses with this defect usually don't survive. The defective gene is called the MECP2 gene. Girls with Rett's usually show completely normal development for several months to a year or more, and then they regress into autism. They also display uniquely characteristic hand-wringing movements and other neuromuscular problems such as unsteady walking, tremors, and muscle spasticity, and they often have seizures. These girls also show decelerated head growth (after the head had been growing normally).

Angelman syndrome. Defects in the UBE3A gene on chromosome number 15 cause Angelman's syndrome, resulting in severe mental retardation, seizures, muscle spasticity, a happy facial expression, unusual bouts of laughter, and symptoms of autism.

Neurocutaneous disorders. These genetically based disorders cause benign tumors to grow in the brain and distinct skin markings. The two most common are neurofibromatosis (NF) and tuberous sclerosis (TS). Infants with these disorders usually begin with normal development, but then benign tumors start to grow within the brain that cause intellectual developmental delay, psychiatric symptoms, seizures, and some features of autism. A thorough examination of the skin will reveal several "café-au-lait" spots (coffee-with-cream–colored flat patches) in the case of NF or "ash-leaf" spots (white patches in the shape of a leaf) in the case of TS. Genetic testing (there is a specific gene-sequencing test for each disorder) and a CT or MRI of the brain, along with the skin findings, are used to make these diagnoses.

Chromosome 16 mutation. A mutation of a certain gene on the sixteenth chromosome called 16p11.2 has been newly associated with autism. This gene can have portions that are either deleted or duplicated. While the developmental and behavioral significance of this gene is not yet known, it has been found in some children with autism.

Bannayan-Riley-Ruvalcaba syndrome. This extremely rare genetic defect in the PTEN gene has been found in a very small number of children with autism. It causes a very large head, increased body size for age, blood vessel growths on the skin (called *hemangiomas*), and small cysts that grow under the skin (called *lipomas*).

Smith-Lemli-Opitz syndrome. This disorder occurs because of a metabolic defect in cholesterol production. The specific gene mutation involved is not yet known. Certain precholesterol mole-cules (compounds that are supposed to be converted into choles-terol) build up in the brain and cause developmental delays and autistic symptoms. These children usually have fused second and third toes, dysmorphic facial features such as droopy eyelids, ears that are small and low set, a split uvula (the tissue that dangles in the back of the throat), small head size, and slow growth. This problem is inherited by a recessive genetic trait, meaning that par-ents can be carriers of the disorder and not be affected at all but pass it along to their children.

Fetal alcohol syndrome. This disorder doesn't have a known genetic basis. It occurs when a pregnant woman abuses alcohol, which has consequences for a fetus's developing nervous system. These babies don't grow well (they are often below the tenth per-centile on a growth curve) and display various features of autism, especially hyperactivity. They have a characteristic look to their faces: the groove between the nose and upper lip, called the *phil-trum*, is flat; the upper lip is thin; the eyes are set close together. The diagnosis is based on known alcohol exposure, developmen-tal delay, and facial features. Even though it's not a genetic disor-der, I include it here because the diagnosis is usually made by a neurologist or genetic/metabolic specialist.

Landau-Kleffner syndrome. This is another disorder without a known genetic basis. The main feature of this syndrome is the onset of seizures between ages three and seven, along with lan-guage regression. It is distinct from autism in that social skills usually remain normal, and the loss of language ability occurs much later than in autism. It is diagnosed with an EEG, which will show a particular type of seizure pattern.

Except for the last two syndromes, each of these genetic problems can be ruled out with genetic or metabolic testing. In chapter 5,

I will explain the types of testing that all children with autism should have and the tests that can be done in special situations to diagnose a genetic cause of autism.

The disorders we do know about, described above, are found in only a very small minority of children with autism. In such genetic disorders, the primary diagnosis is the genetic disorder itself. Autism is simply a manifestation. So, these disorders aren't viewed as clues to what is causing the autism epidemic in children with normal genetics.

What continues to elude researchers is whether there is a single underlying genetic cause of autism that occurs independently of these known genetic disorders. Dozens of minor genetic alterations have been discovered so far in children with autism (many of which I reference in my discussion of the work of Dr. Andrew Zimmerman and his colleagues; see pages 73–77), and each one explains a small part of the spectrum of the disorder. No one has yet to find a major genetic abnormality that is commonly shared by most or all affected children. Will we ever be able to find one such major genetic cause? Since every child's symptoms are unique in their pattern and time of onset, I'm not sure we will find one genetic answer. It is possible that we will discover several genetic associations common to most children with autism. It's also likely that these genetic problems exist on a level that we can't yet detect.

Unfortunately, even as we find more genetic answers, we don't yet know how to repair genetic defects, and we are many years away from such technology. So, finding a genetic abnormality at this point answers why the autism may have occurred, but it doesn't provide parents with more treatment options. However, such information will be invaluable for early screening and diagnosis. If we can identify babies with a genetic risk, we can begin intervention and treatment at an earlier age. It will also give parents a greater incentive to take as many preventive measures as they can if they know their child has genetic risks.

If genetics turns out to be the answer, an even more important question would be, what is causing a rise in genetic problems? Perhaps toxic exposures are responsible for this rise and the ultimate answers may be found in the interaction between these two.

Mitochondrial Disorders

A new theory based on disorders of the mitochondria may end up providing some answers. To understand how, let's briefly look at what mitochondria are. The human body requires energy to function. The sugar, protein, and fat we eat are digested into molecules that flow throughout the body and eventually make their way into every cell. The mitochondria are the tiny factories (like microscopic nuclear reactors) in each cell that convert these food molecules into energy molecules, which are called *ATP*. ATP is what the body then uses for energy.

It isn't known if infants with a mitochondrial disorder are born this way or if something in their environment begins to harm their mitochondria during infancy. They may have low muscle tone and strength, feeding problems, poor weight gain, and developmental delay, basically because their body lacks energy. Some infants may not show any obvious signs at first.

When the body is under stress, for example during a major illness, it requires even more energy. Whole body systems can shut down and the child can become very ill if the mitochondria aren't up to speed. This is often how a mitochondrial disorder declares itself: an apparently healthy infant or toddler shuts down developmentally and neurologically after a major illness.

This issue was the focus of the well-publicized Hannah Poling case. Hannah suffered a severe reaction to her eighteen-month vaccines, which caused the rapid onset of severe neurological and autistic symptoms. Testing found that she might have had a mitochondrial disorder (although this isn't certain) and the vaccine reaction might have pushed her mitochondria, and her entire nervous system, over the edge. She won her case in court.

A variety of mitochondrial disorders have been studied for several decades, going back to long before autism became epidemic. Pediatric metabolic/genetic specialists as well as pediatric neurologists are the types of doctors who study this area. Part of their evaluation for autism includes some special blood and urine testing to look for a mitochondrial disorder, which I explain in chapter 5 (there is no simple blood test that a pediatrician can do). However, only a very small percentage of children with autism who have had such testing have shown a mitochondrial disorder. So, the mainstream medical world believes that this may play a role in only a minority of infants with autism.

Biomedical practitioners, on the other hand, feel that mitochondrial problems may be common in autism. On page 368, I present several studies that demonstrate this. Biomedical doctors believe some children have dysfunctional mitochondria that don't work at full capacity, but such dysfunction doesn't show up on testing. Children may suffer the consequences as if there were a full mitochondrial disorder. There are some treatments that may improve the low muscle tone commonly seen in mitochondrial dysfunction, which I describe on page 298.

This is an emerging area of autism research. We will probably learn much more in the coming years and develop some more promising therapies. Mitochondrial testing may also eventually become part of normal newborn screening so that we can learn which babies may be more susceptible to heavy metals and chemicals (whether their mitochondria are merely dysfunctional or if they have a full disorder) and take preventive measures to protect these children, and their mitochondria, as best we can.

Prenatal and Birth Factors

This is an area that hasn't received much research attention until recently. The theory is that something happens to the baby's brain during early development that sets him up for autism later on. So many factors can affect a baby during pregnancy: chronic maternal medical problems, medications, infections, procedures, and toxic exposures all may have an adverse affect on a baby. Mothers-to-be are careful, but some factors may be out of their control. The age of the mother and/or father and the use of infertility treatments may also play a role. Research has shown that the use of high doses of oxytocin to speed up labor may increase the risk of neurological disorders. Other complications during delivery may result in minor brain injury that sets a baby up for autism. The theory of prenatal and birth factors certainly makes a lot of sense, but we don't have much information yet. On pages 75–76 and in the Resources (page 362) I provide some studies that have shed preliminary light on these possibilities.

Differences in Brain Structure in Autism

Researchers have discovered several structural abnormalities within the brains of children with autism. It makes sense that since autism is a neurological disorder, there may be some detectable differences in the structure or function of the central nervous system of these children. Some of these differences are seen with the naked eye on brain imaging studies, while others occur at the microscopic level. If we can find some common variations in children, this may lead to further understanding of treatment and prevention. We don't have any idea just yet what might be causing these differences, and prevention will rely on that knowledge as well. On pages 76–77 I list several studies that have increased our understanding of brain structure in autism.

Autoimmune Problems

Autoimmune reactions occur when a person's own immune system attacks his own body tissue. Classic examples in medicine include diabetes and rheumatoid arthritis. Numerous studies have demonstrated that many children with autism have dysfunctional immune systems that attack various sections of the brain (see Resources, page 365), and the mainstream medical world is beginning to acknowledge this. Researchers in the biomedical approach to autism have long believed that autism is partly an autoimmune process. I will expand on this on page 86.

AUTISM IS A NEUROBIOLOGICAL DISORDER

For decades doctors viewed autism as a psychiatric disorder. They believed that there wasn't anything biologically wrong with these children and adults. It was "all in their head." Treatment involved medications, some behavioral intervention therapy, and often institutionalization. When the epidemic began in the late 1980s, most doctors continued to believe that there wasn't anything structurally wrong with the brain besides imbalances in neurochemicals that control behavior.

We now know better. Research over the past twenty years has proven that autism is a medical condition, with structural and functional abnormalities within the brain and body. Hundreds of scientists have demonstrated numerous problems with nerve structure, function, and degeneration, defects in cellular metabolism, problems with neurochemical production, numerous genetic defects, hormonal imbalances, immune dysfunction, and inflammatory problems. And these factors not only affect the brain, they create medical problems throughout the body.

Dr. Andrew Zimmerman, a developmental and behavioral specialist from the Kennedy Krieger Institute and Johns Hopkins University, has gathered together many of the brightest minds in the field (from such renowned medical institutions as Harvard, Cambridge University, University of California at Davis, Rutgers, University of Louisville, University of Washington, California

Institute of Technology, Mount Sinai Medical Center, New York, and the University of Pittsburgh) to publish the most up-to-date collection of articles that presents all of this research. His book, *Autism: Current Theories and Evidence* (Humana Press, 2008), references over a thousand research articles. It is definitely a scientific read that would tax the understanding of the average layperson.

While most of the research I refer to throughout this book is in the Resources section in the back, I discuss Dr. Zimmerman's work in detail here to emphasize the point that autism is a neurobiological disorder. Understanding the defects will eventually lead to the discovery of the causes, and hopefully a cure, of autism. Here is a brief look at some of the articles that Dr. Zimmerman presents.

Genetics

EN2 gene and the cerebellum. Rossman and DiCicco-Bloom present evidence that the EN2 gene, which helps regulate the development of the cerebellum (a section of the brain that helps control attention and language), is dysfunctional in autism. In addition, children with autism have been found to have abnormal growth of the cerebellum.

Abnormal activation of maternal genes. Johnson and colleagues present the concept of *teratogenic alleles,* which they describe as genes that the mother carries that turn on during pregnancy and cause abnormalities in fetal brain development. Thirty-three such genes have been identified so far that are thought to play a role in a variety of neurodevelopmental disorders, including spina bifida, Down syndrome, PKU, stillbirth, and autism.

Known genetic disorders. Kaufmann and colleagues explore other genetic disorders that cause autistic symptoms, such as

Rett, Fragile X, and Down syndromes, and how furthering our understanding of these disorders may result in new insights into autism.

Neurotransmitters

Serotonin dysfunction. Blue and colleagues discuss evidence that production of the brain hormone serotonin is decreased in autism. Nerve pathways that generate serotonin are among the first to develop in a fetus, and they extend to many areas throughout the brain and spinal cord. Thus, a disruption in serotonin would have widespread effects on brain function. Treatments that enhance serotonin action can improve symptoms of autism.

Glutamate excitotoxicity. Evers and Hollander offer the theory and evidence that the brain chemical glutamate, which is responsible for activating numerous nerve pathways throughout the brain, is hyperactive in autism (as it has been found to be in other neurological disorders). This overstimulation leads to degeneration and dysfunction of these pathways. Medications that suppress glutamate activity have been shown to improve symptoms of autism in several small studies.

Fetal adrenaline receptor dysfunction. Connors presents evidence that the receptors on cells that are supposed to receive messages from adrenaline-secreting nerves are defective. These B2AR receptors form early during fetal development and are responsible for many body functions. If they are not working properly, many of the signals that one part of the brain sends to another part, as well as to various body organs, won't register properly. This can result in dysfunction in the following areas: brain growth, growth hormone production, methylation metabolism (see page 87), serotonin activity, and immune function, as well as oxidative stress and gastrointestinal problems.

Hormonal and Metabolic Factors

Testosterone effects. Auyeung and Baron-Cohen present evidence that elevated testosterone levels during fetal development may be a risk for autism. They discuss studies that demonstrate that many neurodevelopmental conditions are more common in males and many of the symptoms of autism are extreme exaggerations of male-type behaviors.

Male hormones and loss of certain nerve cells. Keller and colleagues further explore the testosterone theory by discussing animal research that shows that male, but not female, mice lose a certain nerve cell type (called Purkinje cells) in the cerebellum region of the brain, which may explain some of the symptoms of autism. Higher estrogen levels in females are thought to be protective against this loss.

Growth hormone and brain dysfunction. Riikonen presents evidence that growth hormone is deficient early on in autism. Research indicates that this might affect brain growth and development of the cerebellum (including Purkinje cells). Therapy to prevent this deficiency may play a role in future treatments.

Oxidative stress and dysfunctional metabolism. James presents research on how genetic and environmental factors interact to create dysfunctional methylation metabolism and oxidative stress in autism. She offers insights into the implications for early detection and treatment. This is perhaps the most thoroughly researched discussion of the metabolic pathology of autism (see page 87).

Immune System

Immune system and autism. Heuer and colleagues explore research and evidence of immune dysfunction as a contributor to autism.

They discuss three critical areas: autoimmunity (in which a child's own immune system attacks the body), maternal antibodies that attack the fetal brain, and overall immune dysfunction in autism.

Fetal brain inflammation. Patterson and colleagues discuss inflammation within the mother and the placenta during pregnancy and how inflammatory chemicals build up within the amniotic fluid and the fetus. Certain infections during pregnancy may further increase this inflammation. These chemicals can adversely affect brain development.

Maternal antibodies. Morris and colleagues describe the evidence that demonstrates that certain antibodies produced by the mother may cross into the fetus and affect brain development. They also discuss implications for future screening and treatment.

Brain inflammation. Pardo-Villamizar presents evidence of inflammation (from an overactive immune system) within the brain and spinal fluid of patients with autism. He presents ideas for future treatments.

Brain Anatomy

Nerve structure in the brain. Casanova describes research that demonstrates abnormalities in how nerve cells are lined up and dispersed within certain areas of the brain in patients with autism (found on autopsy).

Brain size in autism. Dager and colleagues discuss MRI data that show that children with autism have brains that are 10 to 15 percent larger than normal on average. They also present research demonstrating that the nerve cells within the brain are more widely spaced in children with autism.

Disconnected nerve pathways. Minshew and colleagues present evidence that various nerve pathways don't properly connect one area of the brain with another, which explains some of the behavioral and functional challenges that are seen in autism.

Environmental Factors

Interactions between toxins and genes. Pessah and Lein present theories and evidence that show how various toxins such as pesticides and organic pollutants can cause mutations that directly affect nerve function and cellular metabolism in a manner that may cause some of the neurobiological problems seen in autism.

Putting It All Together

Herbert and Anderson provide a comprehensive review of many of the major findings on causation and tie them all together into a theory that combines prenatal genetics, early environmental exposures, genetic alterations, ongoing environmental influences, and the resulting brain and body dysfunction.

While you might feel discouraged to learn that so many abnormalities could be affecting your child, I would ask you to take heart for two reasons: First, every one of these scientists acknowledges that autism affects every child in different ways and to different degrees, and not every child will have each of these challenges. Second, young brains are moldable; they can heal. Aggressive therapy can improve and reverse many of these abnormalities (that's what this book is about). These and other scientists are bringing us closer and closer to finding the cause or causes of autism. We might be many years away from a clear answer, but countless people are devoting their lives to finding one. I became involved in biomedical interventions to help give hope to children with autism now.

BIOMEDICAL THEORIES

Now I will share with you what the "other side" believes is causing autism. The biomedical approach is a very different world: a world that your regular physician may scoff at; a world that you won't find at most university medical centers; a world not approved by the FDA. But it's a world that I've been involved with since 2000 and one that I will continue to be a part of until it merges with mainstream medicine. Then I won't have to refer to it as *alternative* anymore.

Alternative health care practitioners have been exploring various possible causes of autism, and trying to treat those causes, for the past twenty years with varying results. Many of these providers had been working independently and not collaborating on their work. In 1994 that changed when three physicians who had been investigating autism for many years met to share ideas about what, in their experience, was causing autism. They decided to band together to develop a consensus plan to treat the various causes that they suspected were most responsible for autism. They named their organization Defeat Autism Now.

Dr. Bernard Rimland, a psychologist who founded the Autism Research Institute in 1967 in San Diego, brought his expertise as the pioneer of modern autism research to the table. Dr. Sidney Baker, a pediatrician, graduate of Yale Medical School and former Director of the Gesell Institute of Human Development, has spent decades researching the biomedical aspects of chronic diseases. Dr. Jon Pangborn, a PhD in chemical engineering, former nuclear engineer, and clinical nutritionist, has spent most of his professional life researching the biochemistry of autism and developing various biomedical treatments. These three doctors organized the first meeting in 1995 in Dallas. Thirty physicians and scientists gathered together to share notes and research from the fields of psychiatry, neurology, immunology, allergy, biochemistry, genetics, and gastroenterology. What these doctors found was that many of their patients with autism shared some common medical problems: chronic diarrhea (or constipation in some cases), food allergies, frequent infections, and more. They also shared many common biochemical abnormalities: oxidative stress (an inability to keep up with antioxidant production), an inability to detoxify themselves, and dysfunctional immune systems. And to their shock, many (if not most) of their patients reported a history of normal infant development followed by a heartbreaking regression into autism during the second year of life. The team theorized that something, or some things, must be causing or contributing to this change from normalcy to autism.

Since that time, the group's twice-yearly conferences have grown to include hundreds of doctors and researchers from around the world and thousands of parents. Several other outstanding organizations have formed to research biomedical treatments and to educate physicians and alternatively minded practitioners on how to treat autism. These include AutismOne, the National Autism Association, and the US Autism and Asperger Association. Through trial and error, all of these organizations have developed and expanded treatment plans that they feel have shown the best results in the most children. In chapter 8, I will present the aspects of the biomedical approach that I have had experience with. For now I want to simply introduce you to what the biomedical world (and a growing number of mainstream researchers and physicians) believe are the causes of autism.

We believe that the majority of children with autism are born healthy and neurologically normal but may have some genetic abnormalities that set them up for autism. During the first few years of life, a child is exposed to a variety of factors that work together to trigger autism. While these factors will be harmless to most children, taken together in a genetically susceptible child, they add up and cause a gradual (or in some cases rapid) decline into autism.

We believe that there is no single all-encompassing cause of autism. We suspect that the underlying reason for autism is a combination of genetics and environmental factors. Since we can't change the genetics and it's too late to change the environmental exposures that a child has already had, we concentrate on the suspected causes that we *can* correct. We test and treat the main body systems that seem to go wrong in autism: the gastrointestinal system, the immune system, and the nervous system. Looking for medical problems that can harm these systems, and correcting them, is the focus of the biomedical search for answers.

SOLID SCIENTIFIC EVIDENCE BEHIND BIOMEDICAL THEORIES

In the Resources, I provide over one hundred scientific studies that support biomedical theories on what is causing or contributing to autism. I also list sixty studies that demonstrate the effectiveness of biomedical treatments. Not only will you find these studies of great interest, but you can use them to enlist the support of your own physician in treating your child.

Factors That Result in Autism

The consensus among biomedical practitioners is that autism is caused by a mixture of genetic predisposition and environmental factors. The wide spectrum of severity and timing of symptoms is based on a child's genetics and the degree of exposure to various factors. Here is the theory behind the progression of exposures and problems that may lead to autism (adapted from *Autism: Effective Biomedical Treatments,* Pangborn and Baker; see Resources, page 358).

Genetic predisposition. The theory holds that most children with autism are born normal and healthy, but they have minor genetic or metabolic problems that interfere with their body's ability to eliminate chemicals and heavy metals, fight infections, overcome allergens, and handle stress. These are not the major genetic syndromes discussed earlier in this chapter. Rather, they are minor genetic or metabolic defects that are passed down from the parents. It is also possible that some children don't inherit problems but certain exposures during early life damage their genetics and make them susceptible. These minor genetic problems may be the primary reason that only a minority of children develop autism while virtually all other kids grow and develop in a normal manner, despite the fact that almost all children are exposed to the same factors during infancy. Neurotypical children can handle infections, allergies, toxins, chemicals, and stress because they have the proper metabolic makeup to do so. Understanding the genetics and metabolism of neurotypical kids, and how they differ from those of kids with autism, is one focus of autism research.

Prenatal exposure to heavy metals and toxins. During fetal development, the baby is exposed to various chemicals. Mercury is one such metal that has caused much controversy. It is found in Mom's fillings, used to be found in some brands of RhoGAM (given to mothers with a negative blood type; see page 331), and is present in certain types of fish, most brands of the flu shot (a flu shot is recommended for all pregnant women), and in air, food, and water. But mercury isn't the only pollutant out there. Many other chemicals (such as pesticides and environmental pollutants) may also be found in food and water. The placenta guards the developing baby against much of this exposure, but it isn't a perfect filter. These chemicals may affect more than a fetus's brain development; the most toxic ones (like mercury) can actually damage the very metabolic systems that are supposed to clear toxins out in the first place. Most babies weather this exposure without any trouble, but a small percentage are born with a defective detox mechanism. Some of these babies have inherited a genetically defective detox system from their parents, but some start with a normal system and then experience damage from the chemicals.

Postnatal exposure to toxins. Some exposure to toxins continues after a baby is born. Vaccines used to have a lot of mercury (until 2002), and although that isn't a problem for babies anymore, it is a hotly contested topic in the media, the courts, and the scientific arena. Many parents wonder if their child was affected by vaccine mercury back in the 1990s and early 2000s. Vaccines also have some other chemicals (such as the neurotoxin aluminum and the carcinogen formaldehyde). Research hasn't shown that the amount of chemicals in vaccines poses any risk to babies, but it is an exposure nonetheless. Infant formula has some chemical contaminants, and so does breast milk (though much less, and the benefits of breastfeeding far outweigh any chemicals that might be in there from Mom's diet and body). Nonorganic baby foods have pesticide residue, and some recalls have occurred because of other chemical contaminants. These chemical exposures potentially affect not only the brain development of a young baby but also the immune system, which can increase a baby's susceptibility to infections and allergies.

Antibiotics. I'm not suggesting that antibiotics cause autism. They are very important if a baby needs them. However, antibiotics have the unfortunate effect of killing off the healthy bacteria that live in the gastrointestinal system. These probiotic bacteria play an important role in the immune system, in digestion, and in preventing allergies. A very important branch of the immune system, called the *gut-associated lymphoid tissue* (or GALT), lives in the lining of the intestinal tract. Anything that irritates the intestines will affect the GALT. Killing off the gut's natural probiotics and damaging the GALT can create a susceptibility to digestive, immune, and allergic problems. It can also allow infectious bacteria and yeast to overgrow and thrive in the gut. These germs secrete toxins that further irritate the gut and affect brain function. Most infants receive an antibiotic or three during the first year of life for a variety of reasons (most commonly ear infection, sinus infection, pneumonia, bronchitis, or skin infection). Such treatments are usually well tolerated. But antibiotics can be overused, and the use of too many can cause an infectious and toxic cascade that contributes to autism via intestinal and immune dysfunction.

Food allergies. Food allergies further irritate the gut and immune system. Some babies begin life with exposure to allergic food particles. Proteins from particular foods in a mom's diet can enter the breast milk and irritate baby's intestinal lining. A formula allergy can have an even more profound effect on the gut. Most babies with allergies will show symptoms of colic and intestinal discomfort, and steps will be taken to minimize the allergic exposure by restricting Mom's diet or changing formulas. But this irritation can be one more factor involved in causing damage to the GALT. When a baby begins eating foods directly (which shouldn't happen until six months but often happens at four months), anything he is allergic to will cause even more intestinal damage.

"Leaky gut" syndrome. All of the above intestinal irritants can combine to create a situation called *leaky gut*. The lining of the gut is supposed to be a very effective filter. It thoroughly digests anything that comes in (mainly food) into tiny proteins, fats, and sugars, and keeps all the bad stuff out of the body (by eliminating it in the stools). When the gut lining isn't healthy, two things happen: First, the numerous digestive enzymes that are supposed to be secreted by the gut aren't; and second, the lining of the gut becomes more permeable, or leaky. The result is that proteins aren't completely digested into the tiniest particles possible, so the proteins that are absorbed into the body are larger and more allergenic. In addition, the leaky gut lining lets in more chemicals and toxins (from food and water, as well as those generated by unhealthy bacteria and yeast) than it should. The allergenic proteins adversely stimulate the immune system, and the toxins can irritate the nervous system.

Milk and wheat sensitivity. Another digestive quirk that occurs in some children is the lack of a specific intestinal enzyme called DPP IV, which is responsible for digesting milk and wheat proteins. When DPP IV is absent, the proteins in milk and wheat are digested as larger particles that look very similar to the body's endorphins (natural calming and pain-relieving chemicals). This might not seem like a bad thing, but endorphin mimickers are actually harmful and function like morphine and Vicodin. These suppress brain function, slow down the bowels, and can actually create addiction. They also block pain sensations, which explains why children with autism have very high pain tolerance. The milk- and wheat-derived proteins are called *casomorphine* and *gluteomorphine,* respectively. They can be measured in the urine (just like a normal drug test; see page 114).

There is a second mechanism by which gluten can harm the body. Certain white blood cells have the DPP IV enzyme on their surface, and these will react to gluten in the bloodstream. Unfortunately, these white blood cells may also attack the cells lining the gut because these cells have molecules that are almost identical to gluten molecules. So, an overload of gluten in the bloodstream may trigger an autoimmune reaction against the gut (see the discussion of autoimmune dysfunction on the following page).

Vitamin, mineral, and nutritional deficiency. One result of all of this intestinal dysfunction is that the body can become deficient in various vitamins (especially B and D vitamins), minerals (such as zinc and calcium), and essential amino acids (especially taurine). These and other nutrients are essential for the body's metabolism to run smoothly.

MMR vaccine. Next to mercury, the MMR vaccine has become the most hotly contested topic in autism. The biomedical theory contends that a variety of viruses may play a role in autism by irritating the immune system, which results in inflammation in the gut and the brain (see below). Some of these viruses are contracted naturally. However, the MMR vaccine (given at one year of age) brings three live viruses into the body via an unnatural route. They are injected into the muscle instead of being inhaled or swallowed like most natural viruses. The theory holds that the measles virus may remain living within the body after injection and may be taken up by immune cells that then can carry the virus to the GALT area in the gut as well as into areas of the brain. Other viruses, such as herpes types I and 6 (see pages 104 and 106), can be contracted naturally and can irritate the nervous system.

Inflammation and autoimmune dysfunction. Usually the above factors can be handled by most infants without any ill effects. However, a combination of genetic susceptibility, chemical and allergic exposure, intestinal irritation, germ toxins, and viral infections can add up to two things: inflammation and immune dysfunction. There are three ways the immune system responds:

1. Immune cells envelop and destroy invading germs. That's harmless to everyone (except the germs, that is).

2. The immune system releases inflammatory chemicals into the bloodstream and body tissues to destroy germs. However, these chemicals cause collateral damage: They not only kill germs but also irritate body tissues. This is called *inflammation*. Anything they touch becomes sore and swollen. This wouldn't be bad if it happened occasionally. But the constant inflammation in the gut from all of the above factors, and the resulting

inflammation that can occur elsewhere in the body, especially in the brain, can take its toll.

3. Autoimmune reactions can occur when the immune system mistakes a certain tissue type for a foreign invader. This is the most concerning response. Several studies (see Resources, page 365) have shown that in many children with autism, antibodies generated by their own immune system attack parts of their brain. One study found nine different types of such antibodies.

In essence, the immune system becomes hyperactive and dysfunctional, all because of the cascade of toxic, allergic, and infectious exposures during infancy.

Mitochondrial dysfunction. Alternative researchers believe that mitochondrial problems play a larger roll in autism than mainstream medicine does. Biomedical practitioners believe the mitochondria can be poisoned by heavy metals, such as mercury, lead, and others, and that the resulting dysfunction can rob the body of energy and make a child more susceptible to autism. When combined with inflammation, autoimmune reactions, and oxidative stress (see below), the neurological system becomes overwhelmed.

Oxidative stress. Every cell in the body that is under stress generates byproducts called free radicals. These charged particles literally bounce around in each cell and cause damage to anything they hit. Normally the cells produce *anti*oxidants that continuously neutralize every free radical as it is produced, and any cellular damage that is done is quickly repaired. However, when the body is stressed by all of the above factors, it falls behind in antioxidant production and cells become damaged and dysfunctional. This is a common finding in many chronic diseases, not just autism.

The result of these combined events during the first year and into the second year of life is an inflamed central nervous system and, in many cases, gastrointestinal system. This wouldn't be so bad if the nervous system were already fully developed. But during infancy and toddlerhood it's not. Brain cells are growing and forming connections. Neural pathways that determine every aspect of behavior and ability are being formed. As a result of these potential problems, some of these pathways don't form completely or correctly. The result in early infancy, during the second year of life, or in some cases later on, is autism.

The Biochemistry of the Biomedical Theory

Researchers have been studying the biochemical side of autism for many years. Biochemistry is basically the study of how chemical processes work in the body and what effect they have on body functions. Understanding the biochemical abnormalities in autism has yielded some very useful therapies. While a detailed understanding of this information isn't necessary, I do want to provide you with a simplified explanation of what researchers believe are the basic biochemical defects in autism. This will help you understand some of the treatments I discuss later.

The biomedical theory revolves around the amino acid methionine. The body manufactures many amino acids, but some, like methionine, must be consumed in the diet because the body can't make them from scratch. In the cells, methionine is broken down into methyl molecules and thiols. (I probably just lost half of you who are reading this. You don't really need to understand it yet. It will all come together at the end.)

Methyl molecules are a combination of a carbon atom and three hydrogen atoms. Methyl groups are used to turn on or turn off various cellular functions, such as protein production, creating neurochemicals, reading DNA, repairing damaged cell components, and producing energy for the body. The process by which methyl performs these functions is called *methylation* (remember this word—it's the only important one so far!).

Thiols are sulfur compounds whose primary role is to clean any chemicals and toxins out of the body. Most thiols are converted into a molecule called *glutathione*. Glutathione performs two functions: It detoxifies our cells of any chemicals, and it neutralizes free radicals that are naturally generated by our cells (more on that later). Thiols also hold proteins together and help them function. Thiols that aren't used by the cell can be recycled back into methionine. This recycling requires a methyl group and an enzyme called *methionine synthase* to bind methyl back onto the thiol, thus producing methionine again.

What does all this biochemistry have to do with autism? In most children with autism, methionine synthase isn't working correctly (we don't yet know why, we just know that's the case). The result is that any surplus of thiols can't be recycled back into methionine. Therefore, no reserve supply of methionine is maintained. So if the body needs some extra methyl groups to increase its methylation functions (such as during stress, illness, or any situation in which the body requires more energy), it can't get them from any excess methionine. It would have to get new methyl groups from new methionine in the diet. But that's too slow. The bottom line is that cells need an instant source of methyl groups to function properly. With methinonine synthase broken, no such source exists.

Meanwhile, glutathione that is produced from thiols is performing its usual antioxidant and detoxifying functions. However, when glutathione runs low, where does the cell turn to make more? Methionine. But much of the methionine is being used up by the normal methylation processes in the cell and can't be diverted into glutathione. So, the cells can't make fresh glutathione and they lose their ability to detoxify the body.

A final consequence of this defect in methylation metabolism is that the cells of the body enter a state of oxidative stress. Every cell generates molecules called free radicals as a normal byproduct of cellular metabolism. Free radicals damage proteins and

DNA in each cell. Glutathione instantly deactivates these free radicals before they cause damage, but if any do manage to damage something in the cell, methyl groups will repair it. Well, if there isn't enough glutathione or methyl, these free radicals cause more damage and the cells become dysfunctional. In autism, this dysfunction is apparent mainly within the nervous system.

In a nutshell, because methionine synthase doesn't work to maintain a continuous supply of methionine, the two branches of the methionine biochemical pathway work against each other (instead of supporting and balancing each other), and both sides suffer. The result? Cellular damage and dysfunction. The body can't detoxify, can't repair itself, can't produce enough energy, can't turn genes on and off effectively, and can't produce proper proteins for normal bodily functions. One of the goals of biomedical treatment that you will read about is to improve the body's methylation metabolism and reduce oxidative stress so the whole body can function better.

Understanding the biochemistry of disease is important in almost any illness, and many brilliant researchers have devoted their lives to understanding the biochemistry of autism. I gave you a one-page overview, but if you want to read more, check out *Autism: Effective Biomedical Treatments,* by Pangborn and Baker (see Resources, page 358). It provides a more thorough explanation understandable to the average layperson. If you are a science-minded parent and you want an extremely scientific explanation, Dr. Jill James's article "Oxidative Stress and the Metabolic Pathology of Autism" in Zimmerman's book (see Resources, page 358), complete with about 150 references to scientific studies, is for you.

I have only scratched the surface in explaining the biomedical causes of autism. You will learn much more about each of these causes in future chapters as I explain how to test for and then treat each cause.

Problems and Inconsistencies in the Biomedical Theory of Causative Factors

The biomedical theory is quite a large bite to digest. Many aspects have good research to back them up, but some don't. In the Resources, starting on page 374, I provide you with a list of the scientific studies that have been done to support this theory. But there are some holes in the theory and some aspects that don't fit with all types of autism.

Not all children with autism have been vaccinated. Among the five hundred patients I have worked with so far, six have never had any vaccines. There are also several who had some vaccines but didn't have the MMR. Now, this doesn't mean that vaccine chemicals or the MMR vaccine don't play a role in autism, but to my mind it does show that there is far more involved in autism than just vaccines. As I will discuss in chapter 16, we need to do more research to learn whether vaccines play a role in autism, figure out exactly what that role might be, and, most important, determine which infants are susceptible to being adversely affected by vaccines.

Not all children with autism regress after the MMR vaccine. There are many differences in the patterns and timing of the onset in autism. Some kids show regression in the weeks after the MMR vaccine, but many kids don't. Some infants develop signs in the early months and don't get worse after the MMR. If the MMR vaccine plays a role in autism, it may be only in a subset of children.

Some infants show early signs of autism *before* exposure to most of the biomedical factors, such as allergic foods, antibiotics, and vaccines. Although this is true, it doesn't take away from the validity of the biomedical theory. It speaks more to autism as a spectrum disorder and to the fact that there are many varied causes and patterns of onset. Researchers suspect that an infant who develops early-onset autism may have more significant genetic abnormalities or more pre-natal toxic exposure than infants with later-onset autism.

Not all children with autism have biochemical problems with methylation. Some children have normally functioning cellular metabolism, and some are even what we call *overmethylated:* Their methylation metabolism is working too well. It isn't clear why this occurs, but it's another demonstration of how many factors are involved in autism and how problems can vary greatly from one child to the next.

Some children with autism show no symptoms of intestinal problems. In keeping with the biomedical theory, one would expect that any child so affected would have chronic diarrhea, constipation, or some evidence of intestinal disease. Many children with autism do, but some don't. I have met kids with autism who have, and have always had, perfectly healthy bowels. In my opinion this fact also doesn't take away from the theory. Again, it simply speaks to the varied nature of autism and to the fact that there may be many different causes that affect children differently. In my experience, children with intestinal problems respond more quickly and dramatically to the diet changes and some of the treatments, but even children with normal bowels can benefit.

Some children with autism have never had antibiotics. Most kids with autism have had more than their fair share of antibiotics. Many have had some right before or during the regressive months. But, some of the children I've seen began regressing after age one without ever having had any antibiotics. And some young infants develop autism early on, before they've taken any antibiotics, and when they do get antibiotics for an illness, they don't seem to suffer any ill effects at all. Antibiotics are very important in many situations, but overuse may play a role in autism in some children. However, I don't think that antibiotics are a major cause or contributor to the autism epidemic. They may affect some children more than others, and it's important to limit their use in all children as best as you can.

Some children don't respond to the treatments. One would think that if the biomedical theory were correct, almost every child would respond very well to its treatments. But not every child responds to every treatment. Some don't respond at all to any measures. But the majority of autistic children whom I have known have shown good improvements, and enough children completely or almost completely recover that it's worth trying. Right now, there are no other medical treatments. So any treatment that is going to help some kids recover is much better than nothing.

This is a very different mind-set from the general medical community's when it come to treating disease. Most treatments aren't adopted by mainstream medicine unless they help or cure most patients. Medications aren't approved by the FDA unless they work for most people. Because biomedical treatments lead to near or full recovery in only some children, that's not good enough for most doctors. Never mind that this approach seems to lead to significant improvement in most children. Mainstream doctors will wait until something is discovered that will cure almost everyone.

Moving Forward into Biomedical Treatments

Now that I've told you about these alternative theories, you may be very eager to jump right in. However, there are a few things to do first. In the next chapter, I will discuss testing for mainstream and biomedical causes of autism. After that, there are some critical behavioral treatments you'll need to begin with your child right away. There's a lot to do besides simply jumping into the biomedical treatments, so don't skip ahead. Testing and treatment, both biomedical and behavioral, is a long road, with many avenues to follow simultaneously. I'll guide you through them all.

5

Testing to Evaluate All Possible Causes

You are probably feeling a little dizzy right now after reading about all the possible causes of autism. Various descriptions of medical symptoms and scenarios might sound just like your child, and you'd like to jump right into testing to identify any medical problems that can be treated. Or perhaps your child does not have many of the problems I discussed in the previous chapter and you aren't sure what, if any, medical testing is appropriate. In this chapter I will describe all the testing that is available and offer guidance on how to select, with your doctor's help, which tests to have done.

On page 355 of the Resources, I list the names of labs that provide specialized blood, hair, urine, and stool tests for autism.

COMMON BLOOD TESTS

The following three blood tests are what a pediatrician or neurologist will typically order for every child with autism (in addition to genetic and more complex metabolic/mitochondrial testing; see pages 95 and 98).

Complete blood count. A CBC takes a look at the various types of blood cells. Abnormal findings that may relate to autism could reveal a low white blood cell count (an indicator of a low-functioning immune system), a low red blood cell count (anemia), low iron levels (iron deficiency), and high platelets (cells in the blood that help with blood clotting; if the platelets are high, this may indicate that an inflammatory process is going on in the body).

Complete metabolic panel. A CMP takes a look at various levels of electrolytes, minerals, and proteins that can indicate a variety of problems, such as liver or kidney disease, malnutrition, dehydration, and blood sugar problems. Although the results are almost always normal, this routine test is a good precaution and provides a baseline. It can then be done every year to make sure the body is handling any long-term prescription treatments for autism.

Thyroid hormone levels. This test measures the blood level of thyroid hormone (called *free T4*) produced by the thyroid gland in the neck as well as the thyroid-stimulating hormone (called *TSH*) that is produced by the brain to tell the thyroid gland how much T4 to make. Low thyroid hormone levels can cause the body and brain to slow down. Symptoms include intellectual or motor delay, low muscle strength and tone, dry skin, cooler body temperature, constipation, and low heart rate. Part of the biomedical theory of autism is that the immune system is attacking parts of the body (see pages 75–76). One of the glands that might be affected is the thyroid. Low thyroid hormone function is indicated if T4 is low (which is extremely rare) or TSH is high. This indicates that the gland isn't working well, so the brain has to pump out more TSH in order to stimulate the gland to produce enough T4. It is suspected that the T4 produced by a dysfunctional thyroid gland may not be as active, and the child can suffer from low thyroid symptoms despite normal T4 and TSH levels. Technically the normal range of TSH is between 0.5 and 5. Doctors may see a TSH of 3 or 4, consider it normal, and be under the false impression that a child's thyroid gland is working just fine. In the biomedical world, we worry that a TSH of 3 or higher indicates that the gland may be dysfunctional, since most kids require only a TSH level of 1 or 2 for normal function. So a biomedical doctor may treat a child for thyroid dysfunction in situations where a regular doctor would not. See page 295 for treatment options.

A related blood test looks for antithyroid antibodies, which confirm an autoimmune response against the gland. If a child's initial thyroid tests are significantly abnormal, antithyroid antibodies should be checked (this doesn't change the treatment, but the autoimmune information is good to know).

GENETIC TESTING

As I've discussed, there are various known genetic disorders that can cause symptoms of autism. Most children with autism, however, have normal genetic testing (at least based on today's available testing methods). And that's a good thing, because genetic defects aren't treatable. So, why should you do genetic testing if it won't offer any treatment ideas? There are several reasons. First, having a solid diagnostic cause of the autism can bring some comfort and closure to the ever-present question of why. Second, some genetic problems can be carried by other family members (such as the parents or siblings) and passed down to future children, so it's reassuring to make sure such a genetic risk doesn't exist, and to know about it if it does exist. Third, it adds to the ever-increasing pool of knowledge that neurologists and geneticists are gathering to better understand autism. Here are the genetic tests currently available.

Fragile X test. This blood test examines the chromosomes to see if a child has a repeating pattern of what are called the *CGG nucleotides* in the FMR1 gene. We all have a small number of CGG repeats, but if a child has too many, then that child has a Fragile X chromosome.

Karyotype with high-resolution chromosome analysis. This blood test takes a thorough look at all the chromosomes for any major defects. Although this test virtually always comes back normal, it can miss some subtle genetic defects. More advanced testing techniques are described below.

FISH (Fluorescent In Situ Hybridization) chromosome testing. This blood analysis looks specifically for several known deletions in various genes (meaning part of a chromosome is missing) instead of taking an overall look at every aspect of all the chromosomes. The most common deletions occur on chromosome 15

RECOMMENDED GENETIC TESTING IN AUTISM

Drs. Pickler and Elias, pediatric and genetic specialists, provided an excellent review of genetic testing for children with autism in *Pediatric Annals* (see Resources, page 361). All children with autism should have:

- Testing for Fragile X
- CGH microarray (or high-resolution karyotyping)

Select children with certain characteristics should have:

- Genetic testing for tuberous sclerosis or neurofibromatosis if they have "café-au-lait" or "ash-leaf" spots (see page 66) (for example, in Angelman syndrome, page 66) and are known to cause developmental delay and learning challenges.

CGH microarray. This Comparative Genomic Hybridization test is a new test that provides a more detailed look at all the genes and can pick up minor abnormalities that would be missed on karyotyping or FISH testing. This may become the new gold standard and replace karyotyping.

Genomics testing. Now we are going to completely shift gears into the biomedical world and take a look at a different way to test for genetic anomalies. Instead of looking for major physical defects or deletions in chromosomes, genomics looks for minor problems or dysfunctions in numerous genes that play a role in the overall health of the body. Testing involves a mouth swab sample of cells from the inner cheek. The genes that can be evaluated include those that regulate blood clotting, blood vessel health, antioxidant

- Specific genetic testing for the MECP2 mutation for Rett syndrome in girls with regressive autism, especially those displaying hand-wringing gestures and having seizures (see page 65)
- 7-dehydrocholesterol and total cholesterol blood levels to evaluate for Smith-Lemli-Opitz syndrome in kids with fused second and third toes (see page 66)
- Genetic testing for the PTEN mutation to rule out Bannayan-Riley-Ruvalcaba syndrome in children with very large heads (see page 66)
- FISH genetic testing for Angelman syndrome in kids with a frequent happy facial expression and unusual bouts of laughter, seizures, and tight muscles (see page 66)

production, methylation metabolism, cardiac health, and susceptibility to strokes and cancer. Because research has shown that many
children with autism have defects in their genes that regulate
methylation and antioxidant production, many parents are eager
to find out if their child has one of these genetic anomalies.

However, in my experience, knowing this information does
not change treatment decisions. Most of the reports that come
back on these kids show similar defects, and the treatment recommendations mirror what is in the biomedical protocol anyway.
Although it is interesting to note how these genetic anomalies are
increasing in our population, in my opinion it isn't necessary to
assess every child's genomics (and it isn't cheap). But parents can
discuss this option with their doctor.

MITOCHONDRIAL AND METABOLIC TESTING

As discussed in chapter 4, a minority of children with autism
may have a mitochondrial disorder. An even higher percentage of children may have dysfunctional mitochondria, but that
doesn't really show up on testing. A child with a suspected mitochondrial disorder (autism with low muscle tone and strength,
feeding problems, poor weight gain, and motor developmental
delay) will usually be tested by the neurologist.

Metabolic disorders are similar to mitochondrial disorders.
They are about as confusing, cause similar symptoms, and are
just as rare. There are several metabolic disorders in which a single enzyme or cellular chemical process isn't working correctly in
the body. This results in various other chemicals or acids building up to high levels within the body. These acids then interfere
with cellular function, and the whole body is affected, especially
the nervous system. All newborns are screened with a blood test
to look for metabolic disorders. This test is very accurate and
catches almost all cases at birth.

The tests for mitochondrial and metabolic disorders in a child with autism are the same. They can be ordered by any doctor, but it takes a neurologist or metabolic/genetic doctor to interpret these tests.

Urine organic acid panel. This test measures the levels of various acids in the urine. Very high or low levels of certain acids can indicate a mitochondrial or metabolic disorder. Another type of urine organic acid test is used by biomedical practitioners to look for yeast and bacterial infections. That is a very different test from the one discussed here (see page 119).

Plasma (blood) amino acid panel. These acids are the building blocks of proteins, and various abnormalities may show up that indicate a possible metabolic or mitochondrial disorder.

Lactate and pyruvate blood levels. These two acids are usually abnormal in children with metabolic and mitochondrial disorders and are worth testing in addition to the above panels.

Carnitine blood profile. This is a protein that helps with muscle growth and strength. In mitochondrial disorders it is often low. A low result doesn't necessarily mean that a child has an actual disorder, but it can indicate some dysfunction. If it's low, a child can take a carnitine supplement (see page 298).

Ammonia level. This compound builds up in the bloodstream from certain metabolic and mitochondrial abnormalities. The sample must be put immediately on ice for it to be accurate.

Creatinine kinase. This enzyme elevates within the bloodstream in metabolic and mitochondrial disorders.

The major drawback to these tests is that the results don't show a definite positive or negative result. A specialist has to look at the entire pattern of all the acids, and the tests aren't easy to interpret. A positive result will come back as something like "These results are consistent with a possible metabolic (or mitochondrial) disorder. . . . Clinical correlation is advised" (meaning, Examine the patient's entire case in order to decide). A negative or normal result will read, "These results show a normal pattern." Depending on the type of positive result, a more specific test may need to be done to make an exact diagnosis. This level of evaluation should be done by a pediatric metabolic/genetic specialist.

TESTING FOR HEAVY METAL EXPOSURE

While most chemicals (pesticides and artificial food additives, for example) can't be measured in our bodies, the most toxic forms of environmental exposure—heavy metals—can. Mercury and lead are probably the two most serious ones, and there are several others, such as arsenic, aluminum, and uranium, that our kids are often exposed to. Many testing methods are available to evaluate your child's metal exposure. However, in my opinion and experience, none of these tests are very accurate. The challenge is that metals hide in body tissues (such as fat), various organs, and the brain. And you can't take samples of these areas to measure metal levels. Here are the various bodily samples we *can* test, along with the pros and cons of each method.

Blood test for metals. A doctor can order lead, mercury, and various other metal levels. However, a blood test will find metals only if exposure was very recent (the past few days) or if the body levels are so high that the metals have leaked back into the bloodstream. Very few kids have levels that high. Most of the time these tests come back normal. I do believe that measuring a lead level is prudent, however, since this is probably the most common environmental metal. Some labs offer a test called a red blood cell element profile, which measures the levels of various toxic metals in the blood as well as healthy minerals. In my experience, this type of test rarely shows any significantly high levels of toxic metals. I generally don't order it.

Hair test for metals. This is perhaps the most popular test, since it can be obtained through various labs without a doctor's order. One of the ways the body eliminates toxic metals is by excreting them through the hair follicles. This test measures toxic metal levels in the hair.

Many parents have the misconception that a hair test should be done to see if a child has been exposed to toxic metals. That's not the case. All children are exposed. We don't need a test to tell us that. The primary use for this test is to assess a child's ability to detoxify those metals.

Researchers tested samples of baby hair from children who were later diagnosed with autism (hair that had been saved by the parents as a keepsake). They also tested the infant hair of neurotypical siblings. They found very low levels of mercury and other toxic metals in the hair samples of the children who were later diagnosed with autism, and high levels in the hair of neurotypical kids. This means that during infancy, the babies who eventually developed autism weren't excreting metals into their hair, because they had defective detoxification mechanisms. The metals were staying within their bodies instead of coming out in the hair.

I don't typically recommend this test because it doesn't change my treatment recommendations. The biomedical protocol will improve the body's own detox ability, and knowing the hair results doesn't affect what a child should or shouldn't do with the protocol.

Another way doctors use hair testing is to look at the levels of healthy minerals (a standard hair metal test measures toxic metals as well as healthy minerals). Some doctors believe that the pattern of various minerals in the hair (such as calcium and magnesium) can indicate certain types of heavy metal poisoning.

This type of interpretation is very complicated and hasn't been verified by any mainstream laboratory. I generally don't bother with this aspect of the test.

Urine and stool panels for various toxic metals. These tests are analogous to the tests of hair samples. However, they do have a more clear-cut application. We know the body eliminates metals through the urine and stool during detoxification treatments. So, a parent could do these tests right before a treatment begins and then periodically retest to see if metals are coming out of the body during treatment (hair is not as reliable in this respect). I do not order these tests at the beginning of my evaluations with kids. I save them for when, or if, we do detoxification treatments. See chapter 12 for more on these treatments.

Urine porphyrin or kryptopyrrole levels. These two compounds are thought by some researchers to be generated by our body's metabolism when heavy metal exposure occurs. If this is true, urine levels can be measured as a possible indicator of past metal exposure. However, it isn't clear whether these compounds truly correlate with metal exposure. Urine kryptopyrroles have been studied for many years now, and urine porphyrins more recently. If levels are very high, this may encourage a parent to be more proactive with her child's detoxification treatments. But if the results are fairly normal, it doesn't necessarily mean the child can't benefit from detoxification. I view these tests as optional but possibly useful ways to assess the need for heavy metal detoxification treatments. I usually don't run them right away, though. I wait until the child is further along in the biomedical approach and the parents are considering detox treatments.

Metallothionein (MT) blood profile. This protein/zinc compound moves around in our bloodstream and binds to heavy metals such as mercury to help the body detoxify. Some labs can measure MT levels to make sure the body's MT system is working well. Because the treatment for low MT levels is very complicated and done by only a small number of alternative physicians, I don't advise parents to have this test done except under the guidance of such a physician.

Every new parent I see is very eager to find out if her child has been exposed to heavy metals. Yet because there is no reliable or accurate way to assess this, I usually don't do any of these tests as part of my initial evaluation. I wait until a child has received various other treatments first and see how the child responds. Metal detoxification (called *chelation*) is the most complicated and controversial part of the biomedical approach. There are many other steps to take first. I discuss chelation in more detail in chapter 12.

TESTING THE METHYLATION SYSTEM

As described in chapter 4, many children with autism have a dysfunctional methylation system. There are different ways to test this, but there are no FDA-approved testing methods yet (since methylation problems as a factor in autism is a fairly new, and alternative, idea). I generally like to try kids on methylation treatments (see page 255) without testing first. If they respond well, then I know I made the right choice. Here are the available ways you can have your child's methylation capabilities tested.

MTHFR gene. A genetic test can determine if one of the genes that controls methylation (the MTHFR gene) is normal or mutated. LabCorp (a regular lab, so it should be covered by insurance) offers this test, called a Methylenetetrahydrofolate Reductase Thermolabile Variant DNA Analysis. You can also do a whole genomics panel that looks at a variety of other gene defects along with MTHFR (see page 97). However, I usually don't bother with these tests. Methylation treatments are still worth trying even if the MTHFR gene is normal because there could be other gene defects affecting methylation that we can't test for.

Glutathione blood level. If you ask your pediatrician or family doctor for this test, he or she will probably say, "Gluta-what?" A low glutathione level in the blood generally means that the cells aren't producing enough because methylation isn't working properly (see page 87). Checking a glutathione blood level can help parents and a doctor decide if temporary supplementation with glutathione is needed. A high–normal level may indicate that methylation is working fairly well in a child (although I still try methylation treatments on such children anyway).

Cysteine and sulfate blood levels. Cysteine (an amino acid) and sulfate (a natural chemical compound) are often low in a child with methylation problems. I generally don't order these tests, as I find the glutathione testing more useful.

TESTING FOR INFECTIOUS DISEASES

As discussed on page 85, one biomedical theory about autism is that some viruses get into the body and live within the nervous system. These don't cause an active infection, but they may cause minor irritation or dysfunction. It is also theorized that some viruses or bacteria can trigger an autoimmune response that causes the body's own immune system to attack part of the brain and other body organs. Here is a list of the tests used to detect the viruses and bacteria that are being studied by the alternative community. Some of these viruses and bacteria are treatable, some are not.

Herpes virus type I. This common virus causes canker sores in the mouth. Almost every person contracts this virus at some point in his life. It can be transmitted through saliva anytime there is an active sore. The first time a person is exposed, he may have numerous painful sores, fever, and swollen gums for several days. This is called *herpes gingivostomatitis*. The herpes virus migrates up the nerves of the mouth and face and finds a nice place to rest within the nerves. It lies dormant for months or years until something (like stress or injury to the mouth) lures it back down to the mouth to create another sore (usually just one this time). Once you catch the oral herpes virus, you have it forever. For most people, living with this virus is harmless and only mildly irritating. However, herpes type I can also cause a serious brain infection if a baby contracts it during the newborn period. Such newborn infections are so severe that the baby requires hospitalization and treatment.

In the biomedical world, it is suspected that in some cases the herpes virus may move farther along up the facial nerves and reside closer to, or within, the central nervous system (the brain) and cause minor irritation and dysfunction. During the 1990s a few doctors tried treating kids with anti-herpes medication and found that some showed significant improvement in various autistic symptoms. This protocol has become more popular since then. I have had a couple of patients with autism whose parents described an episode of herpes gingivostomatitis within a few weeks of the beginning of regression into autism.

There is no test to detect the herpes virus directly. What we can test is the body's immune response to the virus; this test is called a Herpes Virus Type I IgG and IgM antibody titer. A positive IgG result indicates past infection. The higher the result, the more significant the possible impact on autism. Positive IgM means a more recent or active infection, and if this occurs without any visible or recent canker sores, it may be an even stronger indication that the herpes is more active within the central nervous system.

On page 271 I will go into more detail on the treatment of herpes and other viruses.

Herpes virus type II. This virus is almost identical to type I, but it causes herpes sores only in the genital area. This virus is therefore extremely rare in children with autism. If a mom has any active genital sores while giving birth, she can pass the virus to her baby. This can cause a very serious brain infection that often results in neurological dysfunction.

I have had a few cases of young children with autism who tested positive for type II. This doesn't mean the child was sexually abused by someone with herpes. It is possible for a parent with genital herpes to transmit the virus when sores are active simply through normal intimate contact with the child.

The titer testing for type II is the same as for type I, and the treatment options are the same.

Human herpes virus type 6. HHV 6 is another common virus in the herpes family. It causes an illness called *roseola* among infants and toddlers, which manifests as three days of high fever and then a rash on the upper back, chest, and head the day after the fever leaves. The rash may spread out to the arms and legs and last a few days. Almost every child catches this illness. Biomedical doctors postulate that this virus might dwell in the nervous system after the infection is over, just as the other herpes viruses do, and irritate the brain. No one has ever proven this theory, but there are two factors that suggest that HHV 6 might be a contributor to autism. First, roseola is the number one cause of febrile seizures. It is generally assumed that the high rate of seizures with this viral illness is due to the high fever. But it is possible that the virus itself may trigger seizures. Another clue is that some children with positive HHV 6 blood test results who are treated with antiviral medications show some improvements, just as with herpes type I.

The test for HHV 6 is a blood titer test (similar to the tests for herpes types I and II). The results will either be negative, borderline positive, or somewhere between low and very highly positive. Of course, we would expect any child who had roseola in the past to test positive for the virus, so is this test even useful? Doctors theorize that a very high titer years after infection may indicate an ongoing effect from HHV 6. This is only a theory, with no proven scientific validity yet. But treating HHV 6 is just another step in the process of pursuing all possible treatments.

Measles virus. I am going to step even farther outside the world of mainstream medicine for a paragraph or two to discuss the measles virus. As of the writing of this book, virtually all scientific research has shown that there is no connection between measles virus and autism. Two research studies showed a possible connection, but they have been discredited and disregarded by the mainstream medical community. So why am I even discussing it?

Some biomedical doctors still suspect that the live measles virus in the MMR vaccine may remain alive in the body after injection and cause a chronic low-grade infection in the gut or brain (see page 85). The only way to detect measles in the brain is to collect spinal fluid via a spinal tap. Measles virus can be found in the intestines by doing a colonoscopy and biopsy. Both of these procedures are invasive and are being done only in research settings by a small number of doctors who are studying this theory. Most children with autism wouldn't have access to this type of evaluation, and some doctors would even argue that such testing is unnecessary.

There is a blood titer test for measles (IgG and IgM) that can be done to measure the child's immune response to the virus. IgG indicates vaccine-induced immunity (or a real measles infection in the past). IgM indicates a recent infection with real measles. We would expect any child who had the MMR vaccine to have a positive IgG titer for measles, but alternative doctors suspect that having a higher-than-expected IgG titer, or a positive IgM, could indicate persistent measles infection from the live virus vaccine. See page 373 for studies that examine this theory.

I have measured measles titers in many of my patients with autism, with a wide range of results. Interestingly, I have found several children with positive IgM titers with no known history of having had a real measles infection. This may be due to lab error, or it may mean that those few children had an abnormal immune response to the MMR vaccine.

On page 270, I discuss the available treatments for measles. You don't have to do testing first; you can go straight to treatment, especially if your child noticeably regressed right after receiving the vaccine.

Strep bacteria. Several years ago a new psychiatric disorder was discovered called *PANDAS* (Pediatric Autoimmune Neuropsychiatric Disorders Associated with Streptococcal Infections; see Resources, page 366). This discovery initially had nothing to do with autism. Several cases were found of children who developed sudden onset of neurological symptoms (such as tics) and psychiatric symptoms (such as Obsessive-Compulsive Disorder) after catching strep throat or a strep skin infection. Testing revealed that these kids had higher than expected levels of antibodies against strep bacteria long after infection. That isn't so surprising. But high levels of antibodies against a certain brain enzyme called DNase B were also found. Mainstream doctors believe that as the immune system attacks the strep bacteria, it also attacks certain parts of the brain that look molecularly similar. This happens with a variety of other autoimmune disorders, so the idea isn't that far-fetched.

Because autism is a neuropsychiatric disorder, it's possible that a child's autism could, at least in part, be due to this autoimmune reaction. Three tests can be done to look for a PANDAS reaction. An ASO (anti-streptolysin-O) antibody titer measures the body's immune response to strep. An anti-DNase B antibody titer measures the degree to which the immune system is attacking the brain. A strep throat culture will show if a child is carrying the bacteria in the throat. Because PANDAS is a new disorder, doctors don't quite know yet what to do for it, and we aren't sure which type of pediatric specialty should be in charge of evaluation and treatment.

If either of the antibody tests is positive, a biomedical practitioner will probably offer some treatment options, such as antibiotics (along with antifungal meds) or intravenous immune globulins (IVIG; see page 280). Parents should also consult with a pediatric specialist familiar with PANDAS. This could be a pediatric infectious disease specialist, a rheumatologist, a neurologist, or a psychiatrist.

Other viruses and infections. Biomedical doctors are researching other infectious agents to look for a connection to autism. These include Epstein-Barr virus (EBV, which causes mononucleosis and chronic fatigue syndrome), Cytomegalovirus (CMV, a virus that hasn't yet been linked to any particular disorder), Lyme disease (transmitted by deer ticks), and others. An association between these and autism has not yet become common thinking among doctors. Lyme disease is being explored by some, and more research may come out that builds on this theory. Blood titer testing can be done for any of these diseases. Anyone living in Lyme disease country should be tested (see page 289).

TESTING FOR INFLAMMATION

As you read in the previous chapter, inflammatory problems may be a factor in autism. There are several blood tests that can measure inflammation. These tests can't, however, tell us which specific part of the body is inflamed.

ESR. An erythrocyte sedimentation rate (also called a sed rate or a Westergren ESR) measures (in simple terms) the time it takes for red blood cells to settle to the bottom of a test tube. Inflammatory substances in the bloodstream will cause this process to take longer. The result is measured in seconds. Ten seconds or less is normal. Anything higher than 15 is very significant.

CRP. C-reactive protein is a molecule that appears in the bloodstream during inflammation. A normal result is 2 or less. Any child with a CRP higher than 2 has some inflammation.

High platelets on CBC. As described on page 94, a high level of this blood cell type may be an indication of inflammation.

Urine neopterin and biopterin. A lab in France (Laboratoire Philippe Auguste; see Resources, page 354) can measure the urine levels of these two compounds. According to researchers at this lab, high levels may be an indication of inflammation. This is not an accepted way to test for inflammation yet, but it may become more widely used if the FDA or other American institutions confirm its validity. I wouldn't recommend this test unless your child is under the care of a physician who is considering advanced anti-inflammatory treatments, which I discuss on page 288.

Myelin basic protein (MBP) blood antibodies. This blood test is often done to evaluate kids or adults with severe neurological problems. It measures the body's own antibodies that are attacking the myelin within the brain (the coating that covers the brain and all nerves in the body). One theory is that when the body's immune system reacts to the measles virus in the MMR vaccine, it confuses the myelin with the measles (the two share similar molecules) and attacks the myelin. This causes inflammation and dysfunction within the brain. These MBP antibodies can be tested by any mainstream lab. A positive result sometimes prompts parents to seek advanced treatments, like IVIG (see page 280), which calms down the autoimmune reaction against the brain. This test almost always comes back normal. Many of the biomedical treatments will help treat inflammation anyway, so I usually don't order this test.

FOOD AND ENVIRONMENTAL ALLERGY TESTING

Part of the biomedical theory is that anything that irritates the gut or the immune system may make autism worse. In chapter 9, I describe in detail how food allergies affect autism. It's important to identify all allergic triggers in any child with autism so that they can be avoided. In this section I will explain how to approach allergy testing in a cost-effective, accurate, and complete way. There are four types of tests that can be done to assess your child's food allergies.

IgE blood testing. Immunoglobulin E is the type of antibody that reacts to a food (or any allergen) during an allergic reaction. When an allergic food is eaten, IgE antibodies release histamine, the chemical that causes the classic symptoms of allergy: skin rashes such as eczema or hives, runny nose, wheezing, itching, or diarrhea. IgE antibody levels can be checked at almost any medical lab through a blood test called an IgE RAST food panel. This test measures allergy to the twelve most commonly allergic foods. Any child with obvious allergy symptoms should have IgE food testing.

IgE skin testing. Another way to identify specific allergens is to inject a tiny amount of each substance into the skin and watch for a reaction. This type of testing is done by an allergist (not a general pediatrician). It is generally thought to be more accurate than blood IgE testing.

IgG blood antibody testing. IgG blood antibodies are very different from IgE. IgG is the type of antibody that the immune system primarily uses to fight infection. A delayed or chronic response to allergies can also produce IgG. IgG levels for more than one hundred foods can be measured through a test called an IgG food antibody panel (available only through blood testing, not skin testing), which can be ordered from some specialty labs.

For each food tested, the results will show either no IgG antibodies or a low, moderate, or high level of antibodies. We know that having high IgE antibodies to a certain food is a definite indication of food allergy. But we aren't sure what the significance of an IgG food reaction is or what effect it may have on the body. Alternatively minded doctors believe that when the immune system has to work to generate IgG antibodies to various foods, it becomes overstimulated and revved up. A hyperactive and dysfunctional immune system can then turn against a person's own body and harm various organs, including the brain (see page 85). Symptoms of IgG food allergies are therefore very different from the symptoms of IgE allergies. IgG food allergies are thought to cause behavioral reactions such as hyperactivity, tantrums, and aggression, or affect intellectual functioning and create developmental and learning delays. Many doctors consider this theory a bit of a stretch, but I have seen many patients show behavioral and developmental improvement when they stop eating IgG-sensitive foods. On page 187, I will go into further detail about how to interpret and act on your child's IgG food allergy results.

Specific gluten allergy blood testing. Because allergy to gluten (the protein in wheat, oat, barley, and rye) has long been recognized as a medical condition, several blood tests have been developed to measure a child's sensitivity. Celiac disease is a disorder in which the gluten allergy is so severe that it causes chronic diarrhea, abdominal pain, growth problems, and sometimes neurological symptoms. Children with celiac disease need to stay away from gluten for their whole lives. Most children with autism are allergic to gluten but don't have actual celiac disease. Many can resume eating gluten once the gut is healed.

Here are the blood tests that check for gluten allergy or can point to celiac disease. These can be done by any regular lab:

- *Gliadin IgG and IgA antibodies.* This is the main way to test for gluten allergy. IgA antibodies are those generated by the intestines in celiac disease. If IgG is positive (meaning allergy) but IgA is normal, then celiac disease is unlikely.

- *Endomyseal antibodies.* This older test has been replaced by the next one (transglutaminase), but I include it here because some doctors still like to use it. A positive result usually indicates celiac disease. Those with simple gluten allergy will have a normal test result.

- *Transglutaminase antibodies.* This new test measures antibodies against an enzyme that is important in gluten digestion. A positive result indicates celiac disease. Virtually all kids with simple allergy will have a negative result.

- *Reticulin antibodies.* This test is sometimes included as part of a celiac testing panel (in which all tests are performed), but it is not as accurate as the other tests. It isn't commonly used anymore.

- *Genetic testing for celiac disease.* Most people with celiac disease carry a gene defect called DQ2 or DQ8, which can be tested for by a blood test called an HLA-DQ celiac disease genetic test. A positive result may mean a person is at risk for developing celiac disease (but this isn't definitive). A negative result means with virtual certainty that a person does not have celiac disease.

However, such a person can still have some sensitivity to gluten. I don't consider this test very useful because the diagnosis of celiac disease is really based on the above antibody testing, and this test doesn't help determine simple gluten allergy.

A child with autism who eats gluten and has chronic diarrhea, recurrent abdominal pain, or bloating should have the whole panel of tests done (minus genetic testing, unless desired), especially if he is shorter and slimmer than normal (if he has what doctors call *failure to thrive*). A child who doesn't have chronic intestinal problems needs only the gliadin antibody tests (see above) to check for gluten allergy.

If your child is already on a gluten-free diet, you shouldn't bother with this test, especially if the diet is helping. Also, a child who has improved on the diet should not go off it just for the sake of testing. If you are not sure if the diet is helping your child, try introducing gluten for a couple months and then have your child tested. After a child has been on biomedical treatments and the gluten-free diet for a year or two, he can try going off the diet. If problems return, restart the diet without testing. If problems don't return, I recommend retesting anyway after several months to be sure gluten isn't causing low-grade allergy.

Urine gluten/casein peptide test. Performed by a few specialty labs, this test measures the casomorphine and gluteomorphine levels in the urine. As you learned on page 84, part of the biomedical theory is that some children with autism can't digest casein (milk protein) or gluten (wheat, oat, barley, and rye protein) properly. These proteins are altered during digestion into a compound that resembles morphine or endorphins (the body's natural relaxers and pain fighters) and may contribute to symptoms of autism. This test checks a child's degree of sensitivity so that parents can decide whether their child should be on a gluten-free or casein-free diet. Once a child is on the diet for several weeks, these proteins should disappear from the urine. Repeat testing isn't necessary, especially if you know the diet is helping.

IgE environmental allergy testing. Nasal, respiratory, and skin allergies among our nation's children have become a growing concern. Just as foods can irritate the immune system (and possibly affect autism), so can things in the environment, such as pets, dust, mold, grass, and pollen. Children who are allergic to these types of things will show symptoms of nasal allergies, wheezing, or itchy skin rashes. Any child with autism who has these symptoms should get a blood test called an environmental inhalant allergy panel. Skin testing for these allergies can also be done by an allergist. On page 297 I will discuss the importance of eliminating and treating environmental allergies.

IgE blood level. The overall level of IgE can be measured to determine to what degree all allergies combined are triggering an overactive immune system. A very high level should prompt parents to be more diligent in preventing their child's allergies.

Ordering the right tests. I like to order both an IgG food allergy panel and the urine peptide test before a child goes on any restricted diet so that I can get a good baseline measurement. If a child is suffering from chronic allergy symptoms such as nasal allergies, asthma, diarrhea, or skin rashes, I will also order an IgE food allergy panel, an IgE environmental inhalant panel, and an overall IgE level, in case the IgG panel misses any allergens. If a child is already on the gluten-free/casein-free diet, I usually don't bother with the urine peptide test or any specific gluten allergy tests. But I will do the IgG panel to see which other foods might still be irritating the intestines and the immune system.

TESTING FOR IMMUNE DEFICIENCY

As you read on page 85, the immune system of a child with autism may not be working properly. In addition to checking white blood cell levels with a CBC test (see page 94), you can have two other tests done to evaluate specific aspects of the immune system.

Quantitative immunoglobulins (QUIGS). This blood test measures the levels of all four antibody types that the immune system generates: IgG, IgM, IgA, and IgE. As discussed on page 111, a high IgE level is a marker for allergies, but a normal level does not mean a child doesn't have food allergies. Low levels of any of the other three classes of antibodies can indicate an immune disorder that may make a child more susceptible to infections. What does this have to do with autism? One of the more advanced treatments for autism is IVIG. This intravenous infusion of antibodies helps correct immune deficiencies and protects a child from infections. A more useful benefit for autism is that IVIG can neutralize some inflammatory or autoimmune reactions as well as some chronic viral infections. But IVIG is very expensive ($1,000 to $2,000 per monthly infusion), and insurance doesn't cover it for the treatment of autism. Insurance will, however, cover IVIG for treating immune deficiencies. So, the main usefulness in checking QUIG levels is to get insurance approval for IVIG. As you will read on page 280, IVIG treatment is not to be taken lightly. I generally check QUIG levels only for children who I suspect may have an immune deficiency or whose autism is moderate to severe and the parents are considering IVIG.

Lymphocyte enumeration panel. This blood test measures the levels of the various types of white blood cells (called *lymphocytes*) that fight infectious diseases, especially viruses. The CBC (see page 94) tells us only the total number of lymphocytes, whereas this panel looks for deficiencies in specific types of these cells. Although there is no direct treatment for this type of immune deficiency (other than the general immune-boosting recommendations I make in the biomedical protocol), any child who has a significant lack of specific lymphocytes is more likely to be affected by viruses, and antiviral treatment should be strongly considered.

TESTING FOR "LEAKY GUT" SYNDROME

As described on page 83, irritation and inflammation of the intestinal lining cause it to become too permeable, allowing food particles and toxins that should otherwise remain within the intestines to be absorbed into the bloodstream. The degree to which a child's intestines are leaky can be measured with an intestinal permeability test in which the levels of two types of sugars—a small sugar and a large sugar—are analyzed in a urine sample. If the gut is leaky, both types of sugars will be absorbed and pass into the urine. If it is not leaky, only the small sugar molecules will show up. I generally don't run this test, because most children with autism have a leaky gut. The few who don't will generally still benefit from the same biomedical treatments to improve overall gut health. Knowing this test result really doesn't change the treatment plan.

TESTING FOR INTESTINAL YEAST AND BACTERIA

As discussed on page 82, intestinal yeast and bacterial overgrowth is a common finding in autism. One of the very first "wow" treatments discovered for autism was yeast elimination. Here is how you can test your child for intestinal yeast as well as related intestinal bacterial problems.

Stool yeast culture and microscopic exam. This test can be performed by either a regular lab or a specialty lab. The advantage of a specialty lab is that it will report the degree of yeast found (from very low to very high levels) and automatically test various antifungal medications and natural treatments to see which ones the yeast is sensitive or resistant to. But this might not be covered by insurance. Any regular lab can examine a sample of your child's stool for yeast, but it won't report if the amount of yeast is high or low or test which antifungal medications the yeast is sensitive to. I prefer to have testing done by a specialty lab. A lab generally wants two separate stool samples from different days to increase the chance of detecting yeast.

The microscopic examination of the stool looks for visible yeast cells and reports results ranging from none to many. In order to identify the species of yeast and the treatment sensitivities, however, the yeast has to be grown for several days in a petri dish. If this is done by a specialty lab, the yeast culture result is reported as a number from 0 to 4, and the medications and natural treatments are reported as resistant, intermediate, or sensitive. It is not uncommon for the lab to see many yeast cells under the microscope but then be unable to get them to grow in the petri dish (thus, a 0 culture result). Such a result (many yeast cells visible with the microscope) is still a useful indication of a yeast problem.

Comprehensive parasitology stool profile. This more detailed examination is performed only by specialty labs. It not only looks for yeast but measures the levels of healthy bacteria (called beneficial flora), harmful bacteria, and parasites. It's useful to know if any bacterial or parasitic problems are present, as these can often be treated at the same time as yeast. Any child with chronic intestinal symptoms should at least get this comprehensive type of test. A regular lab can test for parasites, but it generally won't look for the type of bacteria that a specialty lab will look for.

Comprehensive digestive stool analysis with parasitology. Also known as a CDSA, this very detailed specialty lab test looks for everything the previously described exam does and also evaluates for digestive and inflammatory problems. I recommend this test for any child with chronic diarrhea or abdominal pain. It helps determine the degree of intestinal irritation or damage so that the parents know how strict they need to be with various dietary precautions and treatments. It can also reveal if a child has inflammatory bowel disease (see page 300).

Urine test for intestinal yeast and bacteria. Several of the specialty labs listed in Resources, page 354, offer a variety of urine profiles (called *organic acid* or *organix* tests) that measure various acids, sugars, chemicals, and nutrient levels in the urine. This type of test is a useful backup to the stool test for yeast and bacteria, since a child may have a significant intestinal yeast or bacteria problem but the particular stool sample that is tested might not show it.

Intestinal yeast and bacteria produce various sugars and acids that move through the body and come out in the urine. The primary yeast sugar is called *arabinose,* but there are several others. Levels of these sugars are grouped together under the yeast section of the test results. Children with mild yeast show about twice the normal level of arabinose. Three to five times the normal level indicates a moderate problem, and a tenfold increase over normal means that yeast is very significant. The main acid generated by bacteria is called HPHPA and is listed in the bacterial section of the results. This particular acid is most often produced by bacteria called *clostridium.* Double or triple the normal level means the amount of clostridium may be moderately high. Four or more times normal indicates a severe problem. In chapter 11 I will discuss yeast and bacterial treatments in great detail.

VITAMIN AND MINERAL LEVELS

While there are dozens of vitamins and minerals, not all can be tested for, and testing is not always useful. I generally test only the following:

Plasma zinc level. Zinc plays an important role in the immune and nervous systems. Normal levels in the bloodstream vary from 600 to 1400 (some labs take off a zero and report the normal range as between 60 and 140). Having a low zinc level isn't a cause of autism, but some doctors have found that treating a child with extra zinc to bring the level up to the higher end of normal, above 1000 (or 100), may help improve some symptoms. Any regular lab can run this test. Be sure to specify a *plasma* zinc level (it's more accurate than a whole blood or serum zinc level).

25-hydroxy vitamin D blood level. Of the wide variety of vitamin levels that can be checked in the blood, I believe vitamin D is the most important. All other vitamin levels are almost always normal, and part of biomedical treatment is basic vitamin supplementation, so I don't find it useful to check all vitamin levels prior to treatment. Vitamin D, however, is unique in that it serves many important bodily functions and is almost always low in children with autism. It's important to know how to interpret vitamin D levels. The normal range in standard medicine is between 25 and 100, but new research from the Vitamin D Council (www.vitaminDCouncil.org) has shown that having a level chronically below 50 may cause some problems, and raising the level to 65 or higher is needed to overcome these problems. I will discuss this in more detail on page 222. It's important to get an accurate vitamin D level before starting treatment and then to recheck the level every few months until it is normal. Doctors have to specify a 25-hydroxy vitamin D level (the active form of vitamin D) for the test result to be accurate.

Vitamin A level. This level is usually fairly normal in most children, so I don't often test it up front. I do, however, recommend testing after several months of vitamin A supplementation to make sure the level isn't getting too high.

Red blood cell element profile. As discussed on page 100, this test measures the levels of various healthy minerals (as well as toxic metals) within the red blood cells. This test almost always shows low levels of many of the minerals you will be automatically supplementing with (calcium, magnesium, zinc, selenium, and chromium), so I usually don't bother with it. Some doctors find it useful during follow-up testing.

BRAIN IMAGING STUDIES

Parents and doctors often wonder if there is some abnormality in the brain of a child with autism. There are several ways the brain can be imaged to look for such abnormalities. Some of these tests are more useful than others. The decision on what, if any, type of scan to do depends on the child's individual symptoms.

MRI. Deciding whether your child should have magnetic resonance imaging (MRI) of the brain isn't easy. It's expensive, but insurance usually picks up the bill. It's also invasive; sedation is usually needed to keep the child still, and an IV infusion of dye that outlines the brain's blood vessels is given. Generally, neurologists rather than pediatricians order MRIs. Most MRIs are normal. This can be comforting to parents but ultimately doesn't help them make treatment decisions. In the rare instances where an MRI is abnormal, it usually isn't good news. Here are the three main abnormalities that might be found on an MRI:

- *Brain tumor.* This is often a worry in the back of a parent's mind. However, brain tumors are no more common in children with autism than they are in the general population. And it is highly improbable that a tumor in one part of the brain could cause such a wide range of symptoms.

- *Demyelination.* This is a condition in which the fatty coating that covers the brain and all nerves in the body (the myelin) has degenerated. A small number of children with autism have been found to have demyelination within the brain. This causes those areas of the brain to work more slowly or dysfunctionally. This process is thought to be an autoimmune phenomenon; the body's own immune system attacks the myelin (see page 110). Subtle demyelination can't be seen on an MRI (or any brain scan), but if it's extensive enough, it can. Demyelination indicates significant neurological injury and is often a predictor of poor prognosis for recovery.

- *Congenital malformation.* A child can be born with certain neurological disorders that prevent the brain from growing and forming correctly or cause it to build up too much fluid. Children with congenital malformations often have notable genetic abnormalities or other physical birth defects. I have heard of several children with autism who were found to have a problem called an *Arnold Chiari malformation* near the base of the brain. After undergoing surgical repair, these children showed rapid improvement in many of their autistic symptoms. There is no obvious outward sign that a child has this particular defect, and it isn't appropriate to scan every single child. However, any child who isn't responding well to autism therapy (as is often the case with children who have congenital malformations) should have this possibility considered.

Not every child with autism needs an MRI. The above abnormalities are very rare. The doctors will look for various clues in the child's history and current status that might lead them toward ordering an MRI. Here are some typical clues.

- *Seizures.* Any child who has seizures (regardless of autism) should have an MRI. See page 296 to learn how to determine if your child may be having subtle seizures.

- *Rapid neurological decline.* Any child who goes from neurologically normal to having major features of autism over a short period of time (a month or less) should have an MRI.

- *Serious medical illness with rapid decline into autism.* Some children with regressive autism started their downward spiral during or right after a serious illness. This may indicate autoimmune or infectious demyelination (see above).

- *Severe vaccine reaction with rapid onset of autism-like symptoms.* Although this is rare, there have been reported cases of children becoming severely ill and quickly developing autism symptoms right after a series of vaccines. This may also indicate demyelination. Although the reaction isn't directly treatable, documenting MRI evidence of demyelination may help parents make their case in court.

- *Abnormal neurological exam or skin findings of neurofibromatosis or tuberous sclerosis* (see page 66). Any child with physical exam findings of nerve dysfunction or neurofibromatosis or tuberous sclerosis should have an MRI to look for brain tumors.

A child with normal development during the first year who gradually regresses into autism during the second year and has a normal neurological exam (except for typical symptoms of autism) and no problems with seizures probably doesn't need an MRI. A child who develops symptoms of autism earlier during infancy but has fairly normal motor development and no genetic problems or visible birth defects probably doesn't need an MRI either. Of course, every parent should take the advice of their own doctor regarding the need for an MRI.

CT scan. A CT scan does not show as much detail as an MRI and can miss some important findings. It generally isn't advisable to settle for a CT.

EEG. An electroencephalogram tests the electrical activity throughout the brain. It is done by placing sticky electrode patches around the scalp and measuring the electrical impulses generated within the brain over a period of an hour. The child can be awake or asleep or both during the test. This test is primarily done to look for seizures, which are abnormal electrical discharges within the brain. If a one-hour EEG is normal but a child's case is suspicious for seizures, a twenty-four-hour EEG can be done in a hospital. Some neurologists also offer a portable EEG that a child can wear at home. See page 296 for more on seizures.

PET scan. A positron emission tomography scan (aka single positron emission CT, or SPECT, scan) is like a CT scan, but it measures blood flow through the brain instead of taking a picture of the brain structure itself. An IV solution is infused into the child, and this solution is detected by the scan as it flows through the brain. The main purpose of the scan is to document which portions of the brain, if any, aren't receiving proper blood flow. PET scan research has shown that most children with autism don't have proper blood flow, and the affected areas of the brain may not function properly.

I generally don't recommend PET scans because they are experimental and the results are unlikely to guide therapy. A PET scan may be useful for older children who are going to take psychiatric medications. The scan itself doesn't tell you whether or not meds are needed (behavior will determine that); it just helps the doctor choose the right medications by observing the type of blood flow pattern. You don't necessarily need a scan for this; trial and error and observation will also reveal which meds are best suited to your child.

DECIDING ON TESTING

I have developed my own preferences for which tests I order, but this doesn't make my testing panel better than another doctor's. You should follow the advice of your personal biomedical physician, your pediatrician, or your neurologist. I list my suggested testing for you to use as a starting point. If your doctor is fairly new to the biomedical approach, you could ask him or her to read this section and help you decide what to do. All of the following are blood tests unless otherwise indicated.

Regular lab tests. Here are the standard tests that can be run by a regular lab with an order from your doctor:

- CBC with differential (see page 94)
- CMP (see page 94)
- ESR (see page 109)
- CRP (see page 110)
- total IgE (see page 111)
- lead (see page 100)
- plasma zinc (see page 120)

- free T4, TSH (see page 94)
- Fragile X chromosome analysis (see page 96)
- CGH microarray (see page 97)
- measles IgG/IgM (see page 107)
- herpes types I, II, and 6 IgG/IgM (see pages 104–106)
- ASO titer (see page 108)
- anti DNase B antibodies (see page 108)
- gliadin IgG/IgA (see page 113)
- carnitine profile (see page 99)
- 25-hydroxy vitamin D (see page 120)

Specialty tests. The following tests require a kit to be mailed to you from a specialty lab company and your doctor's signature on the lab slip. Most of these tests are probably not covered by insurance (see Resources, page 354, for contact information for each company):

- IgG food allergy panel (see page 115) for about one hundred foods without diet plan from Alletess or any of the listed lab companies

- Glutathione blood level (a simple level, not the complex detoxification panel; see page 104) from Genova or other lab

- Micro OAT or Organix urine testing (see page 119) from Great Plains, Metametrix, or a company of your choice

- Comprehensive parasitology profile of the stool or comprehensive digestive stool analysis with parasitology (be sure to send two stool samples in your kit; see page 119) from Doctor's Data, Genova, or a lab of your choice.

- Urine gluten/casein peptide test (see page 114) from Great Plains

Blood for the specialty tests is drawn by the lab at the same time as all of your child's regular blood tests. The lab should use the blood collection tubes that come with the kit, then mail the sample along with any paperwork to the specialty lab. For urine, stool, or hair testing (which I don't recommend), collect a sample yourself at home, place it in the kit, and then mail it to the specialty lab. Don't involve the regular lab in this process at all. Your pediatrician may be able to give you urine collection bags if your child is still in diapers.

Tests to be done in certain situations. Review the following sections to decide whether to do these tests:

• QUIGS and lymphocyte enumeration panel if your child has frequent illnesses, you suspect viral problems, or are considering IVIG (see page 116)

• IgE RAST testing for foods and environmental inhalant allergies if your child has chronic skin, nose, or respiratory allergy symptoms (see page 111)

• More detailed genetic testing as indicated (see page 96)

• Urine porphyrins from Great Plains or Laboratoire Philippe Auguste if you are planning chelation (see page 102)

• Standard urine organic acid panel, plasma amino acid panel, lactate and pyruvate, carnitine, ammonia, and creatinine kinase for metabolic or mitochondrial disorders (see page 99)

• IBD Serology 7 blood panel from Prometheus Labs to evaluate for inflammatory bowel disease (see page 300)

HOW MUCH BLOOD CAN BE TAKEN OUT OF A CHILD AT ONE TIME?

Guidelines and opinions differ on this. Laboratories generally limit the amount of blood according to their own policy. In my experience, most children six years and older can have all of the above tests drawn in one day. Younger kids will likely need to have two separate blood draws, at least three weeks apart.

ASKING A REGULAR DOCTOR FOR THESE TESTS

Most alternative doctors are familiar with these tests and shouldn't have a problem ordering them. But most pediatricians and other medical doctors, while understanding and agreeing to order *some* of these tests, won't recognize the connection many of these have to autism and may say no to some of them, in particular the ESR, CRP, IgG food allergy panel, zinc level, measles and herpes testing, vitamin D level, glutathione, stool testing, and urine OAT and peptide testing. Here are ways you might be able to enlist your mainstream doctor's help:

• Find the most open-minded doctor in the practice or the doctor who has known you the longest.

• Make a separate appointment that doesn't involve any sort of checkup or physical exam so you'll have plenty of time to talk. If the doctor already knows your child well and you think your child may be a big distraction to your conversation, go to the appointment alone.

• Do your homework ahead of time and be ready to explain your reasoning behind each test.

- Tell your doctor that you don't necessarily expect him to agree with everything but that you really need his help in getting this information.

- Admit that you realize that some are alternative tests and not recognized as legitimate by the FDA.

- Order your own test kits ahead of time from each specialty lab and have the paperwork already filled out so all your doctor has to do is sign it.

- Be sure to bring any test results that have already been done by a neurologist or other specialist so you don't repeat tests unnecessarily. This shows your doctor you are thinking this through.

- Print out journal articles that I list in the Resources and show them to your doctor. Of course, he won't be able to read them during your visit. But just by reading the titles of the articles, he may be more open to testing and treatment.

- If your doctor really objects to the stool testing through a specialty lab, at least ask for a yeast culture through a regular lab.

- If you have HMO insurance, your doctor may be even more reluctant to run so many expensive (and unproven) tests. Most HMOs do not cover the specialized tests that require kits anyway, so it's better if you don't even ask your doctor to approve any kit tests. Tell him you are going to be paying for these tests yourself, and you only need his signature on the kit order form. He may then be more willing to order the more familiar tests through the insurance plan.

ARE ALL OF THESE TESTS REALLY NECESSARY?

It isn't necessary to undergo such extensive testing. The main purpose of these tests is to look for medical or nutritional problems that might be a factor in your child's autism. The results may provide you with some treatment options, depending on what shows up. However, not all biomedical treatments rely on test results, and there is much you can do without testing. In addition, some of the problems we test for show up as abnormal in most kids with autism, so chances are, the problems exist for your child and can be treated without being tested for.

In part 3 of this book I will show you how to start the biomedical treatments without a doctor's help. I will show you what you can do without any testing and without seeing a biomedical doctor yet. Prior testing is useful for, but not critical to, successful biomedical treatments for autism. You don't need to confirm gluten and casein allergy before trying the gluten-free/casein-free (GFCF) diet. You don't need to confirm yeast in the gut before trying some natural treatments. You don't need to do any vitamin or mineral tests before beginning supplements.

I often meet parents who tell me they've known about the biomedical protocol for a year but didn't start it because they either couldn't afford the testing or couldn't find a doctor to do it. That child has lost a year of potential improvement. What I love to see are parents who have already been doing everything they can without a doctor's help before coming to see me. Any child who fits the classic picture of biomedical causes (chronic runny stools, exposure to multiple antibiotics, and regressive-type autism) should get started the day the parents hear about these treatments.

PART III

Treating Autism

6

Behavioral, Developmental, and Educational Therapies

The symptoms of autism involve problems with a child's development and behavior, so the primary focus of mainstream treatment is utilizing various therapeutic approaches that improve these problems. These programs are a critical part of successful autism treatment, and the earlier a child begins them, the better.

I will start by explaining the various therapies. I can't actually teach you how to use these techniques because that must be done under the supervision of a qualified therapist. She can teach you various techniques to use at home. The purpose of this chapter is simply to show you what's available so that you can make sure your child is getting the right therapy.

Every child with autism is unique, and each therapy program must be individualized to meet that child's needs. If something doesn't seem to be working, it should be changed. New approaches should be added and ineffective techniques discarded. By knowing what approaches are available, you can help your therapists decide what to do for your child and when to make a change. There are some primary therapies that should be offered to all children with autism, and there are some that are suited for a smaller proportion of kids. Therapies generally fall into four different categories: behavioral therapies, language therapies, occupational therapies, and social skills therapies. Most children should receive daily or weekly therapy in each of these four categories.

BEHAVIORAL INTERVENTION THERAPIES

This category covers therapies designed to teach a child with autism how to handle the various tasks and interactions of day-to-day life, and how to suppress the abnormal behaviors and mannerisms. For example, behavioral intervention therapy teaches a child how to ask for food when he is hungry instead of throwing a tantrum on the kitchen floor. It shows a child how to make eye contact when speaking to someone instead of looking away.

Most children with autism should spend much of each day in behavioral intervention therapy in the early years. As chemotherapy is to cancer, and insulin is to diabetes, behavioral intervention is the most important therapy for a young child with autism. Sure, there are other things a child should be working on, but everything should work around the behavioral intervention treatment schedule. Depending on the severity of the autism, young children should spend between twenty and forty hours each week one-on-one with a therapist in a behavioral intervention program.

Several approaches to behavioral teaching are currently being utilized and investigated. Applied Behavioral Analysis (ABA) is the primary method used nationwide, especially between the ages of one and four years. Developmental, Individual Difference, Relationship-based/Floortime (DIR/Floortime) and several variations of ABA, such as Pivotal Response Training (PRT) and Discrete Trial Training (DTT), have also been used successfully.

TEACCH, which stands for Treatment and Education of Autistic and Related Communication-handicapped Children, is commonly used in preschools. Although all the techniques are similar, there are slight variations, and it's important to determine which approach works best for your child. Many children will begin one-on-one ABA therapy in their home or at a center. They may then incorporate one of the variations of ABA, or change over to DIR/Floortime, depending on the response to therapy. Once a child enters a preschool program, he may move on to TEACCH, or remain in a more mainstream classroom setting.

Because each child is unique, I can't offer you specific guidelines on which approach might fit *your* child the best. I will simply describe each one, and it's up to you and your therapists to decide. It's not always easy to know which one to try. I suggest that all parents start with the basic ABA approach, since it has the best track record so far. If your child isn't progressing, try another ABA provider or, in consultation with an experienced professional, consider changing to a different behavioral program. A parent with a child similar to yours who has already been through these therapies may be able to offer you some guidance. It often helps to get two or more independent opinions from unbiased evaluators (not the person providing the therapy) to help you decide which approach to try first. But don't sit around for months trying to decide. Start your child right away in whichever therapy your local state-funded Early Intervention Program provides. Then look into what your other options might be.

If you are seeking insurance coverage for various behavioral therapies and you are having a hard time getting approval, consider narrowing your requests to ABA first. This is considered the standard of care for autism behavioral treatment, and you are more likely to win your case.

Applied Behavioral Analysis (ABA)

ABA is an intensive one-on-one program in which a therapist spends many hours every day working with the child using the principles of stimulus, response, and reward. It follows the classic tenet of operant conditioning, which states that any behavior can be changed by changing what happened just before it or after it, and then rewarding the appropriate replacement behavior. Therapy can take place at a small table with the therapist and child facing each other, on the floor, or pretty much anywhere that is suitable to the current exercise. The therapist begins by providing a stimulus, which may be asking the child to say something, perform a play-related action, or engage in a social interaction. The therapist then demonstrates what the proper response should be. When the child does not imitate the action correctly, the therapist repeats the stimulus and response over and over, or prompts the child physically, until the child does it correctly. Anything the child does wrong is ignored, redirected, or replaced with a more appropriate response. In some circumstances the therapist may physically direct the child through the action and then reward him. Rewards might be praise, a brief celebration (such as a piggyback ride), or a snack (for example, raisins or M&M's). By repeating this exercise dozens to hundreds of times, the therapist teaches the child how to correctly perform the action on his own without needing anyone to provide the stimulus.

For example, a therapist might spend a day teaching a child how to say hello to his mother. The therapist will ask the child to say hello to his mother (the stimulus). When the child doesn't respond, the therapist will demonstrate this by facing the mother, looking her in the eye, and saying hello (the proper response). The child will likely not imitate this action yet, and the therapist will continue repeating the stimulus and response. At some point, she will direct the child by turning his body toward the mother, looking the mother in the eye and saying hello for the child. She will then face the child back toward herself and reward him with a "Good job" (even though he didn't say hello). She is demonstrating the desired behavior and rewarding the child. After this is repeated many times, the child will begin turning to his mother, looking her in the eye, saying hello all on his own, and then enjoying the reward from the therapist. The child will eventually learn that turning to look at his mother and saying hello is a positive experience and will begin doing this on his own outside therapy. The parent will also be taught how to direct the child through these skills at home.

The goals of ABA are to increase desired behaviors (social interaction, playing appropriately), to teach new skills (self-help, communication), to maintain these behaviors (exercising self-control and guiding oneself through tasks), to understand how to move from one behavior to another (working from task to task in a classroom, transferring from one social interaction to another), and to reduce behaviors that interfere with daily life (self-injurious behavior or stimming). Hundreds of everyday communication skills, self-help skills, and educational milestones can be taught one at a time through ABA. It can take many hours each day for several years, but gradually the child is taught how to do everything a child should do in day-to-day life. And the child can be taught to want to do it.

Various forms of Applied Behavioral Analysis, such as Discrete Trial Training (DTT), Verbal Behavior (VB; or Applied Verbal Behavior, or AVB), and Pivotal Response Therapy (PRT), use the same principles as ABA but with minor variations:

• In DTT, skills are taught individually by breaking them down into the smallest tasks possible. In the above example, turning to the mom and saying hello will be taught in two smaller steps. First the child will be trained to turn and look the mother in the eye. Once that is established, saying hello is taught separately.

• In VB, ABA principles are used specifically to focus on teaching speech and communication skills. It teaches very small, measurable units of language one at a time. The child learns to use words to get what he wants (instead of throwing a tantrum, for example). Children are taught to imitate, make requests, label objects, and eventually to converse.

• Although derived from ABA principles, PRT differs significantly from standard ABA in three ways. First, instead of teaching specific individual behaviors one at a time, PRT focuses on several main principles of development and behavior: how to become motivated, how to respond to multiple cues from the environment, how to self-manage behavior, and how to initiate and maintain social interactions. Second, it is child-directed instead of therapist-directed. And third, the rewards are more specific to the behavior. As the child learns these global skills, specific and individual behaviors within these areas are also learned without being specifically targeted. The child generally does not sit at a table (unless he chooses to). Instead, the therapist engages the child in whatever the child is choosing to do on his own. Teachable moments are worked into the child's routine. Rewards are tied more specifically to the behavior; when the child is learning how to ask for a toy, the actual toy is the reward. PRT teaches all the same skills as regular ABA (language, communication, social interaction, academic skills, and avoidance of disruptive behaviors) but it differs significantly enough from ABA that it could be viewed as a separate therapy altogether.

CENTER FOR AUTISM AND RELATED DISORDERS (CARD)

There are many private therapists and therapy centers in every major American city that provide ABA and other behavioral and developmental therapies in addition to state-funded Regional Centers and public schools. Each has its own strengths and weaknesses. In my opinion, one of the most experienced and comprehensive programs is the Center for Autism and Related Disorders, founded in 1990, at the beginning of the autism epidemic, by psychologist Dr. Doreen Granpeesheh. CARD has seventeen locations nationwide, as well as centers in New Zealand, Australia, Dubai (UAE), and South Africa, with more planned in other countries. Any parent of an autistic child who lives within a reasonable distance of a CARD center should strongly consider entering the child in this program. Visit www .CenterForAutism.com for more information.

Developmental, Individual Difference, Relationship-based/Floortime Therapy (DIR/Floortime)

DIR/Floortime incorporates elements of ABA and PRT into a system of teaching that is child-directed and involves teaching specific skills, but the therapist interacts with the child primarily during playtime. It can be taught to parents and other caregivers and is usually done in addition to (not instead of) ABA therapy. The theory behind this therapy is that by engaging the child during his chosen play routines, the therapist (or parent) can teach the child more complex interactions and incorporate language and social skills. This helps the child learn to process experiences, sensations, and interactions, which in turn helps the child develop language, self-help, and social skills.

For example, if a child is sitting on the floor playing with a car, the parent or therapist sits down in front of the child and plays with a car as well. She may move her car in front of the child's, requiring the child to interact with the other car. Does he drive his car around, over, or through the therapist's car? A parent could also place her hand on the floor and drive her car "over the hill," encouraging the child to do the same when she places her hand in front of his car. The parent verbalizes the interaction ("up" or "over"). Such engagements help the child learn to be more interactive with those around him. It's play with a purpose.

DIR/Floortime isn't just random play therapy. It is an organized approach with specific instructions, guidelines, and tools, and it can be a useful adjunct therapy in school-based, home-based, or center-based daily programs. Information on this system, and resources for finding a provider, can be found at www .ICDL.com.

Functional Communication Training (FCT)

This is another supplemental learning system that is done in addition to ABA therapy. It is based on the theory that problematic behaviors are a form of communication for a child with autism (who can't otherwise communicate). The therapist first tries to determine what a child is trying to communicate from a certain behavior (which may vary depending on the setting or circumstance). Then she teaches the child how to communicate, verbally or nonverbally, what he is trying to say, instead of acting out. For example, a child might throw a tantrum to indicate he is tired and doesn't want to perform a certain task. The therapist will then demonstrate more acceptable ways for the child to get the message across, such as teaching him to ask for a break or point to a chair to sit down in to rest. By repeating these lessons over and over, many of the behavioral challenges of autism can diminish, and the child's communication skills increase.

Treatment and Education of Autistic and Related Communication-handicapped Children (TEACCH)

I know the acronym doesn't precisely fit the title, but the creators wanted something catchy. This is a school-based program that emphasizes a very structured approach to learning; it is sometimes referred to as *structured teaching*. Specifics may vary between schools, but the general approach is to set up small classrooms with work stations for each task. Tasks and learning exercises are visually oriented, often with pictures or single-word instructions instead of printed directions. Predictable schedules allow children to move from task to task more smoothly. Children often work alone, but some small group activities also take place. For those children who do well with TEACCH at school, it can also be implemented at home.

IN-HOME THERAPY VERSUS CENTER-BASED THERAPY

Behavioral/developmental therapy for a toddler with autism is a full-time program. The ABA, speech, and OT can often fill eight hours a day. It is obviously more convenient for the family if much of this can be done at home. Many state-funded and private early intervention programs provide in-home therapists. Therapists in some programs, however, may feel they can provide better services at a therapy center. In my experience, most parents feel that their child does better with in-home therapy between ages one and three. I encourage you to start with in-home therapy if you can. You may have to fight for this if the state-funded program is resistant. Of course, certain services, such as group sessions for older children or types of OT that require large equipment, are best done at a center.

One criticism of this method is that it isn't designed to help a child with autism overcome his social or verbal immaturity. It basically accommodates the child in a learning style that he is capable of following, unlike an inclusion approach, which teaches the child to function in a regular classroom. It doesn't stress social interaction and verbal communication. One of the main goals of therapy for a high-functioning child with autism is to integrate him with his neurotypical peers. The TEACCH approach certainly doesn't focus on that. It may be a more appropriate method for children with moderate to severe autism.

SPEECH, LANGUAGE, AND COMMUNICATION THERAPIES

All children with autism have some degree of language difficulty. Some do not speak at all. Many use normal words but not appropriately. Some are unable to form words clearly. High-functioning children may speak in full and normal sentences, but their language might not always fit the social context properly. All kids with autism need some type of therapy to help them communicate properly. A child should spend at least a few hours each week in this type of therapy, preferably in at least two sessions weekly. Following are the three main types of speech and language therapy.

Speech Therapy

Standard speech therapy is mainly for children who can't enunciate words clearly: kids who talk up a storm but can't pronounce various consonants and consonant blends well enough to be understood by strangers. Classic speech therapy works on teaching the proper movement of the mouth muscles: the tongue, lips, and cheeks. While this type of therapy is useful for neurotypical kids, it is not what most kids with autism need.

Language Therapy

This type of therapy teaches kids how to use language properly. Instead of addressing problems with the mouth, it focuses on how the brain processes and creates ideas and turns them into words and sentences. Speech therapists who work with children with autism are trained in language therapy. A child may need some enunciation training, but the majority of the therapist's time should be spent trying to connect with the child through games and interaction and encouraging the child to express himself verbally. A language therapist also works to improve eye contact, which is important for communication. Once the child is using words and sentences, the therapist can begin to address pronunciation problems. Higher-functioning children with near-normal use of language can be taught how to use language correctly in a social setting, have back-and-forth conversations with peers, and build meaningful friendships.

It's important that parents make sure their speech therapist (whether provided by the state or privately funded) is trained and experienced in treating the language processing aspect of autism. A good therapist will also take the time to demonstrate what you, as the parent, can do at home with your child.

As many as 40 percent of children with autism also have childhood apraxia of speech (see page 53). Such kids should receive more intensive language therapy (as many as five hours per day, five days a week) than those with autism alone.

Picture Exchange Communication System (PECS)

This approach is for children who have a good understanding of language but can't express themselves verbally. The child is taught to understand what many different pictures mean. Using a picture board or electronic picture device, the child points to various pictures that communicate what he's trying to say. For example, he might point to the picture of Mommy and then the one for food to indicate to his mom that he is hungry. Many parents of nonverbal children are truly amazed at their children's ability to express themselves using this technique. It's rewarding for them to see that their child's thought processes are there. TACA, at www.TACAnow.org, has a good description of PECS in their section on learning, with information on how to make your own picture cards.

OCCUPATIONAL THERAPIES

Two basic problems that children with autism might have can be addressed by OT: low muscle tone and poor coordination, which interferes with both gross-motor skills, such as running, climbing, and jumping, and fine-motor skills, such as drawing, writing, and manipulating toys; and sensory processing disorder, where a child doesn't properly process sensations (see page 49 for a reminder of the symptoms). Both of these problems can interfere with a child's daily activities and ability to play with and interact with other kids. A child should typically spend one to three hours each week in OT.

Classic Occupational Therapy

An occupational therapist is often one of the first to see an infant or toddler at risk for autism because a delay in motor skills is easier to spot than social delays. An OT provider may begin working with a one-year-old who can't sit up well or crawl yet before autism or any social problems are noticed. OT provides exercises and games that are designed to build muscle strength, tone, and coordination. The therapist works in a space that should look like a cross between a toy room and a gymnasium, with plenty of manipulative toys for fine-motor hand coordination, and climbing equipment, ball pits, and play mats for gross-motor skills. An occupational therapist won't teach a child just how to climb up a ladder and slide down a slide. She will also address day-to-day activities, like putting on clothes, zipping zippers, tying shoelaces, and playing games. Not all children with autism have these challenges, but almost every child is going to qualify for OT services.

Sensory Integration OT

This more specialized type of OT requires additional training. Some sensory OTs will focus only on sensory problems, without addressing issues of overall muscle tone and strength. Classic OT and sensory OT are really two separate types of therapy, and many kids need both. Fortunately, most occupational therapists do provide both, and if you can find one who does both well, you are blessed. Most state-funded programs will provide only one therapist who does both types of therapy. Make sure your child is getting enough sensory OT if that's a significant problem for him. Some children don't have any significant sensory problems. You should tailor the OT to fit his needs.

As you read on page 49, correcting sensory processing problems is very important, and the younger your child is when he starts, the better. A sensory integration OT will use various techniques with brushes, heavy clothing, swings, large objects for pressure, and other items to gradually expose the child to increasing degrees of sensory input in order to desensitize him. Calming down the sensory overload that these kids experience allows the brain to relax and begin processing all the sights, sounds, smells, touches, and tastes of daily life in a more regular manner. It might take as long as six to twelve months, but if the therapy is successful, the child will be calmer and better able to interact with the world around him. This in turn will make other therapies more successful. Visit www.SPDfoundation.net for information.

WHO PAYS FOR ALL THIS THERAPY?

In chapter 3, I discussed the pros and cons of state-funded versus private evaluations, and what may or may not be covered by your state and by your insurance company. Now that your child has had the initial assessments, getting coverage for the numerous therapies he will need in the coming years becomes a very important issue.

In years past, most insurance companies didn't pay for behavioral or developmental therapies for autism because "psychiatric disorders" were excluded from coverage. The government, instead, was paying for these much-needed treatments through the state-funded programs. And when the state couldn't (or wouldn't) provide enough therapy, parents had to hire attorneys to fight the state and the insurance companies to get coverage. Some parents won their battles, but many didn't. These families have borne a huge financial burden as they have tried to get proper treatment for their children.

This has just changed due to two factors. First, we now know autism is really a medical and neurological disorder, and therefore should be covered by medical insurance. Dedicated advocates have worked tirelessly for several years to get laws passed in many states that mandate insurance coverage, and such laws should soon exist in all states. Second, our government is out of money. Many state programs are being cut, and autism therapy is no exception. They are shifting the responsibility over to insurance companies. Some insurance companies are still fighting this change, however, and laws vary from state to state. Your local TACA group (see page 55) should be able to offer you some guidance on your current laws.

Once all the kinks are worked out of this new system, it may end up being a positive change. This will depend on the extent to which the government forces insurance companies to cover autism therapy and how much money the states can utilize to provide some therapies to children without insurance coverage or insurance approval. In addition, there may not yet be enough private therapy centers for the growing population of children with autism. Now that insurance is covering some therapy, many of the children who would have been treated by state programs will need to find a private center. These centers are likely to fill up very quickly. I can't predict how smoothly these changes will be in the coming years. Your best resource for up-to-date information will be your local parent support group.

Another frustrating situation arises when you feel your child needs more hours of therapy or a wider range of therapies than the state program or your insurance approves for him to receive. Even worse is when your child's delays are so mild that no coverage is offered at all. You will likely need to hire an attorney to fight for you, or simply pay for the therapy yourself. Is it worth going this far to get your child's therapy covered? The combination of all needed behavioral and educational programs can cost as much as $10,000 per month for at least several years (depending on how involved the programs are). Even if you need to pay for only some of your child's extra therapy, you may be looking at several thousand dollars per month. Hiring an attorney for $10,000 or more might end up paying for itself many times over in the long run. One of the useful services that TACA (see page 55) provides is legal information that you can use to guide you. Check with your local group. There are also nonprofit organizations that raise money to pay for therapy for needy families. I list some of these in the Resources, page 356.

Feeding OT

Some kids with autism have an oral aversion that makes them extremely picky when it comes to food. They will eat only a handful of different foods (and a certain brand at that) and reject everything else because it just doesn't feel right in their mouths. This can be either a sensory processing problem or an oral problem. Some OTs specialize in feeding techniques to help these kids overcome their aversions. Many classic OTs provide this service as well. If your child struggles with this, and your regular OT sessions aren't helping, find a feeding occupational therapist. Ask your local TACA group or search online for someone in your area.

Gymnastic or Horseback Riding OT

Most regular occupational therapy programs provide OT with a gymnastic twist. There are also some centers around the country that are primarily gymnastic centers but they have OTs there to add a therapeutic effect. This type of program is great for preschool kids and older kids who no longer qualify for state-funded OT but still need help with muscle tone, strength, and coordination.

Some horseback riding centers are taking a similar approach, using riding lessons to help build leg and upper body strength as well as balance. This is called *hippotherapy.*

SOCIAL SKILLS THERAPIES

Teaching children with autism to fit into the world around them, and to enjoy doing so, is a primary goal of therapy. Younger toddlers tend to play alone and seem to care little about what's going on around them. Preschoolers often begin to pay attention to other kids and may try to take part in some games and activities, but they usually have to be prompted to do so. As kids move into elementary school, those who have recovered their language skills and lost many of their autistic behaviors will still miss some basic nuances of social interaction; as their peers thrive socially around them, they can be left behind.

Social skills therapies come in many shapes and sizes. ABA and language therapies begin teaching social skills early on, such as learning to point, making eye contact, and engaging someone in play. As soon as these basic skills are learned, social skills therapy can be incorporated into a child's daily routine to help him expand his social horizon. Here are the various options that will likely be offered to your child or that you can seek out on your own.

Social Skills Groups

The primary method of teaching socialization to children with autism is to have them participate in small play classes taught by an ABA or language therapist (or anyone trained in social skills for autism). These are provided at some public schools as part of the after-school program (your child may be able to attend even if he doesn't attend that school) or at private autism therapy centers.

It is not ideal for your child to be at the top of the class, because he won't have any higher-functioning role models to learn from. He might also learn some negative behaviors and habits from children who are more severely affected by autism. However, high-functioning children can be of great assistance to more severely affected kids. Some programs incorporate neuro-typical kids to fill this gap.

You might not find the absolutely perfect mix of children to group with, or you might not have a choice. Bring your concerns to the attention of the therapist and ask how you can make sure

SOCIAL SKILLS BEGIN AT HOME

It is important to have a trained professional work with your child. But there are some things you can do at home to help develop your toddler's social skills. Here are some basic steps (adapted from the American Academy of Pediatrics' parent guide *Understanding Autism Spectrum Disorders*):

- *Join your child in play.* Point to what he is playing with and talk about what he is doing. Reward any eye contact with a big smile and playful words. Add simple problem-solving steps to the play. For example, during ball play, suggest that he roll the ball into a goal between your hands or legs and cheer when he scores.
- *Teach your child to look where you are pointing.* Point to things your child normally likes to look at and name them. You may need to put your hand on his shoulder or guide his gaze until he learns. Reward success with positive feedback. Then move on to pointing out and exploring new objects. Prepare food together and point to something when it's done, such as the microwave going *ding.* Display facial expressions that fit with the action, such as excitement over a new toy or an "oh, no" look when something spills. When your child mimics these reactions, reward him with a cheer.
- *Teach your child how to point.* Whenever your child wants something, hold his hand and point his finger. Or push the desired object out of reach, and when he tries to reach for it, touch a few wrong objects first, asking him if that's what he wants. As

your child is both serving and benefiting. Find out about other groups on different days or at different times. You might need to try several before you find the right mix. Of course, other children will always be coming and going and changing the group dynamics. You'll have to stay abreast of how the group is doing.

he reaches, move his finger into a pointing position and reward him with the object. Thank him for pointing to it.

- *Teach your child to seek help.* As you pretend not to understand what your child wants, say something like, "Let's go get Daddy to help us." Teach your child how to take Daddy's hand, lead him over to the activity, and have Daddy help. This teaches him to engage his parents.
- *Teach your child to show you things.* A key social skill for any child is to show a parent something fun or interesting by pointing or leading the parent to it so that the child can share the experience. Anytime your child brings you something, take the time to talk about it. He might want help, for example, with opening a container. Pretend you don't understand and keep talking about other aspects of the object. Eventually express happily, "Oh, you want me to open it!" and open the container. If you notice something interesting, like an airplane flying by, but your child doesn't show you, you can show him, make him point to it, get him to make eye contact with you, and reward him with an exciting discussion about it while moving his gaze back and forth between it and you.

Many children with autism can play quietly alone for hours. While you sometimes need a break and time to yourself, it's also important for you to engage your child in teachable moments throughout the day. These activities are simply suggestions for you to try. Every child is different, and your therapists will likely have other ideas that build on, or differ from, these. Follow your therapists' advice.

Relationship Development Intervention (RDI)

The goal of this one-on-one therapy is to correct the core social deficits of autism. It teaches children to understand the joy and value of personal relationships. A child with this foundation will then learn language and social skills—such as friendship skills, nuances of conversation, empathy, and how to share experiences with others—more easily. While RDI can help moderately affected children, it is ideal for high-functioning children, especially those with Asperger's, in whom social awkwardness is the primary problem. It can teach such children to recognize and respond to subtle nuances like sarcasm and humor in addition to everyday conversation.

This is a fairly new approach, and RDI-trained therapists are not yet very common. If you can find one near you, and the price is right, give it a try. It can be an effective adjunct to ABA and other therapies. Visit www.RDIconnect.com for more information and a registry of providers.

Peer Play

Some families won't be able to find an RDI therapist close enough to home to be practical. But one-on-one instructional playtime is very important. One useful approach is to partner your child with a neurotypical child who is about three years older—a friend, family member, or neighbor. Hire him to be your child's playmate for an hour, two or three days each week. Sit down with the child and his parents and explain that your child doesn't quite understand the rules of certain games or how to have fun playing with another child. You want to hire him ($5 an hour sounds like a fortune to an eight-year-old!) to teach your child how to play. You explain that your child might not know how to play fair, how to share, how to stay within the rules, how to understand the rights and preferences of others, and so on. The two kids can play sports games, board games, or pretend games, or solve puzzles or play with action figures or dolls. It's also useful to get suggestions from your child's ABA, speech therapist, or whoever is your child's primary therapist.

SCHOOL-BASED PROGRAMS

If your child is three years or older, the primary place he will receive social stimulation and instruction (besides the home) is school. For most children with autism, the best type of school is one that provides daily therapy. Here are some things to think about.

Private Preschool Versus a Special-Needs Public Program

Most parents like to start a neurotypical child in a private preschool that's close to home, provides a nice mix of structure and independence, and has a teacher who is warm and caring toward children. Parents often spend months researching local preschools (and on waiting lists) in order to find the best one for their child.

Having a child with autism calls for something very different. A private preschool might not be the right place. They generally have one teacher and a teacher's aide for fifteen to twenty children. The teachers simply can't devote the hours of one-on-one time that your child is going to need. For a child with autism, preschool isn't just a place to go for fun, games, and learning. It's therapy. Your child needs to be in a preschool that has almost as many teachers/therapists as there are children with autism. Although public preschools for neurotypical children are not common (most public schools begin at kindergarten), virtually every school district now provides early intervention public preschool therapy programs for autism and other special needs. Some use the TEACCH therapy approach (see page 141). Other schools provide a more mainstream setting with a number of neurotypical children to serve as role models.

There are some situations in which a private preschool may be right for a child:

• A higher-functioning child with mild autism who has decent language skills, good social awareness, and minimal disruptive behaviors may do very well in a private preschool. The neurotypical kids around him will likely be very therapeutic.

• A family that has the financial resources to hire a one-on-one therapist to shadow the child and continuously offer instructions in every teachable situation that arises during the day may find that a private preschool works for them (see below).

• A private school that is designed specifically for special-needs children might work well. These are available in most areas, but they aren't cheap.

Preschool Programs for Special Needs

Most children with autism should enter a program at the preschool age. But some children with severe autism might still require full-time one-on-one behavioral therapy. Even moderately affected children might not be quite ready. Intensive, full-time ABA and other therapies might be the best choice for such children instead of a group preschool program. When you and your therapists believe your child is ready, start by taking a look at what your public school district has to offer.

Special-needs public preschools typically have the following features:

• A special-education teacher trained to teach children with autism and perhaps even more than one such teacher per class

• Several teacher's aides who can help facilitate instruction and spend time one-on-one with the children

- A very high adult/child ratio

- Additional OT, ABA, and language therapists to spend time with each child

A regular private preschool, kindergarten, or elementary school won't have all of these features, so a special-needs public preschool may be your best choice.

Private Preschool with a School Shadow

Children with autism who attend a private preschool may need what is called a *school shadow* (high-functioning children might not need one). This is someone who is hired by the parents to act as a teacher's aide in the classroom, while secretly (secretly to the child, that is, not to the school) focusing most of her time on the one child. This can be a layperson who functions more like an interactive babysitter, or a trained professional who knows how to provide expert guidance for autism. The shadow spends a bit of time with the other kids in the classroom as well. But most of the time she directs the child in his schoolwork, provides extra explanation of instructions when needed, takes advantage of teachable moments involving interactions with the other children, and helps minimize any disruptive behaviors.

Moving On to Kindergarten

Once a child turns five or six, it's time for kindergarten. Many of the same issues around public or private school still apply. Treatment approaches vary so greatly between states and districts that I can't offer you specific information here. But no matter where you live, if you stay in public school, one of the decisions you will need to make is whether your child should be in a mainstream class or a special-needs class.

Mainstream classroom. Getting "mainstreamed" into a classroom of neurotypical kids has its advantages and disadvantages. On the one hand, a high-functioning child may thrive from learning from his peers, may not need a shadow, and can easily and discreetly be pulled out of class for one-on-one language and OT sessions as needed. He can get social skills therapy at an after-school program or a therapy center.

A moderately to severely affected child, on the other hand, might not benefit from such a setting unless there is a school shadow or other type of therapist to facilitate interaction with neurotypical peers. At this age, the other children might not want to play with a child with moderate to severe autism. Five-year-old children are too young to be aware of the need to be polite and friendly to a child with autism unless they are instructed to do so, and they are too old to not notice that something is very different about that child. Five-year-olds tend to be brutally honest without intending any harm.

My own child at age six had a peer with very mild autism in his school. I was watching the children playing a group game one day, and I heard my child say, "Oh, don't try to explain it to Sammy. He'll just stand there and stare at you." When I heard that, I was astonished. But then I realized that my child didn't know what autism is. He was just making an observation. It did highlight for me the importance of trying to educate neurotypical children to be more sensitive to kids in their class "who may not seem to always understand things as well as you do." I put that in quotes as an example of how you can word this for your own child without pointing out any children in the class who you think may have autism.

Special-needs classroom. Many schools retain moderately to severely affected children in the same type of setting as they had during preschool: one with a high teacher/student ratio with lots of therapy time. Some schools will add a few neurotypical kids to the class to act as role models. But such a class might not be the right place for a high-functioning autistic child. There are many different approaches and differences among school districts. You will need to seek advice from your child's therapists who are not affiliated with the school for an objective opinion about what the best setting is for your child. A TACA mentor mom may also be a good resource for advice about your child and the local school program.

Elementary Years and Beyond

I can't provide specifics here, as each child's abilities and level of functioning are so variable. For this age and older, I will need to hand you off to several other authors (see Resources) who have written about their experiences with their own children through the elementary years. TACA also provides various resources and periodic seminars on how to navigate through the public school system and ensure your child is getting the best services possible.

7

Prescription Medications for Autistic Symptoms

For many years autism was thought to be a psychiatric disorder. We now know differently, but the field of psychiatry still provides us with useful treatment options for some children. In my experience, most parents are reluctant to give their children psychotropic medications. They feel that by doing so they are crossing a line they never wanted to cross. There is also the understandable fear of side effects, both short-term and long-term. However, in my experience, these medications can be of considerable benefit for certain children when used properly.

Detailed guidance of psychotropic medications is beyond the scope of this book. Treatment decisions should be made on a case-by-case basis by a qualified physician in consultation with the parents. Most pediatric psychiatrists and some pediatric neurologists understand how to use these meds in autism. Some biomedical physicians do as well. Most pediatricians, however, have very little experience with psychotropic meds and are therefore hesitant to write prescriptions.

This chapter gives you a basic introduction to the various kinds of meds and the types of situations in which they may be beneficial. This information should help you feel more comfortable discussing this option with your doctor. I have seen many young children recover sufficiently with behavioral and biomedical treatments to the point where such medications aren't warranted. I also have some patients who have not recovered enough, and the responsible use of an appropriate medication has led to significant improvements in their behavior and function.

I want to begin with a story that highlights the benefits of psychotropic medication. I worked with one family for about three years, trying a variety of biomedical treatments, and the child showed only minimal improvement. At Thomas's seven-year checkup and autism treatment appointment, he spent the entire hour moving around the room, climbing on the table, throwing tantrums, and banging on the wall and door. His parents told me that this wasn't consistent behavior for him, but that he did spend some hours every day in such a mood. And his sleep was a huge problem. He'd wake up in the wee hours of the morning and not go back to sleep. His parents were exhausted. They'd resigned themselves to the fact that this was how things were going to be. Thomas was definitely one of my severe cases.

We had talked about psychotropic medications in the past, but the parents had been against the idea. I broached the topic once again, and this time they were more open. Now, I would never push psychotropic medications on any family. But I felt that this child's life, and his parents' lives, could improve if the child responded well to a medication. The parents agreed to give risperidone a try. I prescribed a low dose and told the parents to come back in two weeks for a quick chat.

The child they brought back with them was not the same kid. He was calm. He sat in the chair and played with a toy during the appointment. The parents were happy. Nothing about Thomas's autism had improved except that he was calmer, and he slept all night. His parents told me that they remembered my suggesting medication a year earlier and said that they wished they had listened then. They said so not with regret but with a feeling of being at rest, knowing that they could now enjoy some peace every day and night.

I recommend psychotropic medications to less than 5 percent of my patients with autism, usually with positive results. I don't know what the future will hold for Thomas, but I know this was the right choice for him.

BEHAVIORS THAT MAY RESPOND TO MEDICATION

There are many behavioral aspects to autism, and each one can affect a child to varying degrees. Not every challenge can simply be eliminated with a pill, but many can be minimized with appropriate treatment. Here are the most common behaviors that may respond to medication.

ADHD. Some children with autism have problems with inattention and distraction. Many are also impulsive and hyperactive.

Aggression. While many autistic kids are hyperactive, most aren't openly aggressive. But some kids get so revved up that they physically invade the space of other kids to the point that these kids feel threatened.

Irritability. Some children with autism are frequently bothered by something. They often can't tell us why, and they spend hours each day in a foul mood.

Outbursts and tantrums. We expect these behaviors in toddlers and preschoolers, but some children with autism don't mature and gain control over their explosive emotions. They can go from zero to sixty at the drop of a hat. This isn't a big deal if it's only once or twice a day. But some children react frequently and dramatically to any changes around them.

Self-injurious behavior. A minority of children with autism bite their lips, chew the skin on their fingers, bang their head against objects, or take unsafe risks. These behaviors rarely result in serious injury, but they can be a big distraction from therapy and day-to-day life.

Anxiety. Some kids suffer from anxiety. Many high-functioning kids are aware of, and even talk about, their anxiety. Children with moderate to severe autism may not. Anxiety can interfere with social skills and relationships.

Sleeplessness. Some children stay awake until all hours of the night. Some may go to sleep just fine but wake up at 4 a.m. ready to bounce around their room. In general, children (and their parents!) are much happier and do better with behavioral and educational therapies if they get a good night's sleep.

Obsessive-compulsive behaviors. Some kids with autism have OCD challenges. They show some rigidity in their routines, get stuck in repetitive behaviors, and become obsessed with sameness and familiarity. This can interfere with day-to-day living.

Depression. Some high-functioning children notice that they are different from other kids. This can trigger depression, irritability, social withdrawal, and eating and sleeping problems.

DECIDING WHEN TO TRY A MEDICATION

This isn't an easy decision for parents. Some may feel like they are giving up on their child by sedating him and dampening his personality. Such worries are perfectly understandable. In my opinion, though, this isn't what happens with meds. In my office, I approach the treatment of illness in three steps:

1. I identify any underlying causes and then eliminate them if possible.

2. I use natural treatments to help relieve any symptoms that persist.

3. If natural remedies don't work, I use medical treatments to alleviate symptoms that are significantly interfering with a child's life and to treat any causes that can't be prevented by step 1.

Most children improve with the first two steps to such a degree that behavioral or psychiatric challenges diminish and don't warrant medication.

But some children don't reach this point. Their behaviors may interfere with the quality of their home life or social life. Parents need to reinforce at home the behavioral techniques that a child learns at therapy, and a child needs to play with, and learn from, other kids. But parents also need some downtime to recover their emotional and physical energy. If home life and playtime with other kids is chaotic and draining, nobody wins.

Also, their symptoms may interfere with the success of behavioral and educational therapies. Speech, OT, education, ABA, social skills, and other training sessions require a child to pay attention and work with therapists all day long. If a child is hyperactive, aggressive, throwing tantrums, injuring himself or others, or distracted and inattentive, all of these hours, weeks, and years of therapy are not going to be as effective. The hope for every parent is that a child's autistic symptoms respond so well during the early months of biomedical and/or behavioral therapy that these symptoms diminish and the child thrives in therapy. But if a child's aggression, for example, doesn't subside, the hours spent with a therapist might not be so productive. If a medication is used to calm the child down, the therapist might be able to connect better and achieve more in each hour.

If you are considering medication, keep the following two factors in mind:

• *Medication can be used for the short term.* Once your child starts a med, you aren't necessarily committing him to years of treatment. If you see positive results, your child can continue to take it for several months to a year, and then he can be weaned off it to see if it is still needed. Often a child matures or responds to all of his other therapies to the point that medication is no longer needed.

• *Make a written treatment plan.* It's irresponsible to simply put a child on a medication and see what happens. With your doctor, create a written plan, listing the most troublesome behaviors and the ones that should respond to medication. Gather information from therapists regarding these behaviors prior to beginning treatment, then record improvements using periodic updates from therapists. Also document any unexpected benefits. Write down any *new* problematic behaviors or side effects. Your doctor will need this valuable information to help guide ongoing treatment.

FIVE CLASSES OF PSYCHOTROPIC MEDICATIONS

There are five basic classes of medication that can help with symptoms of autism: ADHD medications, antidepressants, blood pressure medications, antipsychotic medications, and antiseizure medications.

These medications work by influencing the levels of various neuro-chemicals that affect mood and behavior. As you learned on page 72, children with autism produce insufficient levels of these chemi-cals. It stands to reason that taking such medications could have a positive effect. Most children should take only one medication, but there are some circumstances in which a child may benefit from two or more medications under the guidance of a well-trained and expe-rienced doctor.

A note about side effects. Because psychotropic medications directly affect brain chemicals, there are more potential risks than with most meds. A particular challenge with autism is that the child will often not be able to communicate a new and uncom-fortable side effect. Parents and therapists must be extra vigilant when such medications are started or changed. An overall negative change in behavior, mood, developmental abilities, or neurological function may indicate an unwanted effect. I have included infor-mation on the most common side effects for each type of medica-tion. Some of these may sound scary; your doctor can discuss with you the potential benefits of the med so that you can decide if the risks are worth taking.

ADHD Medications

There are two basic types of ADHD meds.

Stimulants. Amphetamine and methylphenidate are used to treat attention problems in children with autism. They work by increasing the production of dopamine, a neurochemical that helps with attention and focus. There are several brands to choose from. I don't have a preference for any one particular brand, but I do like to use the long-acting once-a-day formula-tions instead of the short-acting twice-a-day pills.

Atomoxetine (brand name Strattera). This ADHD medication isn't a stimulant. It's a norepinephrine reuptake inhibitor. Norepinephrine is like the adrenaline of the brain. This medication enhances the effects of norepinephrine as it passes from nerve cell to nerve cell, thus speeding up brain function and enhancing attention.

These medications have also been shown to decrease hyperactivity and impulsivity. How can they do that if they are stimulating the brain or speeding up brain function? The theory is that they work on the calming center of the brain as well as the thinking and processing centers. I've had a fairly positive experience with these types of medications in neurotypical children with ADHD, although I use them almost as a last resort. In patients with autism, these meds may help with attention, but they seem to be more likely to cause hyperactivity or aggressive behavior than in neurotypical kids. This might be because the neurochemical makeup of a child with autism is different and stimulant meds have effects in autism that we just don't understand. Despite this, I do believe these meds are worth trying if attention is a big problem in school and during therapy.

The stimulants work better than atomoxetine on attention, and they begin working right away; atomoxetine can take a few weeks to build up to an effective level. However, atomoxetine is less likely than the stimulants to cause hyperactivity or aggression.

Side effects. ADHD meds can cause weight loss from suppressed appetite and increased hyperactivity or agitation. The stimulant meds may cause difficulty sleeping and increased heart rate and blood pressure and may also make existing tics worse.

PILLS, LIQUIDS, GRANULES, AND PATCHES

Every psychotropic medication comes in tablet or capsule form. Some capsules can be opened and put into food or drink. A few meds also come in liquid form and a few are available as transdermal patches. The choice of medications is often limited for younger kids because they won't swallow pills or tolerate the taste of an opened capsule. I can't specify which meds come in which form because this frequently changes. You can search each medication online to see its dosage forms. If you and your doctor feel a particular med is the best choice but your child won't take it in its available forms, a compounding pharmacy (see Resources, page 354) may be able to mix it into a more palatable formulation.

Antidepressant Medications

Selective serotonin reuptake inhibitors (SSRIs) are the type of antidepressant most often used for children with autism. Common brand names are Celexa, Lexapro, Zoloft, Prozac, and others. SSRIs work by prolonging the effects of the neurochemical serotonin as it passes from nerve to nerve (similar to atomoxetine with norepinephrine). Serotonin is a calming neurochemical. It also acts like the brakes for the brain, telling the body to stop doing something. SSRIs can be useful in suppressing obsessive-compulsive behaviors, aggression, and anxiety.

Bupropion (brand name Wellbutrin), a non-SSRI antidepressant, can also be an effective treatment.

A pediatric psychiatrist should guide a family through antidepressant treatment. Once the effects have stabilized and a child is doing well, care may be handed over to a pediatrician. It's much less expensive to have your pediatrician see your child for a refill than to see a psychiatrist every month (and pediatric visits are usually covered by insurance).

Side effects. Antidepressants may trigger sleep disturbances (either insomnia or drowsiness), muscle tremors or incoordination, irritability, and behavioral changes.

Blood Pressure Medications

A particular class of blood pressure meds, alpha-2-agonists, have been found to help with various symptoms of autism. Clonidine and guanfacine are the two available choices. These medications activate certain types of nerve pathways (called the alpha-2 pathways) that control adrenaline levels in the body. When adrenaline is kept at lower levels and adrenaline rushes are minimized, problems with aggression, hyperactivity, tantrums, self-injurious behavior, and sleep can be reduced. Although these medications were initially developed for prescribing by cardiologists, their use in children with autism is generally managed by a psychiatrist.

Side effects. Blood pressure meds may cause agitation, drowsiness, low energy, dizziness, dry mouth, and constipation.

Antipsychotic Medications

The idea of using antipsychotic medications might sound scary, especially since autism isn't a psychotic condition, but they are very effective at suppressing certain "out-of-control" functions in the brain. Although their exact mechanism isn't completely understood, it is thought that they influence the neurochemicals dopamine and serotonin. They can blunt certain behaviors, such as aggression, irritability, or self-injury. They can also suppress hyperactivity and OCD behaviors and help with sleep problems. There are several antipsychotics to choose from, but risperidone is the most commonly used and, as of the writing of this book, one of only two drugs officially FDA-approved for the control of some symptoms of autism. Aripiprazole (brand name Abilify) is the other FDA-approved drug for autistic irritability.

Side effects. Antipsychotics are well known for increasing appetite and causing weight gain. Sedation is often significant at first but then diminishes. Muscle tremors or uncoordinated movements may be seen.

Antiseizure Medications

Some children with autism have problems with seizures and are treated with appropriate medications. An additional effect of these meds is that they are very calming. A child with moderate to severe autism with certain challenging behaviors may benefit from one of these meds even if seizures aren't present. They can typically help with hyperactivity, aggression, irritability, self-injury, OCD behaviors, and sleep problems. There are several to choose from, each with its pros and cons. A detailed discussion of these is beyond the scope of this book. Such meds are often prescribed by a pediatric neurologist, but they can also be managed by a pediatric psychiatrist.

Side effects. The side effects of the different antiseizure meds vary greatly. Some cause weight loss, others weight gain, and still others neither. Most can trigger undesirable mood and behavior changes. Some meds require routine blood tests to monitor how the body is handling the treatment.

A UNIQUE USE FOR RISPERIDONE

This idea comes from my good friend and mentor, pediatrician and biomedical physician Dr. Jerry Kartzinel, coauthor of *Healing and Preventing Autism*. Some kids have very strong OCD tendencies and oral sensory aversions. This combination creates a very picky eater, who will eat only four or five foods (typically Chicken McNuggets, French fries, hot dogs, mac and cheese, and milk). These kids will absolutely refuse to eat anything else. Risperidone can take care of two problems at once. It can calm down the OCD and oral aversion to allow a child to accept other foods, and it can increase a child's appetite so that he will be more open to eating new foods if you take away his favorites. After the diet has been expanded for a month or two, the child can be weaned off the medication.

8

An Overview of the Biomedical Approach

Now that I have covered mainstream interventions and treatment, let's turn our attention to the biomedical approaches. There are many aspects to these treatments, and it will take me several chapters to describe them all in detail. Here is a brief overview of what you and your child will be doing in the coming months.

It takes about three to four months to work through the first four steps, then several more months to incorporate the more advanced therapies in steps five through nine. It's useful to go step-by-step in this manner so that you don't overwhelm your child with too many changes at once. Taking it a step at a time also allows you to carefully track which changes are causing the most improvements and which, if any, are causing problems.

The biomedical approach should be tailored to each child. Decisions should be made in keeping with the child's unique problems, and adjustments should be made along the way based on the child's response to each new therapy. A biomedical practitioner can guide you through this process. However, one of the goals of this book is to provide families with the necessary information to start their child on the treatments without such a doctor, since many parents won't have access to one. So, I'm offering you the next best thing: a protocol that walks you through the process, with instructions on how to make adjustments if a problem arises. I want to stress, however, that it is better to seek professional guidance if you can.

You will be able to work through most of the following steps without a prescription. Almost every step has some over-the-counter treatment options that may help. However, you will most likely come to a point where you need input and prescriptions from a physician. I will show you how to approach your own mainstream doctor for help and provide resources to help you find a biomedical practitioner.

IS A CHILD EVER TOO OLD TO TRY THE BIOMEDICAL APPROACH?

No. It can be started at any age. I have heard numerous success stories from parents and other professionals about teens and even adults showing dramatic improvements from the diet and supplements. The younger the healing begins, the better. But it's never too late to start.

The biomedical treatments that I was trained to use come from what is called the Defeat Autism Now! project, developed by the Autism Research Institute. The information in the following chapters closely resembles ARI's recommendations, but it is not an official description of ARI's treatments. Rather, it is my interpretation of the treatments based on my experience with them. For more specific information on the Defeat Autism Now! project, visit the Autism Research Institute at www.Autism.com.

Step 1: Testing. If you have access to a biomedical doctor, he or she will likely do some thorough baseline testing (see chapter 5) to help create your child's upcoming treatment plan. If not, talk to your pediatrician about ordering tests for you (see page 128 for suggestions on how to approach this). It takes about three weeks for results to come back from the laboratory. As I discussed in chapter 5, you don't have to do any testing in order to take biomedical supplements. You can get started right away.

Step 2: Diet changes to clean up the gut (over a period of about six weeks). If your child has chronic diarrhea or constipation, or alternates between the two, this step should be very rewarding for you. After identifying your child's food allergies and level of sensitivity to casein and gluten, you'll take those factors out of your child's diet. You will also remove artificial ingredients and begin to eat as organically as possible. If your child does not have chronic intestinal problems, he may be less likely to show any "wow" changes from this step. But it is still worth committing to this step. Some kids have casein and/or gluten sensitivity without showing any intestinal symptoms.

Step 3: Begin nutritional supplements (over a one-month period). You will start your child on several basic vitamins, minerals, and other healthy supplements. Some are designed specifically to help with neurological function, others are intended to improve intestinal health, and still others are intended to replace deficiencies caused by the restricted diet.

Step 4: Treat yeast and other intestinal infections (for about one month). If your child's test results show excess yeast, he should begin some natural yeast treatments. You will also discuss options for prescription yeast medications with your doctor. Certain intestinal bacteria and parasites can also be treated.

Step 5: Begin methylation replacement therapy. You are now ready for more advanced supplementation. This begins with supporting the methylation system with methyl B12 treatments. There are a few other supplements that help B12 work better. Depending on your child's test results, he may also begin glutathione treatments.

LOOKING FOR A BIOMEDICAL PRACTITIONER?

The Autism Research Institute (www.Autism.com) has a registry of medical doctors and alternative health practitioners (most in the United States, but some international) who are trained in the biomedical approach. Look for a practitioner near you.

Step 6: Treat viral infections. There are natural, nonprescription antiviral supplements I'll share with you, but to effectively treat some viruses, you'll need a doctor to prescribe an antiviral medication.

Step 7: Treat associated medical problems. If you've been able to obtain thorough biomedical testing, your biomedical practitioner will show you how to treat any other abnormalities that have shown up on the results. Various other health concerns that are commonly associated with autism should also be addressed.

Step 8: Detoxification therapy. There are some safe and natural (but very mild and slow-acting) detox treatments that you can explore on your own. I will also review the more advanced prescription treatment options available only through a biomedical practitioner.

Step 9: Hyperbaric oxygen therapy. This is one of the most effective advanced treatments. I will explain how it works and how you can find an HBOT center in your area.

You don't have to work through the entire protocol. If your child responds well and you feel he is on the road to recovery, you can stop where you are at any time and not proceed into more advanced (and possibly more risky) therapies. These treatments are very flexible and should be individualized for each patient.

VISIT WWW.TACANOW.ORG AND GET A MENTOR PARENT

I'll be frank with you. Going down the biomedical road isn't easy. This plan takes a lot of time, work, and money, and a great deal of time and work (yes, I repeated those on purpose). I can tell you how to do it, but actually doing it takes a commitment. But you don't have to do it alone. TACA can help. Talk About Curing Autism is a nationwide group of moms (and dads) who have been following the biomedical plan for many years. Some of them even helped create it. They've been there, done that, lived that, and, most important, they've done it right in your neighborhood. TACA can set you up with a mentor mom (or dad) in your city, or maybe even on your street, who can help you get started. They'll tell you where to shop, how to cook, and how to get your child to take the numerous supplements. They can also help you find the best behavioral therapists in your area and help you work with your local school system. Veteran TACA moms have already done most of the leg work. Let them help you.

9

Diet Changes

The single most common medical problem shared by children with autism is food allergies. During the 1990s, many parents of children with autism reported that their children had chronic diarrhea that began during infancy and continued for many years. Since the most common causes of chronic diarrhea are allergies to cow's milk and wheat, parents began to wonder if there could be a connection between these allergies, chronic diarrhea, and autistic symptoms. Testing confirmed allergies to cow's-milk products and wheat in many children. More specifically, the proteins contained in these foods are the culprits: casein, the protein in cow's milk (and all mammalian milk); and gluten, the protein found in wheat (as well as rye, barley, and oats). Parents started to restrict these foods, and what became popularly known as the gluten-free/casein-free (or GFCF) diet began to help more and more children across the country. One survey of eighteen hundred autistic children revealed that 65 percent of them showed improvement in various symptoms, including resolution of chronic diarrhea.

The majority of patients whom I've helped get started on this diet have reported some amazing results. If chronic diarrhea has been a challenge, it resolves. In many cases, if a child has not yet begun talking, we see the first words emerge. Problems with hyperactivity often diminish. Potty training, which is often quite a struggle in kids with autism, becomes a snap. Children usually begin to sleep better. Eye contact improves. Children seem to come out of a fog.

The general medical community has not yet acknowledged that these allergies can contribute to autism. With regard to casein, there is not much scientific evidence that an allergy can lead to autistic symptoms. Most of the evidence is anecdotal or contained in non-mainstream medical journals. However, there are tens of thousands of such anecdotes. I have seen hundreds of my own patients improve on the GFCF diet.

There is some scientific evidence that gluten proteins can affect neurological function. It is a well-known scientific fact that adults with celiac disease (a form of severe gluten allergy) can experience psychotic and neurological symptoms when exposed to gluten. These adults also suffer varying degrees of intestinal irritation and chronic diarrhea when they eat gluten. A new study in *Pediatrics* (see Resources, page 365) revealed an increased risk of autism in children whose mothers have celiac disease (as well as other autoimmune diseases, like rheumatoid arthritis and type I diabetes).

Some large medical university research studies are currently testing the GFCF diet theory, and I look forward to seeing the results (which I will post on www.TheAutismBook.com).

"I'VE ALREADY TRIED THE DIET, AND IT DIDN'T HELP."

If you've already tried the GFCF diet and didn't see any improvement, you might be wondering if you should bother trying it again. I recommend that you try it while on the supplements in the next chapter. Many parts of the plan are synergistic: Each part helps other parts work better.

Some children with autism never have chronic diarrhea. Some have normal stools, and some have problems with constipation. A few children will alternate between all three states. In my experience, children with chronic diarrhea and/or constipation are more likely to benefit from the diet and show faster improvement in their autistic symptoms than children with normal stools, although I have seen a number of kids with normal stools show improvement on the diet as well. I have also had a few patients, even some with chronic diarrhea, who showed no benefit from the GFCF diet. Why the diet helps some kids and not others remains a mystery, but it does highlight one aspect of autism treatment. Every child is unique and will respond differently to various treatments.

A few more advanced diets have been shown to help a minority of children with autism. I discuss these at the end of this chapter, and you can decide if and when you should try them.

THE CHILD IS THE BEST LABORATORY TEST

No food allergy test is perfect. Standard testing methods (IgE skin and blood testing; see page 111) will not detect whether a child is chemically sensitive to gluten and casein proteins. Many parents mistakenly think their child doesn't need the diet because their allergy tests were normal. The best way to know if your child is sensitive to a food is to take it out of his diet and see what happens. Then reintroduce it and observe. If you consistently see good things happen without the food, that's all the evidence you need.

HOW CASEIN, GLUTEN, AND OTHER FOOD ALLERGIES CAN MAKE AUTISM WORSE

I introduced you to the theory of food allergies in chapter 4 and described how to test for food allergies in chapter 5. But there's more you need to know about this theory and how it may apply to your child.

According to the theory, there are three distinct ways that food proteins can contribute to autism:

1. through direct allergic irritation of the intestines
2. through internal allergic stimulation of the immune system
3. through chemical effects on the nervous system

Children suffer these reactions to varying degrees.

Allergic intestinal irritation. Any food that a person is allergic to will irritate the lining of the intestines. When these food proteins come into contact with the immune cells in the intestinal lining, allergic antibodies and chemicals are released in an effort to neutralize the offending proteins. Unfortunately, this allergic response does some collateral damage to the intestinal lining, and repeated allergic exposure eventually thins out the lining. A thick, healthy lining is necessary for proper food digestion and absorption. So, a child who continues to eat allergic foods may lose his ability to properly digest even foods he is not allergic to. Some infants and children with severe food allergies experience chronic diarrhea and sometimes bleeding in the stools. Others may have minor allergies that cause only minimal irritation.

How does this allergic irritation affect autism? Due to poor digestion, some children may suffer from vitamin and mineral deficiencies, which can affect neurological function. Some may experience stomach pains that cause behavioral outbursts, since they can't verbally explain that their tummy hurts. But the most serious way that a thinned-out and irritated intestinal lining may lead to autistic problems has become known as *"leaky gut" syndrome.*

"Leaky gut" syndrome. A leaky gut can allow the absorption of many pesticides, metals, and chemicals that otherwise might have simply passed out harmlessly in the stools. These chemicals then travel to the nervous system, where they can cause damage. Perhaps even more serious is that many partially digested proteins and other food substances can be absorbed into the body without being fully broken down. It is theorized that these improperly digested food particles are treated by the immune system as foreign substances. This daily activation of the immune system may cause it to become more hyperactive and dysfunctional. Foods that would otherwise be harmless to a child can become allergic irritants simply because the intestines aren't processing them correctly. It is thought that the disease-fighting side of the immune system may then become depressed, as all of its energy is being directed to fighting allergies. A hyperactive and dysfunctional immune system is thought to be one of the key underlying factors that cause the brain of a child with autism not to work correctly. This process by which our own immune system attacks body organs and systems is called *autoimmune dysfunction*. Throughout this book I discuss various ways in which autoimmunity may play a role in autism.

Doctors believe that when a child has a leaky gut, the larger food particles that are absorbed into the bloodstream trigger an IgG response. This isn't technically an allergic response, so we don't say that these kids are allergic to these foods. If the gut weren't leaky, and if these foods were being properly digested into smaller proteins, they probably would not trigger an IgG response. So, IgG food sensitivities aren't really caused by the foods themselves but rather by the dysfunctional intestinal lining. But in order to help heal the gut and calm down the immune system, children need to go off these foods for several months. Once healing has taken place, the foods can be gradually reintroduced one at a time. An IgG test result can stay positive for years after a child stops eating a particular food, but behavioral improvements can be seen within just a few short weeks.

Casomorphine and gluteomorphine effects. Some research has shown that when casein and gluten are improperly digested (due to the lack of the digestive enzyme DPP IV; see page 84) and absorbed into the body, their chemical structure is altered slightly. These altered proteins have a chemical structure that seems to be a combination of gluten or casein and the endorphins that our body creates naturally as opiates for pain relief and sedation. Morphine and codeine are artificially created forms of endorphins.

This daily exposure can suppress brain function. The three most commonly described improvements when children go on a GFCF diet are that they seem to come out of a "brain fog," their eye contact improves, and their language acquisition and facility increase.

Doctors suspect that some kids with autism suffer chronic constipation because these morphine-like proteins are shutting down their bowels. Kids with allergic irritation *and* morphine effects may alternate between diarrhea and constipation.

One final note about the test results. A common finding on the IgG panel is that a child will show a reaction to some casein foods but not to others. For example, a child may show a high reaction to

---

READ MORE ABOUT THE GUT/BRAIN CONNECTION

For better or worse, the brain and the gut are affected more by nutrition than any other organs of the body, and this is why the biomedical approach focuses so heavily on nutrition. For more in-depth information on how nutrition affects brain function, I suggest you read the most recent book in the Sears Parenting Library, *The NDD Book: How Nutrition Deficit Disorder Affects Your Child's Learning, Behavior, and Health, and What You Can Do About It—Without Drugs*, by Dr. William Sears.

milk but no reaction to cheese. Does this mean your child can eat cheese? No. It's important to do the entire casein-free diet and go off all milk products for a while. The same thing can happen with gluten grains as well. A child may show a high reaction to wheat but perhaps not to oats. But all gluten grains should be eliminated.

STARTING THE GLUTEN-FREE/CASEIN-FREE DIET

Putting your child on the GFCF diet may seem like an impossible task. The American diet is based on dairy products and gluten grains. Milk, cheese, yogurt, butter, bread, crackers, pasta, and cereals are what most of us eat for breakfast and lunch every day.

What makes it even more challenging is that children with autism are often fixated on a very limited diet. Many kids on the spectrum have oral sensory problems that make them shun various textures and flavors. These kids often subsist on milk and bread alone (or so it seems to their parents). Also, the caso-morphine and gluteomorphine compounds are addictive for some kids. Just as a morphine addict would crave the drug, a child with autism has got to have his "fix" of casein and gluten every day.

If your child's test results show a clear indication of gluten and casein sensitivity or allergy, then it's pretty clear what you need to do. However, the results are not always so cut-and-dried. A minority of kids with autism don't register any gluten or casein IgG reaction, IgE reaction, or urine peptide levels. Should these kids try the diet? In my opinion, yes, especially if they have a long history of chronic diarrhea and/or constipation. No test is perfect, and these tests can occasionally come back normal even if a child has a sensitivity.

If you want to start your child on the diet but can't afford the testing or can't find a doctor to order the testing, go ahead and start.

Going Casein-Free

I recommend you remove casein from the diet first. This can be easier than removing gluten because there are various milk substitutes that are usually well accepted by kids, and there are fewer foods with hidden sources of casein than there are foods with hidden gluten. Going casein-free usually involves making only a few changes to the diet. And, in my experience, parents usually see benefits sooner when their kids go casein-free than when they go gluten-free. This serves as a nice encouragement to move on to the more challenging GF diet.

Here are the main sources of casein that you will remove:

- cow's milk and goat's milk
- cow's milk–based formula
- cheese
- yogurt
- butter
- ice cream
- whey protein (read labels)
- casein and caseinates (read labels)

You'll have to do a lot of label reading to detect casein everywhere. In fact, you should empty out all your food cabinets into two piles, a casein pile and a casein-free pile. You'll do the same when you go gluten-free. This helps you figure out which foods you will need to stop buying (or start hiding from your child!).

Here are some replacement foods you can begin giving to your child:

- rice milk (not really milk at all; it's more like rice water)
- almond or hazelnut milk
- potato milk (the Irish are really creative!)

- coconut milk
- milk-free yogurts, cheeses, butters, and ice cream

A note about soy milk: Some specialists believe soy has casein-like properties, so it isn't an ideal replacement.

WHAT! TAKE MY KID OFF MILK?

American parents have the misconception that their child must drink milk in order to thrive. While milk is a very healthy drink, the main two factors in milk—calcium and fat—that are required for a child's growth can be found elsewhere. So, as long as you make sure your child is getting adequate amounts of fat and calcium in other foods, he will be completely fine without milk. In the biomedical approach, we supplement with calcium. We also supplement with healthy fats and oils. And children who really love to drink something milky have plenty of alternative choices. In the end, if your child doesn't take to any of the other "milks," don't worry, he'll be fine (although Grandma might throw a fit!).

Going Gluten-Free

Parents find the GF diet more of a challenge mainly because gluten-free foods taste much different from their gluten counterparts. It's a lot easier to trick children into drinking almond milk instead of cow's milk than it is to convince them that gluten-free bread is the same as the usual bread. Here are the main sources of gluten grains that you will need to weed out of your child's diet:

- wheat
- oat
- barley

- rye
- spelt
- semolina
- triticale
- kamut

These grains are used to make virtually every standard type of bread, cracker, cereal, baked good, and instant mix or meal. Label reading is again very important. Here are grain alternatives:

- rice
- tapioca
- rhubarb
- bean flours (garbanzo, garfava)
- lentils

FOOD SUPPLEMENTS

The combination of diet restriction and picky eating habits puts a child at risk for various nutrient deficiencies. The supplements in the next chapter are designed to prevent that, but it's useful to add in some natural food–based supplements as well. Numerous products are available that provide a plethora of fruit and vegetable components mixed in with various other nutrients. Some that I'm familiar with are:

- Juice Plus + fruit and veggie capsules that you open into food
- Garden of Life's Perfect Food powder or capsules
- Amazing Grass SuperFood powder
- Garden of Plenty powder (from www.DrBoWagner.com)

You can find these products online.

- corn
- gluten-free prepared products

Because gluten sensitivity is a growing concern among adults, you can find gluten-free foods in a dedicated section of most large grocery stores. This can make shopping easier. You can also find GFCF foods online.

Additional Tips

I've given you enough information to get you started on the GFCF diet. But there is more to living these diets than can be contained within the scope of this book. You can find more information, recipes, sample daily menus, and prepared foods online. My favorite websites for GFCF information are www .TACAnow.org and www.GFCFdiet.com. Perhaps the best book written on the GFCF diet is *Special Diets for Special Kids,* by Lisa Lewis, PhD. She also wrote a follow-up book, *Special Diets for Special Kids Two,* with additional recipes. Here are a few additional tips:

Take one step at a time. I recommend you go casein-free first, then institute the gluten-free aspect of the diet. This avoids overwhelming your child with too many changes at once.

Don't go cold turkey. Take a couple weeks to ease into each of the two aspects of the diet. If your child is experiencing the morphine effect and you take away his drug too quickly, you might have one cranky kid on your hands. Two to three weeks for each of these two steps is ideal.

How strict do you really need to be? The answer to this question depends greatly upon each child. Some children can handle the occasional infraction, while others show extreme behavioral regression with even the slightest exposure to casein or gluten. It is often a well-meaning grandparent or alternate caregiver who finds out the hard way that maybe you aren't so crazy after all.

You will learn how strictly you need to follow each aspect of the GFCF diet. You might find through trial and error that you can cheat a little on casein but not on gluten, or the other way around. You might find that your child cannot even eat a food that has been made on machinery shared with other foods that contain gluten or casein. Such equipment is cleaned in between batches, but a tiny trace may be left over. There are other everyday products that contain gluten or casein, such as soaps, lotions, or craft materials, and your child might be sensitive to these. With time, you will learn how careful you need to be.

Don't go it alone. Find a mentor who has had experience with the GFCF diet. One of the ministries of the TACA group is to provide a mentor for parents with a newly diagnosed child. These mentors have been living the diet and the biomedical interventions for years. A mentor can take you shopping, show you how to cook, and teach you all the tricks of the trade that will help you get your child successfully onto the diet. Visit www.TACAnow .org for information on how to find a mentor.

Address oral sensory problems. If your child has strong oral sensory aversions and is fixated on certain foods and textures, he may refuse to eat many of the gluten-free and casein-free alternatives, no matter what you do. Such kids need a feeding occupational therapist to help them overcome their aversions (see page 148).

Noncompliant children. Children without strong sensory aversions who are simply stubborn about the diet changes may respond to a little bit of tough love. Stop buying his favorite gluten and casein foods and see what happens. The key here is that you can't force your child to eat. Prepare healthy foods and eat them yourself in front of your child. Don't put any pressure on him to eat. He will likely begin snacking as hunger sets in within the first day or two. Make sure he is drinking enough fluids to stay hydrated. If he doesn't come around and begin eating within three days (or if he begins to show symptoms of low blood sugar, such as extreme irritability or low energy level), you will need to back off and allow him to eat his favorite foods again. After several days of reenergizing, you can try again, using a different approach: Begin the basic nutritional supplements discussed in chapter 10 first (digestive enzymes, cod liver oil, calcium, taurine, and multivitamins/minerals), and then give the diet another try. If your child continues to refuse, you will have to limit gluten and casein foods to a degree that you can reasonably attain. Your doctor will be able to offer you more guidance. An appointment with a nutritionist familiar with the GFCF diet can also be helpful.

How long to continue the diet if it doesn't seem to be working. I like to see a child try the diet for at least six months before the parents decide it's not helping. Using the rest of the biomedical supplements is also important during this trial period. Children seven years of age and older should try it for at least a year, since they may take longer to respond to the diet.

OTHER NUTRITIONAL CHANGES TO MAKE WITH YOUR CHILD

The GFCF diet is only the first step. There are a number of other nutritional adjustments to make.

Eliminate other sensitive foods. After your child is gluetin-free and casein-free, spend the next couple of weeks eliminating all the other foods that registered as moderate or high on your IgG food test (as well as any that showed up on an IgE test if you had one done). Don't worry about foods that registered at the lowest positive level. You might not notice results as impressive as those from the GFCF diet, but you might see minor improvements, and the benefits of calming down the immune system can help in the long run. Once your child is on all aspects of the diet and has taken the gut-healing supplements in the next chapter for a few months, he may lose his sensitivity to many of these foods. Then you can gradually reintroduce your child's favorite foods one at a time (not the gluten and casein foods, though).

Go natural. Take as many artificial ingredients out of your child's diet as you can, including artificial sweeteners, food colorings, preservatives, and MSG. These chemicals can negatively affect brain function by disrupting neurotransmitters (the brain's natural compounds that control nerve impulses and behavior). Neurosurgeon Russell Blaylock discusses the science behind this concept in his book *Excitotoxins: The Taste That Kills.* As you learned in chapter 4, various neurotransmitters already aren't functioning properly in many children with autism. Avoiding these artificial food additives is very important.

Go organic. Chemicals and pesticides in food may contribute to autistic symptoms. We know that pesticides are harmful to the nervous system and immune system. We hope that most kids can handle the small amounts in foods and get rid of these chemicals by detoxifying themselves. But we suspect some kids can't. It is best not to take the chance; switch to an organic diet, including organic fruits, veggies, meats, grains, and drinks. If your child is having compliance issues with the GFCF diet but will eat some nonorganic gluten-free or casein-free foods, then you will need to allow that in the interest of nutrition. Going 100 percent organic isn't critical. In my book *HappyBaby: The Organic Guide to Baby's First 24 Months,* I provide a complete guide on how to help your whole family go green, not just with your diet but with your whole lifestyle.

Limit sugar. Foods high in refined sugar can affect behavior, suppress the immune system, and feed yeast. It is especially important to limit sugar at breakfast, since your child needs to be at his best for school and behavioral therapies.

Limit animal fats. While meat is a good source of protein, the fat that goes along with it causes low-grade inflammation in the body. As you learned on page 85, inflammation is not our friend. Standard beef is perhaps the worst, but even poultry fat is bad. Free-range animals that are allowed to roam the pastures and graze on organic grass, grains, and seeds are much better, so when your child eats meat, choose free-range and organic if possible. Wild game is another good option.

FOODS THAT ENHANCE THE BIOMEDICAL APPROACH

Healing autism is not all about restricting foods. There are also foods that should be eaten. Here are a few foods that you should try to incorporate into your family's nutritional lifestyle:

Phytonutrients. These healthy plant chemicals have potent antioxidant, anti-inflammatory, and anticancer (pretty much anti-anything bad) properties that can improve many of the immune and metabolic problems in autism. Most parents know that fruits and veggies are good for their children, but for children with autism, they are essential. The phytonutrients in green veggies and berries enhance neurotransmitter production and function. Try to make raw fruits, veggies, nuts, and berries a routine part of your child's snacks and meals. Juicing can be a convenient and good-tasting way to get more of these into your child's diet.

Anti-inflammatory foods. As you've read, inflammation is a significant problem in autism. Certain foods (in addition to fruits and veggies) can reduce inflammation. These include cold-water fish (especially wild salmon, trout, and herring), flax seeds (ground or as an oil), olive oil, nuts, wild game meat (such as venison), onions, garlic, chili peppers, and certain spices (such as turmeric, cinnamon, thyme, cilantro, oregano, rosemary, and ginger).

Glutathione-inducing foods. As you learned on page 88, glutathione is one of the body's primary antioxidants and detoxifiers. We can get it in supplement form (see page 266), but it's much better if we can enhance a child's innate methylation metabolism to generate its own glutathione. Dr. Sidney Baker reported on this emerging idea in his 2007 supplement to *Autism: Effective Biomedical Treatments.* The theory is that certain "super foods" contain natural toxins that, when consumed, send a message to our body to increase its detoxification metabolism. As the body then detoxifies the minor plant toxin, more harmful toxins (such as pesticides, chemicals, and metals) are also eliminated. These foods include chocolate, rosemary, ginger, turmeric, garlic, onions, pomegranate, black currant, spinach, blueberry, broccoli, Brussels sprouts, cabbage, cauliflower, collard greens, kale, kohlrabi, mustard, rutabaga, turnips, bok choy, arugula, horseradish, radish, wasabi, and watercress.

For most of you, many of the foods mentioned in the above three categories are probably not on your shopping list. And your child is probably not going to eagerly dig in when you start offering them. In order to send the right message to your child, however, such a natural diet needs to be a lifestyle change for the whole family. And that's not easy. But there are so many changes taking place in a family with autism that one more might not be too bad. Take baby steps. Change or add one or two things at a time. If your child resists, ask your ABA and/or OT providers for assistance in getting your child to be more compliant with these foods. The supplements listed in chapter 10 can help fill in a few of the gaps. See the Resources for recommended reading on the benefits of changing the whole family's diet.

MORE ADVANCED DIETARY RESTRICTIONS

The GFCF diet is the mainstay of autism diets, and it has been around the longest. Several other dietary approaches have cropped up. In my view, these more advanced diets don't help as much as the GFCF diet, but they can certainly have benefits for some children. I don't recommend that any parent start these other diets during the initial months of the biomedical protocol. It's more important to go gluten- and casein-free, start supplements, and have any medical problems treated. Then see how your child is doing, and at that point, you might consider these additional measures.

Specific Carbohydrate Diet

The SCD operates according to the theory that certain larger carbohydrates (mainly grains and starches) can be irritating to the intestinal lining, especially if that lining is already thin and inflamed. Such a lining has lost much of its digestive capability. Large carbs sit in the gut and act as food for any bad germs that live within the gut. The worst of these germs is yeast, but bacteria can also be a problem. The combination of carb irritation and yeast and bacterial overgrowth can create chronic diarrhea and contribute to autistic symptoms. Restricting large carbs allows gut healing to take place.

SCD was originally designed for patients with inflammatory bowel disease. When it was discovered that many children with autism also have IBD symptoms, the diet was recommended for them, too, with fairly good results.

In my experience, SCD is most beneficial for kids who are already off gluten and casein, on the biomedical supplements, and have had their intestinal yeast infections treated several times yet continue to struggle with chronic diarrhea and recurrent yeast infections. When I put such children on SCD, the intestinal lining is allowed to recover and become healthy again.

The best resource for SCD is *Breaking the Vicious Cycle,* by Elaine Gottschall. You can continue to go GFCF as you incorporate SCD as well. There is one area of conflict between the casein-free diet and SCD. One of the main carb sources in SCD is homemade cow's- or goat's-milk yogurt. The diet also allows some types of cheeses. While these are great sources of protein and simple carbs as well as probiotics, children who are especially sensitive to casein may have problems digesting the yogurt and cheese. Proponents of SCD believe that once a child has been GFCF for a while and the gut is partially healed, he may be able to tolerate the small amount of casein that is in milk-based yogurt (less than the casein in regular yogurt). They believe, and I agree, that the nutritional benefits from this yogurt may outweigh the casein exposure.

Here is a brief summary of what SCD entails (from Pangborn and Baker's *Autism: Effective Biomedical Treatments*).

Avoid the following sources of irritating carbs:

- fruits: canned fruits, jelly, ketchup, and sweetened dried fruits
- vegetables: potatoes, sweet potatoes, beans (black, pinto, kidney, etc.), and canned veggies

- grains: gluten grains, buckwheat, corn, millet, rice, amaranth, quinoa, and tapioca (and pasta, bread, and cereals made from these grains)
- protein foods: processed meats (hot dogs, bologna), fish sticks, canned meats, and processed cheese
- nuts: roasted and sweetened nuts
- drinks: milks (cow's, goat's, rice, soy, canned coconut) and soda

Here are some examples of what your child could eat instead:

- fruits: almost all fresh, frozen, and dried fruits
- vegetables: almost all fresh, frozen, raw, and cooked veggies
- protein foods: most fresh or frozen meats, poultry, and fish, eggs, some specific cheeses, some cottage cheeses, and homemade yogurt
- nuts: nut flours (instead of grains), natural nut butters, and most raw nuts
- drinks: fresh-squeezed fruit or veggie juices, weak herbal teas, goat's milk–yogurt shakes with honey, tomato juice, and natural fruit juices

If you are going to go SCD, you can't do it simply by following this list. There are a lot of details that are beyond the scope of this book. If your child fits the profile and you want to try the diet, read *Breaking the Vicious Cycle.* There are also several websites that discuss SCD. One of the best is www.SCdiet.org.

Some parents have reported that their children's intestinal symptoms and autistic behaviors worsen during the early weeks of the diet. This die-off reaction is thought to occur because the dying intestinal yeast and bacteria are releasing all their chemicals, which can be very irritating. This can happen when a yeast medication is used, too. I encourage parents to stick with the diet. Some gains should be noticeable after the die-off is over.

Parents have also reported periodic worsening of symptoms and behaviors every few months, followed by improvements that bring the child to a higher level of recovery each time.

Some people advocate an extremely strict adherence to SCD rules, which limit even the types of vitamins and nutritional supplements your child should take. They call acceptable supplements *SCD legal.* I don't usually have my patients go that far. I think it's fine to stay on whatever supplements you feel have been working for your child, even if they aren't SCD legal.

Phenol and Salicylate Restrictions

Phenols are natural chemicals that occur in a variety of foods. Salicylates are aspirin-like chemical compounds that exist naturally in some foods as well as artificially in a number of products. These two substances can irritate the nervous system and trigger behavioral problems. This was originally discovered by Dr. Benjamin Feingold, and he developed what is known as the Feingold Diet as a way to improve allergic medical conditions and behavioral disorders. It is thought that some children with autism may be affected by phenols and salicylates. While these foods and chemicals don't cause intestinal irritation like other foods do, they can affect the nervous system in a way that results in unwanted behaviors such as unusual outbursts, hyperactivity, and drunk-like behavior. In my experience, most kids with autism don't show noticeable reactions to foods containing phenols and salicylates. But a minority can be helped by restricting these foods. There is no good test to see if a child is phenol/salicylate sensitive. I first put my patients on the main diets, supplements, and treatments. If various behavioral problems persist, then I have the parents consider phenol and salicylate restriction and see if some behaviors subside.

There are hundreds of healthy foods that have phenols or salicylates in them. An excellent and comprehensive list that provides a complete breakdown of these foods from very low to extremely high levels is at www.GFCFdiet.com/SalicylatesGFCF food.htm. A more manageable list can be found at www.KirkmanLabs.com on the Phenol Assist Enzyme page (look under Products, then Enzymes).

You should see behavior improvements within a week or two of stopping (or significantly limiting) these foods. If you don't, your child might not be sensitive to phenols and salicylates. If you aren't sure, you could try having your child take a phenol-digestive enzyme (see page 200) to see if that helps. If the diet does help, then stay away from the foods for several months as your child continues through the rest of the biomedical plan. Once you are doing everything there is to do, try allowing some phenol foods and see what happens. Your child may be able to tolerate a certain level of phenols. You can also see what happens when you give him a daily phenol enzyme. He might be able to enjoy more of his favorite phenol foods.

Low Oxalate Diet

The natural chemical oxalate, which occurs in many foods, can cause inflammation and may inhibit glutathione production. A low-oxalate diet is a fairly new idea. It isn't clear what percentage of children are affected by oxalates, or whether or not oxalates affect children with autism more than they do other kids. I would offer the same advice for deciding whether and when to restrict oxalates as I did for phenols. You can find a list of high-oxalate foods at www.LowOxalate.info. Click on the Recipes and Food Lists icon on the left, then download the Oxalate Status Food Chart.

One of the urine tests that I recommend is the urine micro OAT test (see page 119). The expanded test, called the full OAT test, measures the level of oxalates in the urine. It would make sense that if a lot of oxalates are coming out in the urine, they are high in the body, but we are not sure that this is the case. The test also doesn't tell us if oxalates are affecting a child. If more information comes out on oxalates or testing, I will post an update on www.TheAutismBook.com.

MONITOR YOUR CHILD'S GROWTH

Restricting your child's diet may result in a temporary reduction in calorie intake. While this may slightly affect his weight, it shouldn't affect his rate of height gain. One goal of the GFCF diet is to heal your child's gut so that he will regain a good appetite and begin eating well again. When the diet is successful, any short-term lack of calories isn't a worry, and the benefits of a healthy gut and nutritious eating should be worth it in the long run. Your pediatrician and/or biomedical practitioner should check your child's growth at least every six months to be sure that he is getting adequate nutrition. On page 299, I offer tips on nutritional supplements that can help if a child isn't thriving. You and your doctor will need to decide if your child reaches a point where diet restrictions are doing more harm than potential good.

10

Vitamin and Nutritional Supplements

I hope you aren't jumping right to this section to start the vitamins first, hoping that your child shows amazing improvement from magic pills. I jest, but I'm also serious. The GFCF diet is challenging, and it would be much easier to just give your child a few vitamin supplements. But the biomedical approach doesn't work that way. The goal of general supplements is to provide nutritional support and improve the health of the intestines (*in addition to* what the diet is doing). Most children who respond well do so because they heal the gut through diet as well. Children who begin the vitamin supplements without also starting the diet rarely show much response.

There are two schools of thought regarding when to start the supplements in relation to the diet. Most believe that the diet should come first so that parents can see if the child is responding positively without any supplements to confuse the observations. Some feel that adding a few of the simple supplements (such as calcium, cod liver oil, taurine, digestive enzymes, and a multivitamin/mineral) provides better nutritional support during the initiation of diet restrictions, and that this benefit outweighs the need for objective observations.

I decide when to start the supplements based on how easy the transition into the diet is. If a child takes well to the new food selections, then his nutrition is adequately covered and the supplements can wait a month or two while parents watch for dietary benefits. But it's a good idea to have the initial supplements on hand when starting the diet so that if your child is slow to warm up to the new food choices, you can cover his need for calcium, vitamins, minerals, fats, and taurine, and you can enhance his digestion with enzymes. On page 231 I provide specific instructions on how to start these at the same time as the diet if that is your preference.

GENERAL GUIDELINES FOR TAKING SUPPLEMENTS

Many parents worry about whether giving their child multiple supplements is safe. I have never seen or heard of a child harmed by regular doses of the supplements discussed in this chapter. Although I suggest a particular order and some particular brand names, you can start any brand in any order without fear of harm. Here are some guidelines to follow as you get started:

Keep a written diary. It's important to keep a written record of the date you begin each supplement and your child's response. Some children won't show any changes, some will have a negative reaction (such as hyperactivity, increased stimming, worsened tantrums, or changes in bowel patterns), and most will respond in a positive way. I've had patients come to my office with vague reports like this: "Well, we started all the supplements, but now Sammy is more hyper." But they don't know when the hyperactivity increased. A parent who has kept a diary might report, "We started the first two supplements and noticed a few improvements. But when we began the multivitamin, Arnold started having some serious tantrums beyond what we are used to." With this family I can easily change over to another vitamin. An accurate diary makes the whole process much easier.

Try out liquids, capsules, powders, and chewables. Supplements come in all shapes and sizes. Because each child is unique in his taste and texture preferences, it's hard to predict which type your child will take most easily. Older kids who swallow capsules should take them if they are available. Capsules can also be opened and mixed into food or drink. Liquids are a good starting place for younger kids, but some have a very strong flavor. Powders mix well into food or drink, but some may leave a grainy texture. You will go through a lot of trial and error as you implement your child's supplement program.

Buy sample bottles or borrow from a friend. Before you shell out $50 for a large bottle of vitamins, see if the company offers a small sample bottle or packet for a few dollars. Or even better, see if another child in your TACA group (or other support group) is taking the vitamin you want your child to try and ask for a few days' worth. Once you determine that your child will take the product, you'll feel better about buying it.

Mix supplements together. You can mix virtually any of the regular supplements together. Whenever there is an exception to this rule, I will tell you. There are only two exceptions in this chapter:

1. Digestive enzymes may break down probiotics, so give probiotics at least an hour before or after digestive enzymes.

2. High doses of zinc may interfere with the absorption of other vitamins or minerals, so it's best to give any extra zinc supplements two or more hours before or after them.

Mix supplements into food and drink. You can put any type of supplement into any food or drink. I don't know of any exceptions to this rule. The food can be warm or cold. Do not cook any supplements into food.

TEACH YOUR CHILD TO SWALLOW CAPSULES

Capsules and tablets are often flavorless (unlike liquid and powder supplements), and graduating to pills can make a significant difference in successful supplementation. I have seen patients as young as five learn to swallow capsules. An occupational therapist is often the right person for the job. You can also ask moms in your local TACA or other support group for tips. The Center for Autism and Related Disorders (CARD, see page 139), with seventeen locations nationwide, offers periodic training sessions to teach children to swallow pills. This is worth a road trip if it will make your child's supplement life easier.

THE FIRST FIVE SUPPLEMENTS TO START

There are five basic supplements that every child with autism should start with, regardless of the child's unique health problems. I recommend you start your child on the supplements in the order in which I present them. Start a new supplement each week so that after five weeks your child is taking all five supplements. This allows you to track how your child is responding to each one.

Digestive Enzymes

Chronic diarrhea, irritation from food allergies, and yeast and bacterial imbalances can all thin out the intestinal lining. When this healthy lining is lacking, the digestive enzymes needed to break down and absorb protein, fat, carbs, vitamins, and minerals won't be produced. Even children without any apparent intestinal symptoms may lack these enzymes. The end result is potential deficiency in a number of important nutrients. Digestive enzymes help children better absorb their foods as well as their vitamin, mineral, and oil supplements. Better digestion may also result in less irritation from foods that a child's gut might otherwise be sensitive to.

Other supplements can be mixed into the food or drink simultaneously with digestive enzymes, with the exception of probiotics (see page 223). These live organisms may be broken down by the enzymes.

Understanding digestive enzyme ingredients. Many different enzymes are needed to assist with digestion. Each food has its own set of enzymes. Here are the types you will find in most multi-enzyme supplements:

- *Dipeptidyl peptidase IV (or DPP IV).* This is probably the most important enzyme for children with autism. It specifically digests casein and gluten proteins. Even children who are on a strict GFCF diet should take this enzyme to help protect them from any dietary accidents.

- *Protease.* This enzyme digests proteins.

- *Lipase and amylase.* These enzymes digest fats.

- *Lactase and other sugar "-ases."* These enzymes are for sugar digestion.

- *Bromelain and papain.* These natural enzymes come from pineapples and other tropical fruits and are incorporated into various products to help with certain aspects of digestion.

Choosing a specific brand. Many brands claim to be the best or to have some unique ingredient. I have used several brands over the years and have not developed a preference. Some formulations contain a mixture of enzymes to digest protein, fat, and sugar; others are more specific for a certain type of food. I prefer those that incorporate all the necessary enzymes into one supplement. It's less expensive and easier to administer. Here are some good choices (see Resources, page 351, for a list of the companies' websites):

• *EnZym-Complete/DPP IV with Isogest from Kirkman Labs.* This provides all of the necessary enzymes.

• *TriEnza from Houston Enzymes.* This is a complete multi-enzyme. Houston Enzymes also makes individual enzymes for specific food groups.

• *Digest Right from Learner's Edge.* This combination is similar to the others.

• *KHP Enzymes from Kartner Health.* This combination is similar to the others.

• *SerenAid and Vital-Zymes Complete from Klaire Labs.* SerenAid doesn't have as wide a range of enzymes as the rest, but it may be a good choice for children who react to other brands. Vital-Zymes Complete is similar to other multi-enzyme supplements.

• *Pancrecarb or Creon.* These prescription digestive enzymes contain only amylase and lipase for fat digestion and general protease for protein digestion. They were initially designed for children with cystic fibrosis. Children with autism who don't tolerate other digestive enzymes can try one of these.

• *No-Fenol from Houston Enzymes and Phenol Assist from Kirkman Labs.* These specific enzymes help with digesting phenols. I don't recommend trying these during initial supplementation. I recommend them mainly for parents who determine that their child is sensitive to phenol foods (see page 194) and want to allow their child to eat these foods occasionally.

Dosing digestive enzymes. Virtually all of these digestive enzyme products come in capsule form only. I suggest you follow the manufacturer's suggested dosing. If dosing isn't specified for your child's age, follow these guidelines: Any child old enough to swallow capsules should take one at the start of each meal. Children too young to swallow capsules should take about half a capsule opened into their food at the start of each meal. Kids five and older can increase to one whole capsule opened into food after being on the half dose for about one month. As soon as a child can swallow pills, you don't have to open them into food anymore.

Side effects of digestive enzymes. Most children don't report any side effects. The following may occur, however: abdominal pain, bloating, worsened diarrhea, increased tantrums, and hyperactivity. There are two possible reasons for these:

• A die-off reaction is occurring (see page 193).

• The DPP IV digests casein and gluten proteins thoroughly, so fewer morphine-like chemicals get into the body. The child may go through withdrawal and show worsened autistic symptoms.

These effects should be temporary. They may even be considered a positive sign, in that they show that the enzymes are inducing some changes within the gut. Most kids improve again after a couple of weeks of therapy. If symptoms are intolerable, stop the enzymes for a few days and then restart them at a lower dose. You can eventually work up to the full dose. If your child continues to have bothersome symptoms, change to a different brand. If that doesn't help, hold off for now. If your child doesn't have chronic diarrhea, digestive enzymes may not be a critical supplement, and you should move on to the next supplement. If chronic diarrhea is a problem, after a month or two, try a prescription enzyme (Pancrecarb or Creon).

WHERE TO FIND SUPPLEMENTS

Throughout the following chapters I recommend a variety of supplements. In many cases I suggest a specific brand because I have had good experience with it. When there are several brands that I like equally, I provide you with choices. In the Resources, page 351, I list the websites where you can find these supplements. I tell you when I feel that any brand you can find online or in a store will do. In some cases I provide a website within the text of the book.

Taurine

This amino acid plays an important role in many body functions: It helps with digestion and absorption of fats and vitamins, acts as an antioxidant, assists with detoxification and methylation (see page 255), and is used to form various brain neurotransmitters. It has also been shown to inhibit seizure activity in some patients (see page 296). Some of the more advanced supplements used in autism rely on the body's having a good supply of taurine.

Choosing a brand of taurine. Numerous companies make and sell taurine, and of course each one believes it makes the best. There is probably very little difference from brand to brand,

and the most important factor is finding one that your child will easily take. I usually start with Kirkman Labs' brand of taurine capsules.

Dosing taurine. Children age five and under should take 100 to 250 mg once daily. Children six years and up can take about 500 mg daily. Doses do not have to be precise to the exact milligram; if opening a capsule, don't worry if the dose varies slightly day to day. Side effects are virtually unheard of.

Cod Liver Oil and Fish Oil

Sounds yummy, right? Cod liver oil (CLO) is a specific type of fish oil taken from the livers of cod fish, whereas most fish oils are extracted from several parts of different kinds of fish. All fish oils contain the two omega-3 fats that our bodies need for a healthy cardiovascular system, neurological system, immune system, and intestinal system: DHA and EPA. They also contain a variety of other healthy fats. For children with autism, these extra fats help heal the gut, lower inflammation, act as antioxidants, and help with brain function. An additional benefit of CLO (as opposed to fish oils in general) is that it contains a natural source of vitamin A. This important vitamin helps with brain function and vision. Kids with autism who tend to study objects while looking at them sideways may improve in this behavior with CLO. CLO also has vitamin D, which is important for various body functions (see page 120).

Should you start with cod liver oil or fish oil first? I usually start children off with CLO because it contains vitamin A. CLO and fish oils come flavored to hide the fish taste, so most kids will accept them. If your child won't take CLO, move on to a fish oil (see below) and add vitamins A and D separately (which I describe below as well).

Choosing a cod liver oil. This is another arena in which everyone claims to make the best one. I believe the best for each child is the one that he will easily swallow without protest. Virtually all CLOs come flavored with natural lemon, orange, or strawberry oils and don't taste fishy. Here are a few that I've used over the years (see the Resources for a list of the companies' websites):

• *Nordic Naturals.* This is the first one I was introduced to and I've continued to recommend it as a good place to start. Their Arctic Cod Liver Oil comes in liquid or gelcaps, and they also have one with extra vitamin D added (this saves buying and giving a separate dose of vitamin D). Other companies are likely to begin adding extra vitamin D, too.

• *Carlson Labs.* This company makes a good liquid CLO for children and gelcaps for older kids.

• *Kirkman Labs.* This company makes its own CLO (liquid and gelcaps) and also sells some other brands.

ARE FISH OILS CONTAMINATED WITH CHEMICALS?

Parents often express concern that fish oil supplements might contain mercury or other pollutants from the ocean. After all, some fish contain mercury. Fish oil supplements are carefully tested (usually by independent companies as indicated on the product label or the company's website) to make sure they don't contain contaminants. I believe these companies are trustworthy and that the benefits of omega-3 fish oils are so significant that this concern shouldn't keep you away from CLO or fish oils.

Choosing a fish oil. Fish oils come from a variety of different types of fish. They generally don't contain vitamin A or D, unless it has been added, as indicated on the label. Here are fish oils I have had good results with (see the Resources for these companies' websites):

• *Metagenics EPA-DHA High Concentrate Liquid*. This one tastes fine and its high concentration means the volume of each dose is very low. Metagenics makes a variety of other formulations as well.

• *Coromega Brand*. This company makes convenient squeeze pouches.

• *Nordic Naturals*. This company makes a wide variety of fish oils in all types of dosing forms, including a concentrated liquid.

• *Kirkman Labs*. Kirkman Labs sells a variety of fish oils on its website.

• *KHP Omega Oils*. Kartner Health sells a good-tasting fish oil liquid.

• *Dr. Sears Family Essentials Brand*. Our family business makes some tasty liquid and chewable fish oil supplements.

• *Moxxor Brand*. This unique blend of fish and mussel oils with grape seed extract comes in a small, easy-to-swallow gelcap. It's a more potent anti-inflammatory than most brands.

Choosing between liquid, chewable gelcaps, and capsules. Wouldn't it be nice if every child would just swallow his daily CLO or fish oil without any complaints? Some kids do, but for many it's a challenge. You might need to try several options before you find one your child will take. Here are some guidelines:

- *Liquid.* This is the standard for every child who can't yet swallow pills. The usual dose is about ½ teaspoon, so it shouldn't be too difficult to hide it in food or a smoothie drink if your child won't take it straight. I like to start out with liquids. Some children with bionic taste buds, however, detect hidden fish oil and won't have anything to do with it. A chewable may be a better choice for such kids.

- *Chewable gelcaps.* Some companies make fish oil or CLO in very small gelcaps that can be chewed up. The taste and oily texture are the same, but some kids enjoy the fun of popping through the gelcaps. The main drawback is that a child has to eat anywhere from five to ten of these to equal a comparable liquid dose. But for a child who likes them, these are a good choice.

- *Fruit chewable fish oils.* This may be an easier way to get omega fish oils into a child. The only drawback is the fairly low dose of oils in each chew.

UNDERSTANDING CLO AND FISH OIL LABELS

The package usually lists the following information for each dose of the product (a dose usually equals 1 teaspoon or 1 to 3 capsules): (1) the total number of mg of fats (or oils); (2) the mg of specific types of fats (such as DHA and EPA); (3) the mg of other types of fats; and (4) the mg of total omega-3 fat. Percentages of DHA, EPA, and other types of fats will vary among products. These differences don't really matter at the beginning. I make my dosing recommendations based on the total number of milligrams of omega-3 fat. If the total isn't labeled, just add up the DHA, EPA, and "other omega 3s."

• *Adult gelcaps.* These are for older kids and adults. They often come flavored, so an option for younger kids is to poke open the gelcaps and squeeze out the oil. Adult gelcaps may be more concentrated than the straight liquid, so the amount you have to get into your child's mouth may be easier to handle.

Dosing cod liver oil and fish oil. Dosing doesn't have to be precise. Here are some guidelines:

• *Starting dose.* The best dose to begin with for any child two years and older is about 500 mg of total omega-3 fat once daily (if you're using Moxxor brand, the starting dose is only 150 mg, since it is so potent). The amount that equals this number of milligrams should be clearly indicated on the label. Infants and young toddlers should start with about 250 mg once daily and progress through the increases below at half the suggested doses.

• *Increasing dose.* After three weeks on the starting dose (during which time you will have added a few other supplements), increase the total omega-3 fat to about 500 mg *twice* daily (or 150 mg twice daily with Moxxor). I suggest morning and midafternoon. Supplements taken near bedtime (except those I specifically advise you to give at night) may keep a child awake.

• *Eventual target dose.* To avoid overloading on vitamins A and D, it's probably best to limit CLO to about 1000 to 1200 mg of total omega-3 fat daily (the above dose). But there will come a time in the protocol when I will recommend that you add even more omega-3 fat (see page 267). You will do so by adding a separate fish oil (which doesn't have vitamin A; a little extra D is okay) so that the total daily amount of omega-3 fat is about 2000 mg (divided into about 1000 mg twice daily). In general, this will mean about ½ to 1 teaspoon of CLO and of fish oil every day, or 2 to 3 capsules of each daily.

Side effects of fish oils. Side effects are uncommon. But children with autism can have behavioral reactions to a variety of supplements, and CLO and fish oils are no exception. The main unwanted reactions are hyperactivity, increased tantrums, and overall unusual behavior. These may be due to sensitivity to the particular flavor or other added ingredients, or to the proportions of DHA and EPA fats in the product. While most kids do very well when given equal amounts of these two fats, a minority of kids with autism have a deficiency in one and plenty of the other. This type of child would need to be supplemented with a higher proportion of the deficient fat. However, most parents aren't going to know their child's specific omega-3 metabolic profile, so it really comes down to trial and error. I start each child with supplements that have close to equal amounts of DHA and EPA. If your child reacts with negative behaviors, make the following changes one by one until you find a good match:

• Buy similar products but with a different flavor.

• Look at the websites for the companies I have provided and find a supplement that is higher in DHA and lower in EPA (see page 351).

• Try products that have more EPA than DHA.

• Look for soy lecithin in the ingredients. Some children are very sensitive to soy.

• Try going back to the starting dose and don't increase it.

Vitamins and Minerals

Many children with autism lack various vitamins and minerals because of intestinal problems and diet restrictions. Each vitamin and mineral plays an important part in body functions, so it's important to support a child's nutrition with recommended daily amounts. Some vitamins should be given in higher-than-normal doses for a while in order to correct deficiencies. Others are known to be therapeutic for certain neurological problems when given in high doses. The world of vitamin and mineral supplementation can be very confusing, but I will make it simple for you by suggesting specific brands and exact doses to give your child (see below in this chapter). If your child is already taking a basic multivitamin (not specifically designed for autism), switch to a specialized multivitamin/mineral supplement.

Here is a list of essential ingredients you should look for in a multivitamin/mineral supplement:

Vitamins	Minerals	Other
A	calcium	folinic acid
C	iodine	choline
D	magnesium	inositol
E	zinc	glycine
B1 (thiamine)	selenium	DMAE
B2 (riboflavin)	manganese	N-acetyl-cysteine
B3 (niacinamide)	chromium	taurine
B5 (pantothenic acid)	molybdenum	
B6 (pyridoxine or P5P-pyridoxal-5-phosphate)		
B7 (biotin)		
B12 (methylcobalamin)		

What does each ingredient do? Sometimes too much information is a bad thing, and trying to understand the many purposes of each vitamin and mineral can give anyone a headache. For those of you who are curious, I've laid it out for you here:

- *Vitamin A:* helps with general neurological function and vision; may suppress measles virus

- *B vitamins:* help with neurological and immune function; assist in various metabolic processes in the cells

- *Vitamin B6:* helps with overall neurological function and specifically assists with methylation metabolism

- *P5P:* is the active form of B6; the body converts B6 into P5P (see below)

- *Vitamin C:* acts as an antioxidant

- *Vitamin D:* regulates calcium levels in the body; stimulates the body's natural detox system

- *Vitamin E:* acts as an antioxidant

- *Calcium:* builds strong bones; essential to efficient cellular functions

- *Iodine:* is used in the production of thyroid hormone

- *Magnesium:* assists in many aspects of cellular metabolism and helps move the stools

- *Zinc:* important in various cellular processes; boosts the immune system

- *Selenium:* helps detoxification; boosts the immune system

- *Manganese and molybdenum:* help with various cellular functions

- *Chromium:* assists with immune function

- *Other ingredients:* perform a variety of functions

Is it safe to take high doses of vitamins? Almost all of the vitamins and minerals in the multivitamins that I recommend are in standard RDA amounts, or slightly higher. Some of the B vitamins and vitamin C are several times higher than RDA. This is perfectly safe; anything the body doesn't need passes out harmlessly in the urine. Vitamin B6, however, is often provided in extremely high doses, sometimes as much as 100 times the RDA (labeled as 10,000% of RDA). There's a good reason for this. B6 is necessary for proper methylation. Many children with autism don't process B6 very well, so normal dietary amounts may leave them deficient. As a supplement, B6 needs to be taken in very high doses for enough to get into the cells and the nervous system of a child with autism. Decades ago researchers discovered that institutionalized children and adults with autism showed significant improvement when given very high doses of B6.

One vitamin that could create a potentially harmful overdose with long-term use is vitamin A, because it is found in both multivitamins (about 5000 IU per dose; IU stands for *international units*) and cod liver oil (about 1000 IU per dose). There is some controversy over how much vitamin A should be taken daily. Doctors are taught that the maximum daily amount for adults is 5000 IU and for children, 2500 IU (1250 IU for ages two to three). Most alternative-minded health care practitioners believe we can take about three times that amount without any problems and enjoy potential benefits. Children with autism need extra vitamin A to aid in neurological and visual function. It is my opinion that children aged two to three can safely take 2500 IU daily, aged four to six can take 5000 IU, and children aged seven to twelve can take 7500 IU daily. If you follow my dosing guidelines for the multivitamins and cod liver oil that I recommend, safe levels of vitamin A won't be exceeded. As a safeguard, vitamin A levels can be tested a few months after beginning these supplements to ensure the blood level is normal (see page 281). Some companies make a multivitamin/mineral without vitamin A (and some without D) for those parents who want to add lower doses separately.

Take multivitamins/minerals with a meal or snack. It's best to take these supplements with breakfast and then again in the midafternoon with a snack. Do not take a dose with dinner or near bedtime, as this may cause sleeplessness.

Understand the difference between vitamin B6 and P5P. There is a very important distinction between these two. B6 is an inactive vitamin; it doesn't do anything within the body as it is. The body has to convert it to its active form, P5P, in order for it to perform its functions. As you have already learned, various aspects of body metabolism don't work very well in some children with autism, and the conversion of B6 to P5P is one of these aspects. There's no test that can be done to determine how each individual child handles B6 conversion. Some companies put only B6 and others only P5P into their products. But many companies put in both B6 and P5P. I suggest parents start with a product that provides both. If your child becomes hyperactive (or more so than he already is), you might need to switch to a different formulation. See the discussion of side effects below for information on how to find a formulation that fits your child. P5P comes in much lower doses than B6. That's because the active form is much more potent.

Proper dosing of vitamin B6. Every child's metabolism is different. Some kids have severe methylation inefficiency, which requires higher B6 doses, and some have only minor methylation defects (or normal function) and may need very little extra B6. Some children convert B6 to P5P less efficiently than others do, so they may do better when given P5P directly, to bypass the conversion step. Here are some guidelines to help you find the right dose:

• The maximum daily amount of B6 any child should take is 8 mg for each pound of body weight, not to exceed 500 mg. For example, a thirty-pound three-year-old can take as much as 240 mg a day, divided into 120 mg twice daily. However, that dose may be much more than is actually needed. This is simply the maximum.

• The maximum daily dose of P5P isn't known, but since it's more potent than B6, I suggest limiting P5P to no more than 2 mg per pound of body weight, or a maximum of 100 mg daily.

• If you are using a combination of B6 and P5P, I suggest limiting each to about half of their maximum for your child's body weight.

• The goal is to provide gradually increasing doses of B6 or P5P (or both) up to the maximum until you see what dose your child does best with (see page 218).

Getting the most vitamins for your money. Pay attention to the "serving sizes" in various products. In one liquid product, 1 teaspoon may contain a certain number of milligrams of each vitamin, and in another, it may takes 6 teaspoons to equal the same number of milligrams. This can help you determine the quantity your child will have to swallow and the cost of a month's worth of product.

Choosing a multivitamin. I recommend beginning with one of the following multivitamin/mineral products, all of which have a combination of B6 and P5P. These brands contain the most important ingredients. None of these multivitamin/mineral supplements provide the full dosing of everything your child will need. Individual vitamins and minerals will have to be added (zinc, extra B6, calcium, magnesium, vitamin C, and vitamin D; see page 220). Websites are listed in Resources.

• *Spectrum Support from BrainChild Nutritionals.* This company makes several formulations that vary slightly in certain vitamin levels and ingredients. They make only liquid preparations. Their B6 and P5P levels are lower than other companies' products, so an additional B6 or P5P supplement will likely need to be purchased.

• *Super-Nu Thera from Kirkman Labs.* This company makes numerous products in liquid, powder, and capsule form. They make some without vitamins A and D (for those who prefer to get these from other sources). They provide B6 doses ranging from fairly low to very high (don't start with the highest one; change over to it later if your child ends up doing well on maximum B6 doses). They have combination B6/P5P choices as well. They also make a standard multivitamin (by the name of *Spectrum Complete*) that contains regular doses of all vitamins and minerals, including regular amounts of B6. They also make a separate high-dose B6 in both capsule and chewable form and a B6/magnesium combo (as well as P5P options) that can be added so parents can adjust the B6 or P5P doses individually. I generally recommend their Super-Nu Thera with vitamins A and D that has both B6 and P5P.

• *Child Essence by Learner's Edge.* They make a capsule multi-vitamin with P5P only. Additional B6 may need to be added.

• *Basic Nutrients Plus and P5P with Magnesium from New Beginnings.* This brand comes in capsule form only in two separate products: Basic Nutrients Plus, which contains regular doses of all vitamins and minerals, and a separate P5P plus magnesium so that P5P dosing can be adjusted up or down as desired.

• *VitaSpectrum by Klaire Labs.* This product comes in capsule and powder form. It is similar to the other brands except that it contains only slightly higher than normal B6 and P5P levels. They also make separate B6 and P5P plus magnesium products.

• *KHP Vitamins & Minerals.* Kartner Health makes one powder form with slightly higher than normal B6.

Dosing multivitamins/minerals. Many parents get confused and shy away from these products until they receive exact dosing suggestions from a doctor. Most products come with suggested dosing for adults (such as two capsules twice daily) but don't specify doses for children. Parents worry about overdosing. In reality, it can be very simple. Here's what I suggest:

• Begin with half of the serving size listed on the label once each morning (as long as it doesn't exceed any of my dosing parameters). This is not the suggested dosing; rather, it is the number of capsules, teaspoons, or ounces of powder or liquid that contains the listed milligrams of ingredients. For example, a product might say, "Recommended dose: 1 to 2 teaspoons per day or as directed by your physician." That is not the dose I suggest you follow. The label will also state, for example, "Each serving size of 1 teaspoon contains the following milligrams of vitamins," then list these ingredients. It is that "serving size" that I recommend you base your dosing on.

• For two- and three-year-old children, continue that dose (half the serving size once daily).

• For children four years and older, after three weeks, increase to the same dose twice daily (half the serving size in the morning and again with a midafternoon snack). Watch to see how your child tolerates it (see side effects, below). Children four to six years old should stay on that dose.

• Children seven and older, after three weeks of that twice-daily dosing, can then work up to the full serving size twice daily.

• Don't exceed any suggested dosing that you find on the label without a doctor's permission.

Increasing to higher B6 doses. Once you determine that your child is doing well on a multivitamin/mineral, it's time to try some extra B6. Many of the above companies make a plain B6, sometimes with magnesium. It's fine to use B6 from a different company than the one you use for your multivitamin brand. Add an extra 12.5 to 25 mg of B6 to each dose of the multivitamin. Every week increase by this much again until you reach a total dose of 4 mg of B6 per pound of body weight (count both the multivitamin and the additional B6), or a maximum of 250 mg (divided into two daily doses). This is half of the eventual maximum of 500 mg daily (or 8 mg of B6 per pound of body weight) that I will work your child up to in chapter 12. Observe for side effects such as hyperactivity, increased stimming, or aggressive behavior. The optimal dose is whatever seems to create improvement in your child's behavior or abilities without causing side effects.

If unwanted side effects occur, go through the checklist below.

If you decide to change to P5P for your child's high-dose form of B6, start with about 0.5 mg per pound of body weight (12.5 mg of P5P for a twenty-five-pound child) per day. Slowly increase by 12.5 mg increments each week until you reach half of the maximum dose (50 mg, or 1 mg per pound of weight, including what's in your multivitamin). As with B6, in chapter 12 we'll maximize dosing to 2 mg per pound of weight.

Side effects of multivitamins/minerals and making adjustments. Serious reactions are virtually unheard of. In experimental studies involving extremely high doses of B6 (more than 500 mg daily), some patients developed peripheral neuropathy, a condition in which the nerves in the face, arms, or legs become dysfunctional. Weakness and lack of coordination are the main symptoms. This resolves when the vitamin is stopped. I have not heard of any child developing this symptom from dosing within the guidelines I've provided.

The main unwanted reactions, which occur in about 10 percent of children, are hyperactivity, stimming, and aggressive behavior. These resolve quickly when the product is stopped. Here are the various theoretical reasons that a child might react to these products (or react to the high B6 within the product) and the changes you can make to eliminate these reactions:

- *Sensitivity to the flavor in a liquid or powder.* Change to a different flavor.

- *Sensitivity to a particular added ingredient.* Change to a different brand with fewer or different ingredients.

- *Stomach upset.* Be sure to take it with food.

- *Zinc deficiency.* Zinc is needed to help convert B6 to P5P. If a child is severely zinc-deficient, the amount of zinc in these products might not be enough. Try stopping the vitamin, adding extra zinc (see page 221) for two weeks, and then restarting the multivitamin again (as you continue the extra zinc).

• *Inadequate magnesium intake.* See page 221 to make sure your child is getting enough magnesium.

• *Hyperactivity.* B6 requirements vary, but if a child receives more than he needs, he may become hyperactive. Switch to a lower B6 multivitamin/mineral formulation.

• *P5P and B6 imbalance.* As you have already learned, some children do better on P5P than on B6. If you are giving your child a B6 multivitamin/mineral formulation, switch to a P5P-only brand, or vice versa. If you are giving your child additional B6 and you see unwanted symptoms, change over to P5P.

ASK TACA

TACA has many experienced parents who know what they are talking about when it comes to supplements. If you have any questions, visit www.TACAnow.org. They have a live chat room (staffed by trained parents, not doctors) and are happy to provide support, answer questions, and offer suggestions to parents.

Giving extra individual vitamins and minerals. The multivitamin/mineral supplements don't provide enough of several items that are important for kids with autism. Here are some vitamins and minerals that you should give twice daily in addition to the multivitamin/mineral:

- *Calcium.* Children who go on a casein-free diet can become calcium-deficient. Alternative milks are usually fortified with calcium, but it might not be enough. Children need about 800 mg of calcium each day. Calcium not only helps build strong bones, it plays a role in many aspects of cellular metabolism. Unless your multi already has enough, I recommend supplementing with 250 mg of extra calcium twice daily. You can easily find liquid, powder, or capsule forms of calcium on the same websites that provide the multivitamins. You may find it convenient to buy a calcium/magnesium combination if your child needs more magnesium, too.

- *Magnesium.* Magnesium works synergistically with B6. The actions of one are dependent on adequate supplies of the other. Children should get between 2 and 4 mg of magnesium for every pound of body weight. A thirty-pound child would need between 60 and 120 mg daily. Most multivitamin/mineral products provide enough magnesium, but if yours does not, find a supplement. A child who does well on high-dose B6 will probably do well with the high end of magnesium dosing (4 mg per pound of weight). Magnesium can cause diarrhea (it is actually used to treat constipation, page 294), so reduce the dose if this occurs. Any brand is fine.

- *Zinc.* Most children with autism are deficient in zinc. This mineral helps with methylation, boosts the immune system, and improves intestinal function. Most multivitamins/minerals supply between 5 and 20 mg of zinc per dose. This may not be enough, and supplementing with additional zinc so that the total daily amount adds up to the following doses is helpful: One- to three-year-olds need 15 mg daily; four- to six-year-olds need 30 mg; and older children should take 40 mg. It's best to divide the dose into two daily doses and to give them with a snack about two hours before or after other supplements (zinc can interfere with absorption of other supplements). Try to find either zinc picolinate or zinc monomethionine.

- *Vitamin C.* This is an important antioxidant for kids with autism, and it assists with various metabolic functions. But multi-vitamins/minerals don't supply enough vitamin C. Various forms are available in stores or online. I happen to like Kirkman Labs' vitamin C powder because the dose volume is very small. The total daily amount a child should take (the amount in the multivitamin plus a separate vitamin C) is as follows: Two- and three-year-olds should take 250 mg daily; four- to six-year-olds should take 500 mg daily; and older kids should take 500 mg twice daily.

- *Vitamin D.* Recent studies have shown that a large percentage of our population is deficient in vitamin D. Vitamin D is actually a hormone that is produced in our skin from sunlight exposure, and it plays an important role in many bodily functions. Our society's sun phobia may be causing more harm than good. Experts believe that in order to bring the body's level of vitamin D up to normal, about 1000 IU for every twenty-five pounds of body weight should be given once a day. This is much higher than the RDA amount, but I've reviewed the research, and I believe it is very important. Many brands are available to supplement the amount in your multivitamin. I like Carlson Labs' vitamin D drops. Some cod liver oils and fish oils are now being supplemented with high-dose vitamin D (1000 IU per dose), so this may be a convenient option for your child.

- *Iron.* Infants normally become slightly deficient in iron around one year of age. As the diet expands to include more iron-containing foods in the second year, this deficiency usually corrects itself. However, persistent low iron can lead to anemia, which in turn can contribute to intellectual developmental delay. Your doctor can screen for iron-deficiency anemia with a CBC (see page 94) or a specific iron and ferritin level. If iron is low, supplement with daily iron according to your doctor's recommendations (I suggest Floradex brand; it's better absorbed and easier on the stomach than most forms of iron).

Probiotics

Probiotics are healthy bacteria that live in the intestines. They help with digestion, protect against infections and allergies, and prevent yeast overgrowth. As you learned in chapter 4, antibiotics destroy the natural gut probiotics. As a result, yeast and harmful bacteria can take over and cause chronic diarrhea, constipation, and digestive problems. Replacing these missing organisms (even in children without intestinal symptoms) helps the gut healing that began with the GFCF diet.

Types of probiotics. There are hundreds of different probiotic products on the market. Each claims that its own unique blend is the best. I don't have a particular preference. There are, however, five types that experts believe provide the most benefit. These are incorporated into many products:

• *Lactobacillus acidophilus.* This is the most common type used in supplements and has been around the longest.

• *Bifidobacterium.* This is another common one that has been used for many years.

• *Lactobacillus rhamnosus and Lactobacillus GG, a strain of L. rhamnosus.* These specific strains of lactobacillus bacteria have recently been discovered and are thought to be more potent than L. acidophilus. Whether this is true is hard to say.

• *Streptococcus.* This probiotic is different from the strep throat type. It interacts with other probiotics to help them grow.

• *Saccharomyces boulardii.* This is actually a yeast germ (whereas the others are bacteria), but it doesn't take hold within the intestine and cause infection. Instead, it kills other yeast germs, especially Candida albicans. It also helps other probiotics grow. Unlike the other probiotics, it isn't designed for continuous use. On page 236, I describe how to use it.

Choosing a probiotic. While some probiotics may be better than others, there's really no way to know which ones are going to be best for your child until you try them. I recommend that you start with a probiotic that incorporates most or all of the above types (except S. boulardii; that comes later). If this, along with diet and other yeast treatments, helps resolve your child's intestinal problems (if he had any to begin with) and your child is showing overall improvement in other aspects of his autism, then it's probably the right choice. If your child has persistent or recurrent intestinal symptoms or if yeast keeps coming back (as determined by repeat testing), a change in probiotics is warranted. While any brand is fine, here are some of the specific choices that I've recommended over the years (in no particular order of preference). These come in a variety of forms: capsules, powders, liquids, and pearls (small, easy-to-swallow balls). See Resources, page 351, for a list of the companies' websites:

• *Lactobacillus and bifidobacterium combination (any brand).* Most health food stores and online supplement companies carry this basic probiotic combination. Any brand you can find is okay to start with as long as it is milk-free (some probiotics contain milk products).

• *Ther-biotic Complete from Klaire Labs.* This broad-spectrum probiotic contains many of the standard types. I have found it to be well tolerated by many of my patients. I start kids of any age at ⅛ teaspoon once daily and increase to ¼ teaspoon twice daily as tolerated. Klaire Labs makes a variety of other probiotics for specific situations.

- *ThreeLac.* This unique blend of three types has become quite popular. It comes in single-dose packets. Kids two and up can take about half a packet twice daily (or a full packet once daily). Infants should take half that amount. It is available from numerous online sources.

- *Pro-Bio Gold from Kirkman Labs.* This probiotic blend is an effective mix of various types.

- *Culturelle.* This is a single probiotic type, Lactobacillus GG, which is thought to be one of the most potent probiotics. It is available in stores and on numerous online sites.

- *KHP Probiotics.* This is a blend of various standard types of probiotics from Kartner Health.

Dosing probiotics. Dosing varies greatly from brand to brand and type to type. I have provided a specific dose for some brands I am familiar with. For the others, I suggest you follow the dosing guidelines on the label if a dose for children is specified. If the label provides a dose for older children (such as 6 and older) only, give your one- to five-year-old about half that amount. If your brand gives a dose for children twelve and older (or adults) only, give half that amount if your child is six to eleven, and one-quarter if your child is under six. If your probiotic suggests a range of dosing, start off low and see how your child does. Increase to the highest dose over a few weeks as long as your child tolerates it. It's best to give probiotics in two daily doses, but it's okay to give them only once a day if giving supplements is a challenge. Do not give probiotics at the same time as digestive enzymes (the enzymes will break down the probiotics). Separate them by at least one hour.

Side effects of probiotics. The main side effects are abdominal pain, gas, bloating, and worsened diarrhea. These can mean that the probiotic is working, killing off some bad germs in the gut, which release their toxins and cause these symptoms. If side effects are tolerable, hang in there. They should subside within a week or two. If symptoms are too uncomfortable, or mild symptoms persist for more than two weeks, stop the probiotics and let the reaction subside. Then restart at half the dose and see how that goes. If problems persist, change to a different probiotic.

GETTING THE MEDICINE DOWN

The very idea of trying to get several supplements into your non-compliant child may seem overwhelming. Coaxing your child to take his supplements twice a day won't be easy, but almost every parent whom I've worked with has been able to get her child on a manageable supplement routine. Here are some tips:

- *Don't try to hide them.* Although hiding supplements in food and drink works well for some children without oral aversion who will eat and drink pretty much anything, many kids with autism are the opposite. Their bionic sense of taste and smell will detect everything. It's hard enough to feed these children; you don't want them to begin rejecting food and drink because they don't trust what's in it. Be open with the fact that it's medicine time.
- *Be firm.* This isn't the time to be Ms. Nice Guy and beg and plead with your child to take his supplements. Be very straightforward about it. Don't ask in a nice cute little baby voice; tell him it's medicine time in your stern (but not angry) voice.
- *Use rewards.* Choose a daily activity that your child enjoys (such as TV or eating a treat) and lay down the law: He doesn't

See page 243 for more information on how to minimize yeast die-off symptoms.

Varying probiotics over time. Some physicians advise switching probiotics every three to six months. Periodic exposure to new strains of probiotics may do a better job of fighting off harmful intestinal bacteria and yeast. If your child's intestinal or yeast symptoms keep returning, switching probiotics is a good idea. But if you find a probiotic that consistently works for your child,

get to do it until after medicine time. Repeat over and over, day after day, "You can watch TV (or whatever the reward is) after you take your medicine" or "Do you want to watch TV? First, take your medicine." Be consistent and never waver. A smile and a hug should also accompany the reward.

- *Use ABA therapy time.* Ask your ABA therapist to teach your child how to take his supplements. Once your child complies, continue using the same technique.
- *Mix supplements into a small serving of pureed foods.* Pear, peach, and apple puree (or baby food) have a slightly tart flavor that can mask supplements. Experiment with varying amounts (1 to 4 tablespoons per round of several supplements) to see what your child will take. Don't try to hide it; let your child know it's medicine time. Add a drop of Stevia or other natural sweetener if needed. Small bites of GFCF ice cream may also work.
- *Mix supplements into a small quantity (2 tablespoons) of strong-flavored liquid.* A smoothie works well, as does pear, orange, pineapple, or grape juice. Mix it in a bowl, then draw it up into a syringe or medicine cup. Add Stevia if needed.
- *Ask around at your next TACA meeting.* You'll hear many unique approaches from other moms.

my attitude is, if it ain't broke, don't fix it. It's okay to stay on the same one for years.

Getting It All Started

I gave you a lot of information to "digest" in this chapter, but what it really boils down to is about seven different supplements given twice daily using the dosing that I've supplied. There are two basic approaches to starting supplements. I don't have a preference; each has its advantages and disadvantages. Let's explore both of them and you can decide.

The one-at-a-time slow approach. This is the most scientific way to begin supplements because you will carefully observe each individual response along the way. It also takes the longest to get on the whole treatment plan. You start the supplements one at a time, some at full dosing and some at a lower dose that you will then gradually raise. You observe your child for anything positive, negative, or neutral along the way and keep a careful diary. Begin each supplement in the following order according to these guidelines:

1. *Start the GFCF diet.* I know you've already done so, but this is just a reminder. After you've taken a month or so to observe how this diet affects your child, move on.

2. *Digestive enzymes.* Begin these according to my dosing guidelines on page 203. If your child has a die-off reaction, as described on page 226, hang in there. The reaction should subside in a week or two and you can move on to the next step. If there is no die-off reaction, you can move on as soon as you see some improvement in the health of the stools or in your child's behavior or after a week has gone by without anything positive or negative occurring.

3. *Taurine.* Follow the dosing guidelines on page 205. There shouldn't be any negative effects, but if any adverse behavioral reactions do occur, stop the taurine. Move on to the next step after one week of taurine.

4. *Cod liver oil or fish oil.* Begin the starting dose (page 209). As soon as you see positive changes, go ahead and increase to the next dosing level. If you don't see any benefits within two weeks, go ahead and increase. If negative behaviors occur, stop the oil and buy a different flavor and try again. If the same negative behaviors recur, follow the suggestions on page 210. You might need to try a fish oil instead. Once your child is on the increased dose level and you've observed benefits or no change at all for more than a week, move on to the next step. There is a third level in fish oil dosing that you will come back to in a couple of months (see Eventual Target Dose, page 209).

5. *Multivitamin/mineral supplement.* Use the dosing guidelines on page 217. After three weeks (or sooner if you see positive changes), increase to the next dosing level. If you see negative changes, decrease to the previous dosing level or stop the product. If it's necessary, restart the process with a different mix of B6/P5P, a different flavor, or a different brand. Don't worry about working up to high B6 dosing just yet. Try to bring your child up to a moderate level of B6 and see how he does. Once your child is taking this and doing well for two weeks, move on.

6. *Probiotics.* Hold on to your hats. If anything is going to cause a die-off reaction, this is it. Begin your probiotic according to the dosing guidelines on page 225. If uncomfortable die-off occurs, stop the product and purchase some activated charcoal capsules and Epsom salt baths. Follow the instructions on page 244 for beginning these anti–die-off treatments, and after a couple of days, resume the probiotic at half the dose you previously

used. Slowly work up to the target dose over a few weeks. As soon as you see positive changes in the health of the stools or behavior improvement (after die-off has subsided, if it occurs), move on to the next step. If two weeks go by without any positive or negative changes, move on.

7. *Other single vitamins and minerals.* Begin calcium, magnesium, and vitamins C and D together. If you observe any negative changes, you'll have to start them over one at a time to see which is the culprit. If there are no more negative reactions, add zinc according to the dosing on page 221.

There are two main advantages to this approach:

• You can accurately observe how each individual supplement is helping your child so that you can feel better about continuing it long-term.

• If there is a negative reaction, you can immediately know the culprit. Negative reactions are less likely when treatments are introduced gradually, especially in sensitive children.

The drawbacks to this approach are:

• It takes a very long time to get on the full spectrum of supplements. Not including the initial diet changes, it should take about three months to get up to full speed with everything. This isn't such a bad thing for younger children, but parents of an older child may feel like they want to get everything going more quickly.

• It delays some of the more potent treatments, like yeast medication and methyl B12, which often create bigger "wows" in children than the initial supplements do.

The fast-track approach. With this method, children begin about half of the supplements at the same time. They begin with very small doses and gradually increase everything over a few weeks. They then begin the other half and slowly work those up. This takes half the amount of time and it isn't necessarily more likely to cause a negative reaction, since everything is introduced slowly. The main drawback is that you won't know which supplements are responsible for improvements. However, if you get some nice "wows," you might not care! Follow these guidelines:

1. During introduction of the GFCF diet, begin basic vitamin supplementation with digestive enzymes, taurine, cod liver oil, multivitamins/minerals, calcium, and vitamin D, but start these at one-quarter my suggested dosing and slowly increase to regular dosing over three weeks. Do not proceed to separate high-dose B6 or an additional fish oil yet. If you see a die-off reaction, begin charcoal and Epsom salt baths to try to push through it while sticking with the supplements (see die-off instructions, page 243). We expect to see some die-off reactions as many changes occur within the gut, especially with probiotics in step 2, below. Another option is to start the diet first, and then, after two weeks, begin all of the supplements in this paragraph as stated.

2. After your child has been on these first supplements for about two weeks, add in the second half in a similar manner: Give one-quarter the dose of probiotics, vitamin C, magnesium, and zinc, and slowly work up to the full dose over two weeks.

3. Wait two more weeks and then begin additional B6 or P5P dosing according to the instructions on page 218 until you reach half the maximum dosing.

The decision about which approach to take is based largely on the age and past sensitivity level of the child, what the parents have tried in the past, and how eager they are to get everything going as quickly as possible.

Letting It All Soak In

Once you have your child on this first stage of treatment, allow a few weeks to go by while you observe how it's all working together. If you see good things, great. If you don't see much, that's okay. Some children don't respond until more advanced stages of treatment are implemented. If your child has worsened and none of the suggested adjustments have helped, take a step back and stop the supplements. You can move on to yeast treatment without them. See if yeast treatment leads to any great strides. You can always come back to try basic supplements again once the gut is cleaned up.

SUPPLEMENT UPDATES ON WWW.THEAUTISMBOOK.COM

Companies make changes in their products and develop new supplements from time to time. The choices I offer in this book were available at the time of this writing. As I come across other brands or newer supplements, I will post these recommendations on the website.

11

Treating Yeast and Bacterial Infections

Doctors who first worked with children with regressive autism back in the early 1990s found that one of the biggest "wows" came from treating intestinal yeast overgrowth, and this benefit holds true today. Children whose diarrhea doesn't go away with the GFCF diet usually show resolution with yeast medications. They also show improvement in the areas of language, tantrums, hyperactivity, and stimming. In chapter 4, I explained that many children with autism have yeast overgrowth in their intestines. In chapter 5, I showed you how to have your child tested for yeast. Now let's talk about treatment.

The best way to rid the body of yeast, and keep it away for good, is to use a three-pronged treatment approach: dietary changes to prevent yeast growth; natural treatments to suppress yeast growth; and prescription medications to periodically kill off yeast overgrowth. This third step is often the easiest, but it causes the most wear and tear on the body. The most successful families are those that incorporate all three approaches. I usually start with natural treatments to reduce yeast followed by a round of medical treatment to flush it out. Then I continue natural treatments while yeast-preventing diet changes begin.

One note before we start: We all have yeast in our bodies. It's supposed to be there. That's why most mainstream medical professionals scoff at the idea that intestinal yeast can cause problems. But yeast (like all living organisms) generates waste products. Some people are sensitive to these chemicals. So, there are two questions to answer:

1. How much yeast does your child have?

2. Is your child affected by the yeast's toxins?

Some children have a lot of yeast, but treating it doesn't seem to lead to any improvement. There is no medical test that measures whether or not a child is sensitive to yeast toxins. Since most children are sensitive, it's worth going through treatment and prevention measures to see if your child benefits.

SYMPTOMS OF INTESTINAL YEAST OVERGROWTH

Symptoms vary among children, and it's useful for parents to identify a child's unique signs so that they can know when repeat courses of treatment may be needed. In addition to looking for the obvious intestinal symptoms of abdominal pain, bloating, and diarrhea, also watch for night waking, unusual laughing, drunken-like or foggy behavior, lowered energy level, increased tantrums, stimming, or aggression, constant chewing on objects or teeth grinding, anal redness or itching, hand flapping, and toe walking.

NATURAL YEAST TREATMENTS

Some of the supplements you have already started giving your child may help with yeast. Probiotics fight yeast by competing for space and nutrients in the gut. Digestive enzymes may reduce yeast by allowing fewer nutrients (which yeast feeds on) to pass undigested into the colon. Vitamin C, in doses of 500 mg or more, may kill yeast. Below are several additional supplements that act more directly on yeast. Your child can take one or all of the five I list here. They work in different ways that may complement each other. You can begin these treatments even if your child has never been tested for yeast, especially if he has received numerous antibiotics, the number one cause of yeast overgrowth. For specific name brands that I refer to, see Resources, page 351, for website information.

Colostrum. This is the milk produced by mammals in the first few days after they give birth. Human colostrum is very beneficial to babies. It is filled with immune boosters, healing agents, anti-inflammatories, and natural germ fighters, and it is just the thing for healing up an irritated gut and keeping any unwanted yeast or bacterial germs at bay. The problem is, human colostrum isn't available as a nutritional supplement. So, we turn to the next best thing...cows. Various companies collect colostrum from cows during the first days after they give birth before they begin producing mature milk. The casein proteins are removed and the colostrum is processed for use in children (and adults). Dosing varies according to the product. I recommend you follow the instructions on the label. If dosing for a child isn't specified, give half the adult dose. Here are some brands that I've had some experience with:

- *Colostrum Gold.* Kirkman Labs makes this liquid form.

- *Ora Mune Gold Liquid Colostrum.* Ora Mune makes several liquid products, including colostrum. Transfer factor and beta glucan are other components of their colostrum products, which boost the immune system and may fight off yeast.

• *Transfer Factor Multi-Immune.* Researched Nutritionals makes this blend of colostrum with other immune-boosting agents.

Grapefruit seed extract. This natural product comes as concentrated drops that you place in food or drink. I've been using the NutriBiotic brand with good results. Kids two to four years old should take about two drops once or twice daily. Kids five years and older should take three to five drops once or twice daily. They also make capsules for older kids.

Saccharomyces boulardii. This yeast kills other yeast and bad bacteria in the intestines. It isn't designed for continuous use. Courses of ten days to three weeks are helpful in flushing out yeast as often as needed. Search online for various companies that make it and follow the manufacturer's dosing recommendations. Typical dosing is about two billion organisms once or twice daily for children of any age.

Candex. This unique digestive enzyme, made by Pure Essence Labs, breaks down fiber, a major component of the outer capsule of yeast germs. It should be taken at least an hour before or after meals and other supplements. Follow the dosing instructions on the label or on the manufacturer's website.

Monolaurin. This is a type of fat found in breast milk and other places in nature. It has antifungal, antiviral, and antibacterial properties. Forms manufactured from coconut milk are available online. I like the Lauricidin brand. It comes as tiny pellets that can be swallowed or crushed into food. The company's website provides specific dosing instructions for children.

Long-term use of these natural products. The supplements that I discuss above can be taken indefinitely (with the exception of

S. boulardii). I suggest, however, that you take a break for a few weeks from each product (one at a time) at least every six months. This allows you to observe your child to see if "yeasty" behaviors return. If they do, this is a sign that ongoing use of products is important. More important, this means that yeast toxins do have an effect on your child and that some level of underlying yeast is persisting in your child's gut. A course of antifungal medication (see below) may be useful in cleaning out the yeast more thoroughly before you restart the natural products. This may bring your child's behavior up to a whole new level.

YEAST-FREE DIET

The term *yeast-free* is a bit misleading. Changing the diet to help reduce yeast doesn't simply involve avoiding foods with yeast in them (this yeast, by the way, is invisible to the naked eye). That's only part of it. The primary goal in a yeast-free diet is to limit foods that feed yeast. And yes, you guessed it; this may mean all of your child's favorite foods. A more advanced type of yeast-free diet, the specific carbohydrate diet (SCD), was presented in chapter 9.

A simple yeast-free diet can be useful in two ways:

1. If you find that your child has recurrent yeast problems, following these diet precautions can help lower yeast levels.

2. You can use this diet as a way to diagnose yeast problems. Spend a week strictly following these guidelines, and if you notice improvements in your child's behavior or intestinal symptoms, your child likely has yeast. You can then treat it. If you don't want to follow the diet long-term, you can at least periodically come back to it to check how your child is doing. If he responds well

every time he spends a week on the diet, that tells you he needs further yeast treatments (and/or to stay on the diet).

What your child can't eat. Let's start with the bad news. Limit or avoid the following foods:

- foods with mold: most cheeses, dried or cured meats, mushrooms, olives, peanuts, soy sauce, berries, malt, canned tomatoes
- foods made with yeast (leavened): breads, baked goods, vinegar (and sauces/dressings/condiments that contain it)
- starches: corn, potato
- sugary foods: refined sugar, sweet fruits (grapes, raisins, dates, figs, citrus), dried fruits, most juices, sugary drinks, honey and syrup, chocolate, high-fructose corn syrup

What your child *can* eat. Feel free to feed your child anything that isn't on the above list (unless it breaks the rules of other dietary precautions). Here are some major food groups that don't pose a yeast problem:

- fresh meat, fish, poultry, pork
- almost all vegetables (your child will be thrilled!)
- mozzarella and feta cheese, butter, milk (if your child is not on the CF diet)
- beans
- eggs
- freshly pressed (at home) juices: apple (without the peel) and orange
- whole-grain nonbaked foods like cereals and pasta (these would need to be gluten-free if your child is on the GF diet)
- breakfast foods cooked without yeast (use baking soda or powder instead), such as biscuits, muffins, pancakes, and

waffles (these would have to be gluten-free if your child is on the GF diet).
- nuts (except peanuts) and seeds
- fresh fruits not on the above list (don't overdo them), especially banana and pineapple

YEAST MEDICATIONS

Oral antifungal medications are available only by prescription in the United States. Following are the different types of medications.

Mild Antifungal Medications

There are two choices that are safe, have virtually no risk of serious side effects, and can be used for months or even years at a time. The reason these two are so safe is that they aren't absorbed into the bloodstream. Once swallowed, they go into the intestines, killing anything yeasty in sight, then pass out in the stools. Therefore they don't need to be processed by the liver, so they can't cause any internal wear and tear on the body.

Nystatin. This medication is the mildest and safest of all choices. It is commonly used in pediatric medicine and is the med that your mainstream doctor will most likely be willing to prescribe for you. I have seen a growing number of pediatric gastroenterologists also prescribe it for their patients with autism, as this specialty is seeing more and more children with autism and chronic diarrhea. The typical dose is 1 teaspoon of liquid (or one tablet swallowed) four times daily. A monthlong course does a good job of significantly reducing yeast levels. After that, twice-daily dosing can be continued for months to keep yeast away. One drawback to nystatin is that we are now seeing resistance to it in some yeast stool cultures. This is what happens when any antibiotic or antifungal medication is widely used in our society. Amphotericin B may now be a better choice (if you can get it; read on).

Amphotericin B. Let me give you a little heads-up. Don't ask your pediatrician for this medication. Its primary use in pediatrics is intravenous treatment of severe fungal infections for hospitalized patients, and it causes some very bad side effects when given via IV. However, it also comes in an oral form that is perfectly safe. But your regular doctor won't believe that. You are more likely to get fluconazole (see below), even though it has more side effects. A biomedical practitioner may be willing to prescribe amphotericin B. It does a better job of killing yeast than nystatin does. Amphotericin comes in capsules, but a compounding pharmacy can mix it into a liquid for your child. It is dosed four times daily for about three weeks:

- children 2 to 3 years: 125 mg per dose
- children 4 to 6 years: 250 mg per dose
- older kids: 500 mg per dose

Like nystatin, amphotericin B can be taken fewer times each day for long-term yeast-suppression therapy, the same doses as above but only twice daily.

YEAST LOVES CONSTIPATION

Stools are a natural breeding ground for yeast and bacteria. Emptying the colon every day is a good way to help keep yeast away. Children who are constipated may not respond well to yeast treatment, or the benefits may be short-lived. If yeast treatments aren't doing anything for your child, consider constipation as a possible reason. See page 291 for tips on how to diagnose and treat constipation.

Strong Antifungal Medications

Again, your regular pediatrician might not be willing to prescribe these drugs for you, but an alternatively minded doctor will. Your pediatrician will at least be familiar with these meds. They are used in pediatric and adult medicine to treat oral or vaginal yeast infections as well as fingernail or toenail fungal infections.

Fluconazole (brand name Diflucan). This is the most commonly prescribed strong yeast med for children with autism. It is approved for use in infants of any age to treat oral thrush (Candida in the mouth). It comes in capsule or liquid form. The typical dose is 3 mg per kilogram of body weight per day, given once daily for two to four weeks. A double dose is supposed to be given on the first day to bring the medication up to effective levels in the bloodstream right away.

Ketoconazole (brand name Nizoral). This medication is pretty much the same as fluconazole, it just hasn't been around as long. It is the second-most commonly used strong yeast med in treating autism. It comes as capsules only, but it can be compounded into a liquid. Its main purpose is to offer an alternative treatment to a child whose yeast is resistant to fluconazole. Other than that, it doesn't work any better or worse than fluconazole or any of the other strong meds. The typical dosing for ketoconazole is 4 mg per kilogram of weight once daily for two to four weeks.

Itraconazole (brand name Sporonox). This is the newest of the three strong "-azole" meds. Like ketoconazole, it is used primarily as a treatment for fungi that are resistant to the other meds. It comes in capsule or liquid form. Typical dosing is 5 mg per kilogram of weight once daily for two to four weeks.

Terbinafine (brand name Lamisil). This is a different class of antifungal medicine from the "-azole" drugs and is rarely used in autism. It comes as capsules and sprinkles. The usual dose is 5 mg per kilogram of weight once daily for two to four weeks.

COMPOUNDING MEDICATIONS: IS IT WORTH THE EXTRA MONEY?

The best choice for any child who can swallow pills is the capsule form of supplements or medications. But most younger children with autism can't swallow pills, so either a liquid is needed or capsules must be opened (or tablets crushed) into food or drink. The powder inside the capsules or tablets, however, generally tastes quite horrible. Most parents have to rely on the liquid forms of these meds. The two most commonly used antifungal medications, nystatin and fluconazole, come in liquid form. However, these liquids have sugar, artificial flavors, and other chemical ingredients that children may react to. Plus, the sugar may feed yeast and interfere with the med's efficacy. These confounding factors can make it difficult for a parent to determine if a yeast medication is helping. Enter the compounding pharmacy. These specialty pharmacies can mix medications into liquid form with non-yeast-promoting natural sweeteners (like Stevia) and without any bothersome chemicals. But this isn't cheap. In my office, I try the regular form of a liquid medication first (if available) and see how the child does. I treat any worsened behaviors as a die-off reaction (see below). If this helps, then we know that compounding probably isn't needed. If, on the other hand, a child worsens, and die-off precautions don't help, I stop the med and start a new liquid prescription compounded without sugar or anything artificial. If that goes well, we know the child needs future prescriptions compounded. See Resources, page 354, for a nationwide list of compounding pharmacies that are familiar with autism treatments.

Choosing the Right Antifungal Medication

If your child had a comprehensive yeast stool analysis (see page 118) and the sample grew some yeast, the lab probably did a sensitivity test to determine which meds the yeast would be susceptible to. These would be labeled on the result as sensitive (which means the med will work), intermediate (the med might work), and resistant (don't bother trying that med). You can use this information to help you know which med to ask your doctor for. Some stool tests won't grow yeast, but yeast might have been visible under the lab's microscope (this is labeled under the microscopic section of the stool result). In such cases, you know yeast is there, but you have to guess which med to try.

If you don't have these kinds of results, and you want to try a milder yeast med, I suggest amphotericin B if you can get it. If not, go for nystatin. If a stronger med is your preference, fluconazole is the best place to start. If it doesn't seem to help but you are fairly certain yeast is a problem, ketoconazole would be the next med to try. This is all best decided under the guidance of a biomedical practitioner.

Side Effects of Yeast Medicines

As with most prescription meds, side effects are possible but serious side effects are very rare.

Yeast die-off reactions. Yeast germs store a lot of toxic byproducts, as do any unwanted bacteria that live alongside them. When these germs are killed, they release all their toxins. If a child is sensitive to these toxins (which up to this point have been slowly excreted by the germs and gradually absorbed by the body), the sudden rush of chemicals can be very irritating to the gut and the brain. Diarrhea, bloating, gas, and abdominal pain can worsen. Typical autistic behaviors, especially tantrums and hyperactivity, can become more extreme. This reaction generally subsides after a few days, but it can be a very tough few days. Die-off reactions can occur from any treatment that kills yeast or intestinal bacteria, including probiotics, digestive enzymes, natural yeast treatments, and antifungal medications. Yeast-limiting diets generally don't cause die-off reactions, because they work more gradually. The good news about a die-off reaction is that it may be a sign that the treatment is working. Here are two ways you can help the body process these germ toxins and limit this reaction:

- *Activated charcoal.* This may sound strange, but charcoal capsules are a common poisoning antidote used in emergency rooms. The charcoal moves through the intestines and absorbs pretty much anything it comes in contact with, then passes harmlessly out through the stools. During die-off reactions, charcoal can be taken three times daily. It should be taken at least one hour before or after any other supplements or medications (two hours is better if possible) so that the charcoal does not also absorb and deactivate the other supplements and meds. Children who can't swallow capsules can have them opened and the powder sprinkled into a small amount of food or drink. Mixing it into a few sips of a smoothie works well. Capsules usually come in 250 mg doses; smaller doses can also be found. Give children two to five years old about 125 mg three times a day. Kids six and up can take 250 mg three times a day. Once die-off symptoms subside, you can stop using the charcoal.

- *Epsom salt baths.* This magnesium sulfate product is available in drugstores with products for the feet, as it is commonly used for soaking ingrown toenails. Sprinkle ½ to 1 cup into a bath once a day during die-off times. The sulfur gets absorbed through the skin and acts as a natural detoxifier. You can also add ¼ cup of baking soda to the bath to prevent the skin-drying effects of sulfur. It's okay if a child happens to swallow some of this bath water, though the magnesium may give him diarrhea. Try to prevent him from drinking it.

If your child experiences severe die-off symptoms, you can stop the offending agent for a few days, begin these treatments, and then restart the particular supplement or med at half the dose and work up to full dosing again over a few days. If symptoms are due to an antifungal medication that is prescribed for a certain number of days or weeks, don't start counting those days until your child is back on the full dose.

Liver damage. The most serious side effect with the stronger meds (not nystatin or amphotericin B) is liver damage. These meds (like most) need to be processed by the liver before they move to the rest of the body. Long-term use of strong antifungals can put a strain on the liver, and on rare occasions, the liver becomes so strained that damage can result. This damage can be permanent. Several cases of fatal liver failure have occurred in the many years that these meds have been in use in the general population (I'm talking about millions of prescriptions). I have not yet heard of this happening in the autism community. So, it is a theoretical risk but not a likely one. I believe the potential benefit of taking these meds under the care of a knowledgeable doctor outweighs the risk.

However, it's important for you to know how to identify signs of liver strain when they do occur so that you can immediately stop the medication and contact your doctor. Signs include:

- abdominal pain in the upper right side of the belly (where the liver is located)
- dark, cola-colored urine
- jaundice (yellow in the eyes or skin)

Fortunately, liver strain is rare. I have never seen any of these signs in my own patients.

Blood Monitoring While on Strong Yeast Medications

A blood test can be done to check the health of the liver (called a CMP or a liver panel, page 94). Any strain on the liver will register as an elevated AST or ALT level (two enzymes produced by the liver). Double the normal levels of one or both of these enzymes indicates minor strain. Real liver damage causes levels that are five or more times the normal range. Your doctor will discuss such results with you.

Blood testing isn't necessary during a standard two- to four-week course of a strong med. A child can easily handle these meds two to three times a year without worry. Here are some situations that do warrant a blood test:

- Your child takes a strong yeast med for more than one consecutive month.

- Your child takes a yeast med along with an antiviral prescription medication (see page 271) or a prescription chelation medication (see page 278) for more than a month (these both strain the liver).

- Your child takes a strong yeast med more than three times (two- to four-week courses each time) within twelve months.

These guidelines aren't set in stone. Your doctor may have a different opinion, and you should follow his or her advice.

Supporting Liver Health During Antifungal Treatment

An herb called *milk thistle* (or *silymarin*) can be taken during these treatments to help keep the liver healthy. It isn't known for sure if this actually helps (research hasn't shown a clear benefit), but it is a popular treatment in alternative medicine circles. I generally don't tell my patients to take it during isolated four-week courses, but I do if a patient is going to take meds often enough to warrant blood monitoring. Numerous brands of silymarin are available online. Follow the product's recommended dosing.

Interactions with Other Medications

Strong antifungals can interact with some other prescription meds. They can increase or decrease the potency of other meds, and their own potency can be altered in turn. None of the prescription medications that I discuss in this book fall into this category, with the exception of some psychiatric meds. However, let your pharmacist know about other prescription meds your child is taking (prescription B12 and glutathione are fine) just to be sure. Also, one of the milder antifungals (nystatin and amphotericin B) should not be taken at the same time as a strong one. They can deactivate each other.

STEP-BY-STEP PLAN FOR TREATING YEAST

Now that you have all the background information on yeast, let's put a treatment plan together. If you have a biomedical doctor, then you should follow his or her advice for your child. If you don't have such a doctor, this section will guide you through the steps. You will need to enlist your pediatrician's help for prescription medications.

Step 1: Testing for yeast. On page 117, I laid out the options for yeast testing. If you don't have access to testing or can't afford it, it's okay to try some natural yeast treatments to see how your child responds. You can also try the yeast-free diet for a week and watch for improvement as a way to diagnose yeast. I also think it's fine to try a mild antifungal med without testing, especially if your child has had a long history of antibiotic usage and/or chronic diarrhea that doesn't improve with diet changes and the initial supplements. Testing first may give some useful information, but it isn't critical.

Follow your biomedical doctor's advice on testing. If you don't have one, ask your regular doctor for a stool yeast culture, or you can order the specific specialty test kit that you want and take the kit and paperwork in to your doctor's appointment. Your doctor may be willing to sign the orders. You'll collect the urine and/or stool samples at home (ask your doctor for some urine collection bags if your child is still in diapers) and mail them in to the specialty lab. Most labs require a doctor to be registered with their laboratory so that no one can simply forge a signature. Your doctor is going to have to be willing to register. If you can't get such a specialty test, at least start with a stool test from a regular lab.

STOP CERTAIN SUPPLEMENTS PRIOR TO STOOL OR URINE YEAST TESTING

Stop any probiotics, digestive enzymes, and natural or prescription yeast treatments at least one week prior to testing. This allows yeast to regrow if it's still an underlying problem. If yeast is gone or adequately suppressed, simply spending one week off supplements shouldn't allow it to regrow.

Step 2: Natural treatments. I recommend you start your child on a probiotic and one other natural yeast remedy. I've used a variety of them and haven't developed a preference. After a few weeks, add another natural treatment. You can add on as many natural remedies as you want to try. If your child responds well to these remedies, you can simply continue them for about six months, then retest to see how the yeast is doing. If it's still a problem, you can then try a medication. If, on the other hand, you don't see improvement from natural treatments, or you *do* but you want to hit yeast even harder, try a medication to see if you get better results. Continue any natural treatments at the same time.

Step 3: Yeast medication. Choosing a medication depends on your child's history of antibiotics, past intestinal symptoms, current intestinal status, how much yeast shows up on testing, and a variety of other factors. I can't give you specifics here because you are going to need to have your own doctor prescribe this. My most common approach is to give a strong med (fluconazole is my main choice unless the child is resistant; ketoconazole is my second choice) for four weeks, then provide a mild med twice daily indefinitely to help keep yeast away. You can't keep taking the med forever, though. I usually stop the mild med after six months at the longest and see how the child behaves without it.

As for retesting the yeast, I don't like to overdo it, because it isn't cheap. I decide on a case-by-case basis. Sometimes the parents and I observe a child's behavior and overall well-being and decide on more treatments based on what we've learned about his own unique yeast symptoms (see page 234). I may treat a child with another round of strong meds if his known yeast symptoms suddenly return after being gone for many months. If we aren't sure, I retest (I don't automatically test both urine and stool again; I retest whichever gave the most useful information the first time around). I continue to prescribe the same strong med until it seems not to confer the same benefits it had in the past. I then switch. Yeast stool culture results plus antifungal sensitivity testing may help guide this decision.

Step 4: Yeast-free diet. I usually recommend this for a child if yeast keeps returning despite treatment. The long-term goal is that once the intestines heal and stay healthy for a year or two, the child won't have to stay on the diet or continue any natural or prescription treatments.

Step 5: Specific carbohydrate diet. I presented this diet to you in chapter 9, but I told you not to start it then. Now it's time to decide. For children who struggle with recurrent yeast, especially if chronic diarrhea continues despite the GFCF diet and yeast treatment, SCD is definitely the way to go. I've seen many children do well on this diet. After a child's third round of strong antifungal meds within a one-year period, I'll usually make this recommendation. You don't have to wait that long, though. If yeast treatment really helps but problems come back right away once treatment is stopped, jump right in. It's not easy, but it can be well worth the effort.

AVOIDING YEAST IF A CHILD NEEDS ANTIBIOTICS

The yeast symptoms of a child who has responded well to yeast treatments in the past are likely to worsen if oral antibiotics are needed for an illness. It's best to avoid antibiotics if possible. On page 332 I discuss how to decide if antibiotics are really needed and what natural treatments you can try instead. An antibiotic shot is a good alternative, as it won't affect the gut as much. But if your child does take oral antibiotics, I suggest you also give him one of the mild yeast meds twice daily during that time and then for another month after he's done with the antibiotics. Also restart any natural yeast treatments you have found useful in the past. This will help prevent your child from regressing in his behavior and needing a strong yeast med.

TREATING INTESTINAL BACTERIA

Just when you thought yeast was the only germ you had to deal with, certain bacteria can also pose a problem. They can overgrow in the intestines for the same reasons yeast does, and they can produce similar toxins that affect the brain. The problem is, treating these bacteria with antibiotics can make yeast worse, so if antibiotics need to be used, yeast treatment should accompany them. Most unwanted intestinal bacteria will subside with all the gut healing steps you've taken so far. Probiotics play a big role in this. Monolaurin may as well. When I see some unwanted bacteria show up on a specialty lab stool result, I never go after them right away with antibiotics. I check the stool again six months to a year later and may consider treating them then if bad germs have persisted. Common bacteria that tend to show up in stool samples include Pseudomonas, Klebsiella, Streptococcus, and others. Susceptibility testing is done on these germs to help a doctor decide which antibiotic to prescribe. Next to metronidazole (brand name Flagyl; see below), Bactrim is probably the most common antibiotic course prescribed for intestinal bacteria. Some doctors use vancomycin, a very strong but effective choice. Ciprofloxacin is perhaps the best choice, as it covers almost all unwanted intestinal bacteria. However, it may cause problems with bone growth, so it isn't recommended for children under eighteen.

Clostridium difficile

There is one particular intestinal bacteria that creates more harm than any other. Clostridium difficile, or C. diff for short, is in the same family of germs as the bacteria that cause tetanus, botulism, and gangrene. These germs secrete neurotoxins (chemicals that directly affect neurological function) as well as toxins that irritate the gut. An overgrowth of C. diff in the gut can have as much of a negative effect on a child's autistic behaviors and neurological function as yeast overgrowth. A C. diff infection is usually caused by antibiotic overuse (the same reasons yeast overgrows).

Testing for C. diff. There is no way to directly grow these bacteria to check the degree of infection. The only method we have is to measure the toxins generated by C. diff. There are two ways to do this:

- *The urine micro OAT test* (done mainly to check for yeast) also measures a particular acid secreted by C. diff (not the neurotoxins themselves) as it is excreted in the urine. This acid is called *HPHPA* (listed under the bacterial portion of the test). See page 119 for an explanation of this acid level.

- *A stool test for C. diff toxins A and B* (two toxins that directly irritate the gut) can be done by a regular lab, and your doctor will be familiar with this test. However, this test is usually positive only if the C. diff infection is severe enough to cause bloody diarrhea. I usually don't do this test, since most children with autism don't have bloody diarrhea.

Treating C. diff. There are two ways to treat this overgrowth:

- *Probiotics and colostrum.* Your child is probably already taking these.

- *Prescription antibiotics.* The most commonly used one is metronidazole. A second choice is vancomycin. These are prescribed for a two- to four-week course. Metronidazole comes in capsule and tablet forms only; a compounding pharmacy will have to mix it into liquid for you if needed.

My usual approach to treating C. diff (based on urine micro OAT results) is to prescribe metronidazole according to standard dosing for two weeks while treating yeast with an antifungal medication. I treat simultaneously because if I treat C. diff only, yeast can flare up. C. diff can also worsen if yeast is killed off but C. diff isn't treated. If I am treating yeast with a four-week course of meds, I'll generally have the child begin the antifungal first for a week, add in the metronidazole for the next two weeks (so a child is taking both), then finish the last week with the antifungal med alone. Some doctors treat with metronidazole for all four weeks.

If a child's C. diff acid level on the OAT test is borderline and doesn't warrant treatment but the test does show a yeast problem, I watch out for a worsening of autistic behaviors or intestinal symptoms as I am treating the child's yeast. If die-off precautions don't help and the problems persist, then I suspect I may have triggered a C. diff problem. I might then add metronidazole onto the end of the yeast treatment. I will also use metronidazole with future prescription yeast treatments. Further urine micro OAT tests can be used to monitor this.

Getting help from your regular doctor. Doctors are very familiar with a medical condition called C. diff colitis (severe inflammation of the colon). It is a known side effect of a particular antibiotic called clindamycin that is mainly used for skin infections or abscesses. Although any antibiotic can cause C. diff to overgrow, clindamycin has a particular propensity to do so. Once C. diff takes over, it produces toxins A and B, which damage the gut lining and cause bloody diarrhea. This is the aspect of C. diff that most doctors know about. But they aren't familiar with the neurotoxic properties of C. diff toxins and the impact they may have on autism. So, your regular doctor probably won't agree to treat your child for C. diff based simply on urine micro OAT results. One way you may be able to convince your doctor is to ask for a stool test for C. diff toxins A and B (done through a regular lab), especially if your child has chronic diarrhea. If these toxins show on the test result, your doctor may be willing to treat your child. Convincing him or her to do so is a bit of a long shot, though, unless your child's diarrhea is bloody.

12

More Advanced Treatment Options

Once your child is on the diet and the basic supplements and has started yeast treatments, it's time to consider more advanced treatment options. You can do some of these on your own without a prescription, but you'll need a doctor's help for most of them. Your own open-minded regular physician may be willing to give you prescriptions for certain things, and I'll offer you some guidance on how to convince your doctor to help you. But in many cases you'll need a biomedical practitioner for certain treatments that a standard physician would not be comfortable with. I'll give you some guidelines on how to decide if you should seek out such a doctor.

METHYLATION TREATMENTS

As you learned in chapter 4, the methylation pathway is broken in most children with autism. This pathway is essential for so many aspects of a child's metabolism, including detoxification. Fixing the pathway can lead to amazing improvement in a child with autism. Several of the supplements you've already started are designed to assist with this, but now it's time for the big guns.

Methyl B12 Shots

This is perhaps the biggest "wow" treatment that has been discovered for children with autism in the last decade. B12 shots have been around for decades, but the ones we use in autism aren't your "grandmother's B12 shots." They are a specific type of B12: *methyl* B12 (or methylcobalamin). Most older forms of B12 shots are *cyano* B12 (or cyanocobalamin). This form doesn't do anything for autism. It's the *methyl* part of the B12 that helps correct methylation metabolism.

Who should try the shots? Every child with autism. There isn't a single patient I have not told to try them. There is no useful way to test whether a child should try B12 shots. A blood test is available to measure B12 levels, but it isn't useful because it includes inactive forms of B12. Having a low, normal, or high blood level of B12 has no bearing whatsoever on methyl B12 use. The ultimate test is to simply try it and let your child's response be the "lab test."

What benefits can you expect to see from B12 shots? In my experience, the most commonly reported improvements are increased language and social interaction. Improved attention in school and therapy sessions is also fairly common. Changes can be immediate, but they can also take a month or two to become apparent. Most biomedical doctors recommend keeping your child on methyl B12 for at least two years if you see improvements. They can be continued indefinitely. If you don't notice any benefits, give it at least three months before stopping.

Administering methyl B12 shots. The thought of giving your own child a shot naturally makes you cringe. But I've never had a parent who wasn't ultimately able to do it. Parents with a diabetic child have to give their child insulin a few times every day. B12 shots are given only once every three days. The B12 comes in pre-filled syringes with needles already attached (the same used for insulin), so parents don't have to measure the injection solution (though you can save money by getting it in a vial and drawing out the solution yourself). The needles are the shortest and thinnest made, so children barely feel them. The amount of solution that is injected is only about $\frac{1}{20}$ of a milliliter (just a few drops), so it's very fast. The shot can be administered in the buttock while a child is asleep, and often he'll not even wake up.

To learn to administer the B12 shots, you can view videos online, ask a TACA parent if you can watch her give her own child his injection, or invite a TACA mom over to your house to help you with your child's first shot. Dr. James A. Neubrander (considered to be the guru of methyl B12 shots) has a website (www. DrNeubrander.com) that provides a wealth of information on B12, including video instructions. Here are step-by-step instructions:

1. Wait until your child is in a deep sleep (though some kids do better if they are awake and know it's coming).

2. Roll the syringe between your hands for a few minutes to warm up the solution to body temperature to reduce the pain.

3. Pull down the back of the pajamas (and fold down the diaper) to expose the upper outer area of the buttock.

4. Wipe the area with rubbing alcohol and let it dry.

5. Uncap the needle and place the needle near the skin.

6. Hold the buttock firmly with one hand to keep your child fairly still in case he squirms.

7. Quickly jab the needle in at a 20- to 30-degree angle to the skin (see videos or printed instructions on Dr. Neubrander's website). I say *jab* because it causes less pain if the needle goes in quickly. Here is how to estimate a 20- to 30-degree angle to the skin: Going straight down from directly overhead is 90 degrees; tilting the needle down about halfway toward the skin is 45 degrees; tilting another halfway from there is about 25 degrees.

8. Quickly inject the solution and pull the needle out. You may need to dab away a spot of blood with a cotton ball.

There. That's it. Sounds easy, right? It will become easy for you after a few rounds.

Dosing methyl B12 shots. The dose will be calculated by your physician. The standard dose that is best for most children is about 65 mcg (micrograms) per kilogram of body weight every three days (Monday, Thursday, Sunday, Wednesday, Saturday, etc., for example). Some doctors feel that 75 mcg per kilogram is better. A forty-pound child weighs 18 kg. Multiply this by 65 and you get 1170 mcg per injection for the lower end of dosing. If going with 75 mcg per kilogram, the dose would be 1350 mcg. Here's a hint, though: It's easiest for the pharmacist to measure the doses into your syringes in 250 mcg increments, so it's best to round up or down to the nearest 250. So, in this example, I would give the child 1250 mcg, which falls nicely right between the 65 and 75 mcg per kilogram range. Some doctors, however, feel that precise dosing is important; the pharmacist can give you precise micrograms if you want.

You can't get methyl B12 shots from just any pharmacy. You have to go to a specialized compounding pharmacy that has experience with methyl B12 shots for children with autism. If your pharmacist says, "Hmmm. I think I can figure out how to make this for you," run (politely). In the Resources, I provide a list of pharmacies that will ship methyl B12 nationwide. You need a prescription from a doctor that would read something like this: "Methyl B12; 25 mg/ml: Give _____ mcg subcutaneously every 3 days."

The frequency of the shots can be adjusted by your doctor. Some children need them only once a week, while others benefit from a shot every other day. Watch how long the benefits last with each dose. Your doctor will help you decide how to adjust the frequency.

Using anesthetic cream to numb the skin. You can apply a cream to the injection site about thirty minutes prior to the shot to numb the skin. This can turn a noncompliant child into one willing to accept the shots. Two kinds of cream are used: EMLA is a prescription formulation, and ELA-Max is an over-the-counter version. Try both types to see which works better for your child. Some kids don't need this, however, especially those who stay asleep during the injection.

Red urine. Because B12 is red, some might come out in the urine with the first pee after each shot. Don't worry, this isn't blood. If you see this, it may mean you are injecting the solution too deeply. The solution is intended to go into the fat layer, just beneath the skin. This allows it to be slowly released over three days (and not enough will show in the urine to be visibly red). If the shot goes too deep (into the muscle), it will be released over several hours, not days. There's nothing dangerous about this, and you might actually see even better results for a short period of time. But the effects probably won't last. The slow-and-steady-release method is preferred. If you repeatedly see red urine, try injecting the B12 at an angle closer to the skin.

Other forms of methyl B12. If you (and your child) don't want to do shots, there are four other ways to administer methyl B12.

They don't work as well, but they are much better than nothing. I've listed them in order of efficacy (highest to lowest):

• *Nasal methyl B12 spray* (prescription). This is the next best thing to the shots. One spray in one nostril every other day is the starting dose (you can alternate nostrils). Then, after a few weeks, increase to one spray every day. Most pharmacies put 1250 mcg in each spray. Children six and older can move up to two sprays (one in each nostril) every day. The B12 easily absorbs into the blood vessels lining the inside of the nose. This, and the transdermal cream below, can be purchased from most of the compounding pharmacies listed in the Resources, page 354.

• *Transdermal methyl B12 cream* (prescription, although OTC forms may become available). This solution is applied to the skin (see glutathione dosing, page 266, for tips on areas of the body you can apply creams to). Dosing varies between 500 mcg and 3000 mcg twice daily (start low and work up as you observe the effects). This method isn't commonly used anymore because the shots and nasal spray work much better.

• *Sublingual methyl B12* (over-the-counter). Numerous websites sell this version (search online). Absorption is just okay (it's supposed to soak into the tissues under the tongue), but it's better than not taking any methyl B12 at all. Dosing doesn't have to be precise, but typically it would be about 2000 mcg (or 2 mg) twice daily for children two to five years of age, and up to 5000 mcg (5 mg) twice daily for older kids.

• *Oral methyl B12* (over-the-counter). B12 that is swallowed typically isn't absorbed in the intestines very well, so I don't recommend this.

If you see good things with methyl B12 shots, it doesn't hurt (literally) to switch over to nasal methyl B12 after several months to see if you retain the same benefits.

Side effects of methyl B12. The main side effect is hyperactivity. It isn't clear why this occurs, but there are several approaches that may help prevent this:

- Make sure your child is on taurine (see page 204).

- One of the supporting supplements that work synergistically with B12 (folinic acid, DMG, or TMG; see below) may be needed. Normally I recommend waiting until a child is on methyl B12 for five weeks before adding folinic acid, but if hyperactivity is bothersome, start adding it sooner.

- Methionine and SAM (S-adenosylmethionine) supplements both disrupt the benefits of B12 in about half of children with autism, so stop using them if your child is just starting B12.

- A small percentage of children actually have overactive methylation metabolism; overloading this with even more methyl treatments can cause hyperactivity. There's no good way to test for this, however. You just have to guess.

Getting your mainstream physician to prescribe the shots. Many family physicians are familiar with B12 injections, which are given to adults for various ailments (though typically they use cyanocobalamin, so you would need to specify methylcobalamin instead). Such a doctor may be open to trying methyl B12 on your child. Most pediatricians, however, won't be willing to prescribe it. I can't blame them; ten years ago I wouldn't have prescribed a "weird" shot that I knew nothing about to be given at home "off label" by a parent. But if you have an open-minded doctor, he might be willing.

The best way to approach your doctor is to make an appointment outside of a regular checkup, preferably without your child so you can both concentrate. Tell your doctor a little about what you are doing, then put a small stack of research papers in front of him that describe the use of methyl B12 in autism (see Resources for methyl B12 articles and print out a few that are online). Ask him to glance through just a few of the summary paragraphs and the recommended dosing, which you will have highlighted for him. Tell him you are aware that this is alternative medicine, you aren't sure it's going to help, but you know it isn't going to hurt, and your neighbor's child responded with amazing results (or a friend, or whoever you know who has had a positive response). You just want to give your child the best chance to improve. Beg, plead, bring cookies (that *might* have worked on me)—whatever it takes.

HOW LONG SHOULD YOU CONTINUE SUPPLEMENTS?

Many of the prescription medications have a limited course of treatment, such as a month for yeast medicines or six months for antiviral medicines (see below). The basic supplements from chapter 10 and the methylation treatments above, on the other hand, don't have a designated end point. I encourage you to continue giving these to your child for at least three years, especially if the response is positive. This allows the gut and the brain to heal and your child to catch up in development while benefiting from the effects of the supplements. When you reach a point where you want to see how your child does without the treatments, gradually remove one supplement each week in the reverse order that you introduced them. If your child shows any problems, resume treatments for at least another year.

Folinic Acid

This is the active form of folic acid; the body converts folic acid from any food or vitamin source into folinic acid before utilizing it for methylation. Folinic acid plays an important role in methylation metabolism by helping methyl B12 work more efficiently. We give methyl B12 alone for five weeks first in order to observe how it is affecting a child. But eventually folinic acid will need to be added.

Dosing of folinic acid. Children with autism need higher-than-normal folinic acid doses for it to adequately support methyl B12. The maximum amount is 800 mcg twice daily. Virtually all of the specialized multivitamin/mineral supplements in chapter 10 contain about 200 mcg of folic or folinic acid per dose. Now you should buy a separate supplement and give your child an additional 200 mcg twice daily along with the multi. Over a few weeks, gradually increase the dose until your child is taking a total of 800 mcg twice daily from all combined sources. You can find it online in capsule form or tablets at most of the same websites that sell the multivitamin/minerals. Open the capsules or crush the tablets into food or drink if your child doesn't swallow pills yet.

Side effects of folinic acid. A minority of children become hyperactive on extra folinic acid. If you notice this while working up to the maximum dose, back off to a dose that was okay and stay there. Some children do not need any extra folinic acid.

Different forms of folinic acid. There are four different forms of folinic acid: plain folic acid, folinic acid, FolaPro (from Metagenics), and leucovorin (prescription folinic acid). Each type works slightly differently in methylation metabolism. If your child gets hyperactive on one form, try another. The dosing guidelines are the same.

DOES THE WORD _METHYLATION_ MAKE YOUR BRAIN HURT?

So far I have spared you the pain of trying to understand the complex details of methylation biochemistry. If you've never taken biochemistry, then I recommend you remain blissfully ignorant. But if you love studying pictures of dozens of chemical names all interconnected by arrows and circles, then methylation biochemistry is just your ticket. The handbook _Autism: Effective Biomedical Treatments,_ by Pangborn and Baker (see Resources, page 358), is the definitive guide to understanding the science and biochemistry behind biomedical treatments. It provides detailed scientific information on how the supplements in this section interact with the body and with one another.

DMG and TMG

Dimethylglycine and trimethylglycine are made up of glycine, an amino acid, plus either two or three methyl groups. The methyl in these two compounds helps drive methylation metabolism. As with folinic acid, there's no way to know which one will work better for your child because it depends on which aspects of methylation aren't working properly. It's trial-and-error time again.

Both supplements come in a variety of forms: liquid, capsule, and powder. They also come combined with folic acid or folinic acid plus a little bit of B12 (although the oral B12 really doesn't work well). They are available at most of the same online companies that provide the multivitamin/minerals. I recommend starting with plain DMG. Once you've worked out a good dosing regimen of DMG (see below) and folinic acid separately, you may want to consider a combination product of DMG and folinic acid to suit your child's needs. If you end up switching to TMG, be sure to continue folinic acid. There is no reason to take both DMG and TMG.

Dosing DMG and TMG. There is no set dosing for these two products, as each child's needs vary according to the unique quirks in his own methylation. Starting low and going slowly is important in figuring out the correct dose. More is not necessarily better. Here is what I suggest:

- Start at 125 to 150 mg once each morning.

- After two weeks, add an early-afternoon dose of the same amount (not too late or it may keep your child up at bedtime).

- Gradually increase each dose over a month period until you reach the following maximums: children two to five years of age, 500 mg per day; children six to twelve, 800 to 1000 mg per day; teens, up to 1500 mg per day.

Side effects of DMG and TMG. As with other methylation supplements, hyperactivity can be a side effect. If you see this, back off to a lower dose that worked well and go back to once-a-day

---

VARIATIONS IN METHYLATION METABOLISM AND SUPPLEMENTS

We know a lot about methylation metabolism in autism. But when it comes to each individual child, there are so many factors at play that there's no way to know exactly which mix of supplements is going to work best. Starting the methylation supplements in the order prescribed in this chapter seems to work well with most children. A proper mix of methyl B12, folinic acid, and DMG or TMG that fits your individual child can be found through trial and error. Some children ultimately do well with methyl B12 alone, but most achieve the best results when all three are used.

dosing. If the lowest dose makes your child hyper, switch to the other form. If your child becomes hyper on any form of DMG or TMG, it means he doesn't need this extra help with his methylation metabolism.

Glutathione

This is a protein/sulfur compound that is naturally produced by the cells on a continual basis and acts as one of the body's primary antioxidants and detoxifiers. It also plays a role in reducing inflammation, regulating sugar metabolism, and boosting the immune system. Unfortunately, it is produced by the methylation cycle. So, most children with autism have low glutathione levels. Boosting the methylation cycle with methyl B12 and its supporting supplements can eventually bring glutathione levels up, but adding glutathione in the meantime (for a year or two) is very beneficial.

Dosing glutathione. Oral supplements are available online from a variety of sources, but these are thought to increase yeast growth in the intestines, so they generally are not recommended. Topical cream that absorbs through the skin is the preferred route. The most effective formulations are those prescribed through a compounding pharmacy (see page 354 for a list of these). If you can find a doctor to prescribe it, the usual dose is 250 mg per milliliter of cream: apply 0.5 ml of cream twice daily. Alternate between the following areas of the body: on the inner wrists, in the bend of the elbows, behind the knees, on the instep of the foot, and between the shoulder blades. These body parts can be used for other transdermal treatments as well. Do not apply more than one cream to the same area of the skin on the same day unless directed to by a physician. A good over-the-counter alternative is Kirkman Labs' Reduced L-Glutathione Lotion (www.Kirkmanlabs.com). Follow their suggested dosing.

Side effects of glutathione. These are rare and are usually behavioral, such as hyperactivity or increased stimming. It isn't clear why this occurs in some children. It may be a sign that your child doesn't need any extra glutathione (see page 104 to review information on testing blood levels of glutathione).

Other ways to get glutathione. Children who have persistent low glutathione levels on blood testing despite using the cream and methylation treatments can try some more potent routes of administration (through a biomedical practitioner):

- *Nebulized glutathione.* Inhaling via a vaporizer-like machine (only available by prescription) is very effective at getting glutathione into the body and into the cells. It is already being used in children and adults with chronic lung conditions. If you have an open-minded doctor, you can try getting a prescription (from a regular pharmacy or through a compounding pharmacy). Here is what a typical prescription would look like: "100 mg per ml of solution; inhale 100 to 200 mg (or 1 to 2 ml) once or twice daily."

- *Intravenous glutathione.* This is probably the most effective route, but it obviously has its drawbacks. Once-a-month glutathione infusions at a biomedical practitioner's office can lead to huge "wows " that last for a few weeks.

Maximizing the Dose of B6 and Fish Oils

Remember back in chapter 10 I told you that you would eventually increase the doses of these two supplements to a higher level? Well, now's the time (once your child is on all the methylation treatments and you've determined which mix works best). Follow the guidelines I provided in those sections. Designate two to four weeks for each of these steps so that you can observe how each is affecting your child.

SAMPLE SUPPLEMENT SCHEDULE

All of the supplements I've discussed up until this point are the standard ones that most children should be on (barring any negative reactions). Organizing all of these into a daily program can be quite a task. You can choose between grouping them all together as much as possible or spreading them out throughout the day. Here is an example of what your child's regimen could look like:

Morning (with breakfast)
- digestive enzyme
- multivitamin
- cod liver oil
- taurine
- calcium, magnesium
- vitamins C and D
- extra B6 or P5P vitamin
- DMG (or TMG) with folinic acid
- glutathione cream

Midmorning
- probiotics (these need to be given separately from digestive enzymes)
- natural yeast supplements (if taking)
- fish oil
- zinc

OTHER ADVANCED STEPS

There are literally dozens of supplements and treatments that may or may not help a child with autism. There's no way to try them all. I have shared with you what I recommend in my office on a routine basis. These other treatments can be incorporated into your child's treatment plan in any order.

Lunch
- digestive enzyme

Midafternoon (these ones are given here to avoid interfering with sleep at night)
- multivitamin
- cod liver oil
- extra B6 or P5P vitamin
- DMG (or TMG) with folinic acid
- probiotics
- vitamin C (if taking twice daily)

Dinner
- digestive enzyme
- taurine
- zinc
- fish oil
- glutathione cream

Bedtime
- calcium, magnesium (may help with sleep)
- other sleep aids if needed
- B12 shot (every three nights)

This schedule is definitely not set in stone. Your child's requirements and preferences may vary.

Antiviral Treatments

As you learned in chapter 4, alternative researchers speculate that some viruses may play a role in autism. Children whose lab results show immune dysfunction (see page 85) are more likely to be harboring viruses. I have explored these treatments with numerous patients and have sometimes seen great results.

Measles virus and high-dose vitamin A. You don't need a prescription for this protocol, but it can be very dangerous if not done properly. One of the viruses that theoretically contributes to autism is the measles virus from the live MMR vaccine (see page 85 for a discussion of this controversy). If measles plays a role in autism by irritating the gut and the brain, then suppressing the virus should help. The only known medical treatment for measles infection is high-dose vitamin A. This is an approved treatment for children who are hospitalized with measles and suffering from life-threatening complications. In such situations, vitamin A is given orally or intravenously in very high doses without causing any harm or side effects. It doesn't kill the measles virus; it stuns it so that it stops replicating and causing infection. Its use in autism is considered alternative because we aren't treating an active life-threatening measles infection. However, any child who developed regressive autism within a month or two of receiving the MMR vaccine should undergo this treatment, just to cover the bases.

There is a blood test (called a *titer,* see page 107) that measures how strongly the immune system is reacting to measles. Some doctors believe that a high result may indicate a bigger problem with measles; in this case, a doctor may track the measles titer after vitamin A treatment to see if it comes down. Since we don't know whether a high titer correlates with the degree of measles infection, it isn't necessary to check titers.

Dosing. Because of the controversial nature of this protocol, I am not going to provide you with specific dosing instructions. You should give your child this treatment only with the guidance of a physician. I will tell you that the high doses are given for only two days. This regimen can be repeated every six months (put it on a calendar) to "re-stun" any measles that may be present. Not all children show benefits, but enough parents have reported to me that they've seen improvements in their child's functioning that I use this routinely on my patients.

Side effects. I've heard of no negative reactions when high doses of vitamin A are given for only two days. However, *taking high doses of vitamin A for too many consecutive days is very dangerous.* I heard of one case where a child was given high doses for a few weeks (without a doctor's guidance) and became seriously ill. I also heard about a parent who gave her child the prescribed number in droppers, instead of drops. Such overdosing can be fatal. Doctors are familiar with the toxic effects of vitamin A overdosing, so you aren't likely to get any support from your regular doctor for this step. However, because this is an approved dosing protocol for real measles, I do feel it is safe and worth doing.

Herpes viruses and Valtrex. As you read on page 104, herpes virus types I, II, and 6 are thought to possibly play a role in autism by causing chronic low-grade irritation to the nervous system. Epstein-Barr virus and cytomegalovirus may also play a minor role. Blood titer levels can be measured (see page 109) to see if a child has been exposed to these viruses and to estimate how active the viruses may be. But, just as we don't know exactly how to interpret measles titers, we also aren't sure if the other virus titers are any indication of active infection. However, I have seen enough children show improvement when these viruses (especially herpes types I, II, and 6) are treated with Valtrex that I've made this a routine treatment in my office for any child who tests positive to the herpes virus. Valtrex is an approved medication for the treatment of oral or genital herpes in adults. It doesn't completely eliminate the herpes; it only suppresses it. It is not officially FDA-approved for children. I explain below how I administer it in my office, but you should follow the advice of your own experienced biomedical physician.

Obtaining Valtrex. Valtrex is available only by prescription and comes in caplet form only as 500 mg or 1000 mg. The least expensive way to buy Valtrex (it is almost never covered by insurance) is to obtain a prescription and order it through an online pharmacy. It is also available at local pharmacies. If your child doesn't swallow capsules, you can wash the colored coating off the outside of the caplet (to avoid any behavioral problems from the coloring) and then crush up the medication and place it in food or drink (even if your child normally does swallow capsules, you can still do this if he is sensitive to coloring). A compounding pharmacy can also mix the medication into liquid form at a cost.

Dosing Valtrex. This medication isn't FDA-approved for children, so doses are basically estimates. Adults and children twelve years and older can take up to 1000 mg three times daily. Children six to eleven years should take 500 mg three times daily, and children two to five years should take about 250 mg three times daily. More cautious physicians may cut these doses in half. There are two different courses to choose from: Some doctors advise taking it four weeks on, then two weeks off, then on and off again until six four-week courses have been completed. Others like to do three weeks on and one week off for six months. The reason for the break is to allow the liver and blood cells of the body to rest (see side effects, below). If you don't notice any improvement after the first two rounds (three or four weeks each), then you are unlikely to see it later on. I usually stop therapy at that point.

Side effects. Valtrex is a strong medication. It can put a strain on the liver and suppress the body's blood cell production. I have seen a couple of children develop some signs of this on their blood testing while on Valtrex, but these resolved after the medication was stopped. Outward symptoms of liver strain are discussed on page 245. Blood cell suppression can cause bleeding, bruising, and fatigue. Stop the medication and call your doctor if your child has these symptoms.

Natural treatments for viruses. Those of you who don't have access to a biomedical practitioner will not be able to use Valtrex. A regular physician is almost certainly not going to prescribe this for you, no matter how much you beg and plead. There are numerous natural antiviral treatments that alternatively minded doctors use to suppress or eliminate viruses in the body. Except for monolaurin, these don't work directly on the viruses; rather, they stimulate the parts of the immune system that fight off a variety of infectious germs. While these may not work as well as Valtrex, they are certainly much safer:

- *Monolaurin.* See page 236 for details on this antiviral.

- *Low-dose naltrexone.* As you will learn on page 302, the primary use of LDN is to calm a hyperactive child and to help him sleep. However, after several months of use, this mild medication can specifically boost the part of the immune system that fights off viruses. This is a prescription treatment that only a biomedical doctor is likely to prescribe through a compounding pharmacy (see Resources, page 354, for a list of these). LDN is especially important for children whose lab results show an immune deficiency.

- *Myco-Immune by Thorne.* This blend of mushrooms can stimulate the antiviral parts of the immune system. This, and the following two products, are available online.

- *Larch arabinogalactan.* This herb boosts immunity.

- *Transfer factor.* Several companies, including Oramune and Researched Nutritionals, make this supplement that can boost the antiviral parts of the immune system.

- *Olive leaf extract.* This boosts the immune system as well.

Follow the manufacturer's dosing instructions. Since the last five supplements are designed to boost certain parts of the immune system, it would be prudent not to take more than one of them at the same time without a doctor's guidance.

Detoxification Treatments

Of all the biomedical treatments for autism, heavy metal detoxification (or chelation) is the one that has received the most criticism from the mainstream medical community. Prior to 2002, many of the vaccines we gave to our children had mercury. Biomedical practitioners worried that this mercury could be contributing to autism, so they began using chelation to get the mercury, and any other heavy metals, out of their patients. The idea that vaccines could be contributing to autism didn't sit well with mainstream doctors, so they've come down really hard on this aspect of treatment. Also, since aggressive chelation is the riskiest of all biomedical interventions, doctors (alternative and mainstream) worry about possible side effects (see below).

One child with autism died from a reaction to IV chelation a few years ago when the wrong type of chelation medication was inadvertently given. This tragic occurrence has been used by the mainstream medical community as proof that all IV chelation is dangerous. However, this particular case occurred because a medication that is no longer supposed to be used (disodium EDTA) was accidentally obtained from a pharmacy instead of the proper form (calcium disodium EDTA). Equally tragic was the death of a neurotypical child being chelated for lead poisoning in a hospital (by "regular" doctors), in which the exact same type of error was made. In fact, thousands of patients die in hospitals every year from medication errors. We don't shut down hospitals because of that, yet mainstream medicine tries to put a stop to IV chelation for autism because of one accident.

I've used various forms of transdermal creams, suppositories, and oral chelators, but I've never felt comfortable offering IV chelation in my office because of the complexity of the treatment.

The primary worry about chelation is that we are "stirring the pot." Heavy metals hide in the body fat and the brain. A chelator draws the metals out of hiding into the bloodstream and takes them out of the body through the urine (via the kidneys) or the stools (via the liver). The concern is that when we draw the metals out of the body fat into the bloodstream, metals that don't leave the body settle back down into the body fat and the brain. Metals that had been sitting (somewhat harmlessly) in the body fat may resettle in the brain. The net result could be more metals sitting in the brain than prior to the treatment. We don't know if this actually occurs; it is just a theoretical concern. Also, chelation draws healthy minerals out of the body. We try to compensate for this by giving extra minerals during chelation, but this isn't always sufficient. This may be why some children react negatively to chelation.

If the goal of chelation is to rid the body of metals and toxins, then repairing the body's own natural detox mechanisms should help. But depending on a child's exposure to metals, this might not be enough. Giving an actual chelator might also be necessary. Every child is different, and parents should make a decision with their physician's guidance.

Who should try chelation? The majority of children who received a lot of mercury in their shots respond positively to chelation. Even younger children who did not get mercury often show improvement in their autistic symptoms as other heavy metals are drawn out of their bodies. Because of this, I do think chelation is worth trying under certain circumstances. But the bottom line is that you can't do chelation without the help of a biomedical practitioner. There are no "do-it-yourself" treatments that I can (or would) give you instructions for (besides natural OTC products). Now that mercury is out of vaccines (except for most flu shots), aggressive IV chelation is not as relevant as it used to be. However, many doctors believe that children with autism lack the innate ability to detoxify their bodies of metals, and that even small amounts of heavy metals (like the mercury in a flu shot, mercury from a mom's metal fillings, and other heavy metals absorbed from food, water, and air) can affect children. So, even though mercury isn't much of an issue anymore (except for children who got shots prior to 2002), I do believe that chelation is appropriate in the following situations:

• Any child with moderate to severe autism born in 2001 or earlier (who therefore received a lot of mercury from vaccines) who hasn't shown much benefit from biomedical treatments could try aggressive IV chelation with an experienced physician. In a child like this, mercury detox could be the "missing link" that could lead to some significant improvement. Less aggressive oral or rectal suppository chelation is also an option (see below). The sooner you get the metals out, the better. However, at the writing of this book, children who received multiple mercury-containing vaccines will be nine years of age and older. Should these kids still be treated, or should we just leave the mercury alone? Chelation can be done at any age, but no one knows at what age it is no longer worth the risk. I believe chelation for older children of any age is worth discussing with a biomedical doctor.

• Any child who didn't get an overload of mercury from vaccines but did get a flu shot with mercury (or his pregnant mom did) should receive milder forms of chelation (see below), especially if he seemed to react negatively to that shot or showed developmental regression at the time.

• Any child who didn't get mercury but hasn't dramatically improved on the diet and biomedical treatments should at least try mild chelation and parents should discuss the pros and cons of IV chelation with their biomedical provider. In my office, I save chelation for the last step and decide on a case-by-case basis (along with the parents' input) which patients should try it.

Testing to determine the need for chelation. Testing a child to see if he has been affected by heavy metals is not very accurate (although urine porphyrin testing may show some promise; see page 102). I decide if chelation is appropriate based on the above information.

HOW TO DETERMINE IF YOUR CHILD'S FLU SHOTS (OR ANY OTHER SHOTS) HAD MERCURY

Most flu shots still contain mercury. The nasal spray flu vaccine does not, and neither do most flu shots that come in a single-dose vial. It's the large multidose bottles that contain mercury as a preservative. Most parents aren't going to remember or know which form their child received many years ago. Here's how you can tell: In your child's chart at the doctor's office, the nurse should have written down the lot number of the vaccine and the manufacturer on the vaccine record. Once you obtain this record from your child's doctor, call the manufacturer and give them the lot number, and they will be able to tell you how much mercury (if any) was in the shot. This mercury will be termed *thimerosal,* so it's best to refer to it that way when speaking with the company. They will tell you one of three things: there was 12.5 to 25 mcg of thimerosal; there was "trace" thimerosal (less than 0.3 mcg, which is insignificant); or there was no thimerosal. This information can help you assess the need for chelation.

You can also research this information as it applies to the rest of your child's shots. If your child was born in 2002, it is most likely the doctor's supply of vaccines was already mercury-free, but you can still check to make sure. Any other vaccines given in 2003 or later were almost definitely mercury-free.

Choosing the right chelation treatment. Here are the mild to moderate forms of chelation that I have tried with my patients and that I feel are very safe to use under the guidance of an experienced doctor. These are available by prescription only, usually through a compounding pharmacy (see Resources, page 354, for a list). I have placed them in order of most effective to least effective. Chelation should be administered at bedtime because the body's own detox processes increase during sleep. (Note: When doing chelation, it's important for your child to be on all the main supplements discussed in chapter 10, as well as on methylation treatments and glutathione, to help support the body.)

- *Suppositories of EDTA, DMSA, or DMPS.* These three potent chelators readily enter the bloodstream when inserted rectally, so they are a great alternative to IV administration. They are typically given once a day in cycles, such as three days on and four days off or three days on and eleven days off.

- *Oral capsules of DMSA or EDTA.* Oral forms create more gastrointestinal side effects and put a little more strain on the liver, but they can be effective. These are given in cycles similar to suppositories. Oral EDTA is available over the counter online but should not be used without a doctor's guidance.

- *OSR #1.* This oral chelator is not one of my top choices because it is new. It isn't actually categorized as a chelator but rather as an antioxidant. However, by boosting glutathione, the end result is enhancement of the body's own detox systems. It looks very promising so far; biomedical physicians report that most children show improvements in various areas when on it. Although it's not a prescription, it isn't yet being sold to the general public (as of the writing of this book). It has to be purchased from a biomedical practitioner (who buys it from www.CTIscience .com) to ensure it is used properly. It comes in capsule and powder forms and is taken once daily.

- *Transdermal creams of DMPS or DMSA.* These creams are easy to administer, but absorption into the bloodstream isn't as reliable. Follow your doctor's instructions.

Please allow me to restate a very important point: *Chelation should be done only under the guidance of an experienced biomedical practitioner.* I have listed various choices without providing specific instructions for a very good reason.

Natural chelators. If you explore the world of over-the-counter detoxification remedies, you'll find everything from magnetic pads that go under a mattress to saunas that sweat the metals out to clay baths. While I don't oppose any of these treatments, I've never used them on my patients because I'm not sure they do much. If you read some credible information that leads you to one of these therapies, then it's okay to try it. The proof will be in the changes you see or don't see in your child.

There are two natural detoxifiers that I do feel are worth trying that are available over the counter:

- *TTFD cream.* Thiamine tetrahydrofurfuryl disulfide is a form of vitamin B1 that is derived from garlic. It is available from compounding pharmacies (see Resources, page 354) with a prescription. There is an over-the-counter form called Authia Cream that combines TTFD with methyl B12 into one product (if using this, ask your doctor if you should stop your usual methyl B12 treatments). This treatment is applied to the skin twice daily (see glutathione instructions for areas of skin to apply it to, page 266) for several months or for as long as benefits are apparent.

The major drawback is that the cream's garlic smell is very potent. It goes by the nickname *skunk cream*. Some children can't tolerate the smell and have to stop using it, even if it seems to help. On days when a child goes to school or attends therapy, the morning application can be skipped and two doses can be used later in the day. This cream has become the favorite natural detoxifier among many doctors and is thought to be fairly effective when used in conjunction with glutathione cream (do not apply together on the same body part at the same time).

- *NDF drops.* This is a combination of chlorella (an alga) and cilantro (an herb) that stimulates the body's own detoxification processes. It is available from BioRay (www.BioRayNaturalDetox .com) and comes as a liquid. Follow the dosing instructions on the package. While this product is safe to take, it works very slowly. You may or may not see obvious positive results.

Duration of treatment. Most people continue chelation for one to two years (if it is creating positive results). If you don't see anything positive, it means either that you aren't using the right chelator or that your child doesn't have a significant problem with heavy metals. If you've tried two or three chelators without success, the latter reason may be the case for your child.

INTRAVENOUS IMMUNE GLOBULINS

An IV infusion of antibodies (called *immune globulins*) is a mainstream treatment for children with certain immune disorders, primarily those with an IgG deficiency. It is very expensive (about $1,500 per infusion), but it is often covered by insurance if an immune deficiency is proven by blood work. Children with autism *and* a specific immune disorder can really benefit from IVIG. But it can be helpful for children with autism even if they don't have a specific deficiency (although it won't be covered by insurance). The theory behind IVIG is that the antibodies will deactivate viruses and autoimmune antibodies that may be making the autism worse. The drawback, besides the cost? These antibodies are filtered out of hundreds of donated blood units (it takes that many to obtain enough antibodies for one infusion). Although they are thoroughly screened and cleaned for any unwanted infectious agents, you never know if this process is perfect. Most doctors, myself included, recommend this only for children who are moderately to severely affected for whom all other available treatments don't seem to work well. A child affected by PANDAS (see page 108) may also benefit. IVIG is administered by an allergy and immunology specialist.

REPEAT BLOOD TESTING

There will come a point when your child will need another blood test. The timing of this varies according to the treatments your child receives. In general, I do follow-up blood work once a child has been on the full range of treatments for about three to six months. Some doctors are more aggressive and like to recheck certain tests sooner. I retest anything that was previously abnormal. I look at anything that I am giving a specific treatment for (for example, vitamins A and D, zinc, or viral titers) to make sure I am neither overdosing nor underdosing. I check a CBC (complete blood count) and a CMP (complete metabolic panel) to monitor general body health to make sure prescription medications aren't putting too much strain on the organs. I can't give you specific guidance on this. You and your doctor will decide together what to retest and when.

HYPERBARIC OXYGEN THERAPY

Hyperbaric oxygen therapy (HBOT) has become one of the most popular nonsupplement treatments for autism in recent years. Research has shown some promising results, and in my experience it works in most children. HBOT has been around for decades. It was originally used for decompression when deep-sea divers needed to return to the surface quickly. It then became the standard of care in the field of plastic surgery to help heal traumatic injuries and severe wounds. It has also been used to treat cerebral palsy and brain injury. Numerous HBOT treatment centers are opening around the country to provide this therapy to our growing population of children with autism. Most centers require a prescription from a doctor.

HBOT chambers. There are two types of HBOT chamber. The standard chamber is a *hard chamber,* a ten-foot-long cylinder made of metal that is large enough for an adult and one or two children to enter together. The chamber has windows to see both in and out of. Children can generally sit up, but most adults have to lie down. A chamber made out of flexible material (called a *soft chamber*) is also available, but it can't create pressures and oxygen levels as high as a hard chamber can. Most children, however, don't need pressure or oxygen higher than the standard levels (see below). Some companies rent or sell soft chambers for home use.

How HBOT is done. The child enters the chamber (with toys or some other activity to occupy him) with or without an adult, and the chamber is sealed shut. Air is pumped into the chamber to increase the internal pressure to about 1.3 atmospheres, which is about a third higher than regular air pressure.

This is equivalent to swimming at the bottom of an eleven-foot-deep pool. The child puts on an oxygen mask or helmet that provides about 25 percent oxygen (normal air contains 21 percent oxygen). The adult doesn't need the oxygen unless specifically being treated as well. The treatment session should last about one hour.

The protocol adopted by most centers is to undergo forty treatment sessions over an eight-week period. This means going to a treatment center about five days each week. It's a real time commitment but only for eight weeks. Most children have to set aside some other aspect of therapy while they make time for HBOT, and that's okay. It is thought that concentrating the forty sessions into an eight-week period is ideal, but it is also acceptable to stretch them out over ten to twelve weeks. I wouldn't suggest spreading out the sessions any more than that.

How HBOT repairs the brain. Research involving brain scans (called *PET scans;* see page 124) of children with autism has shown that most (if not all) have decreased blood flow to various parts of the brain. The blood vessels have narrowed. Less blood flow means less oxygen and less function. When extra oxygen under higher pressure is inhaled into the body and absorbed into the bloodstream, that oxygen needs to find somewhere to go so it can be used. It is theorized that the blood vessels in the brain that had narrowed open up again to accommodate this oxygen and resupply those parts of the brain. PET scans done before and after HBOT have demonstrated this effect.

Another theory says that when oxygen molecules are under higher pressure, they diffuse further into body tissues away from the bloodstream, thus reaching areas of the brain where the blood isn't directly flowing. Studies have also shown that stem cells that dwell in the brain tissue are stimulated by HBOT to multiply and differentiate into brain cells to replace any damaged cells, thus improving brain function. HBOT has also been shown to decrease inflammation within the body. I'm sure we will learn more in the near future about why HBOT works. What we do know now is that it does help most children with autism.

Improvements to expect (or hope for) from HBOT. Improved language and social interaction are the big "wows" that many children get from HBOT. Improved intellectual processing and reduction in hyperactivity are also often seen. HBOT can also improve inflammatory bowel disease.

WATCH OUT FOR REGRESSION

For unknown reasons, some children experience a worsening in autistic behaviors, such as hyperactivity and aggression, during the second or third week of treatment. It isn't clear why this happens. Some practitioners believe that HBOT may trigger an increase in yeast growth and will prescribe a course of whichever yeast treatment has done the trick previously. Others recommend just riding it out, as most kids improve again without yeast treatment. You can decide with your doctor what to do.

How long to continue HBOT. The consensus among doctors is that the first forty sessions should be done at 1.3 atmospheres and 25 percent oxygen. Children who respond well should simply continue at those levels for a second or even a third round of forty sessions, with a month or two break in between each forty sessions. Some children will lose some of their gains while off therapy and some will not. The hope is that a child will continue to improve the longer he does therapy. If you don't see any gains after the first forty sessions, your provider may increase the settings. A higher percentage of oxygen (30 percent, 40 percent, or even 50 percent) can be administered. The air pressure can also be increased to 1.5 atmospheres. If you do see gains, however, the settings should not be increased. More pressure and more oxygen aren't always better. Once you reach a point where you don't see any more gains and your child doesn't lose any benefits when off therapy, you should stop.

Some children benefit from occasional maintenance therapy, for example one or two treatments per week. If you feel that your child has reached a plateau of benefit but you lose just a bit when off therapy, a maintenance treatment schedule may work well for your child, especially if you live near a center.

START SAVING YOUR MONEY

HBOT centers are very expensive to establish and run. Most have to charge at least $100 per hour of treatment to stay in business. Some may charge even more. I believe that this is probably the most worthwhile multithousand-dollar therapy that you can spend your money on. It isn't yet covered by most insurance (unless your child also has a diagnosis of cerebral palsy, in which case it might be covered).

Extra supplements to take while doing HBOT. The one drawback to receiving oxygen therapy is that it creates some free radicals within the body (see Oxidative Stress, page 86). So, extra antioxidants should be taken during HBOT months. Most children will already be on about 500 mg of vitamin C once or twice daily. You should also add CoQ-10, an antioxidant that is normally produced within the cells. Kids two to three years should take about 25 mg once daily, kids four to six, 50 mg, and older kids, about 100 mg daily. This is available online or in vitamin stores. It's okay to continue this after HBOT to see if it helps.

Precautions with HBOT. A very small risk of seizures exists with HBOT. A few children with known seizure disorders have had seizures during therapy. I also know of one child who'd never before had a seizure who had one during HBOT. Virtually all children, however, tolerate HBOT without this reaction. It isn't known if HBOT can trigger a seizure, and I still recommend it to my patients with autism and seizures. I just want you to be aware of this risk. It is prudent, in kids who have had seizures, to start off slowly, with oxygen at normal pressure for several sessions, and then gradually increase the pressure over several more sessions until you reach 1.3 atmospheres. Discuss this with your HBOT provider.

Children who are sick with an ear or sinus infection shouldn't undergo HBOT until they are well. The ear and sinus pain when under higher pressure will likely be intolerable. Even a minor cold with some nasal congestion may be uncomfortable. It's also best not to do HBOT when your child is sick with a fever.

You should be able to enter the chamber with your child. Even if you don't get extra oxygen, the pressure may get some extra blood and oxygen to various parts of your body. Most parents report better energy levels and fewer aches and pains when they

---

RENT (OR BUY) AN HBOT CHAMBER

Once you determine that HBOT is a big "wow" for your child, and you know you are going to do it for several months, consider renting a soft chamber. This will likely save you a lot of money in the long run. If you determine that long-term occasional maintenance use may be needed, you might want to purchase a soft chamber to use over the years. Consider pooling your money with other families in your area to share one.

do HBOT with their child. You should check with your doctor first, however, if you have any chronic medical problems.

To find an HBOT center near you, visit www.ihausa.org (International Hyperbaric Association).

AUDITORY INTEGRATION TRAINING

Auditory Integration Training (AIT) is a therapy specifically designed to treat the Central Auditory Processing Disorder (CAPD) aspect of autism (see page 52). Children who recover their language processing abilities through the primary behavioral therapies and the biomedical treatments probably don't need AIT. Children who don't develop near-normal language skills after two to three years of therapy may greatly benefit. The AIT therapist (often an audiologist or speech and language pathologist) identifies the sounds and frequencies that a child is overly sensitive to and those that he seems to ignore. The child then listens to music and sounds through headphones that emphasize the sounds he doesn't normally process. Pitches and sounds that he is sensitive to are filtered out or reduced. This auditory input exercises the brain's processing center to make it more receptive to the language and sounds of day-to-day life. Some nonverbal children may begin to use language, and children with immature language skills often show significant improvement.

There are several styles of AIT. The Tomatis and the Bernard methods are the classic approaches. Fast Forward, Earobics, and Binaural Beat Technology are newer methods. Children typically engage in one-hour sessions every day for a two-week period, but this can vary. Sessions can be repeated periodically to enhance the benefits. AIT is not yet considered a mainstream therapy, but if further research demonstrates its efficacy, it may someday become a standard approach for children with autism.

Other techniques utilized by therapists to improve CAPD include modifying the child's learning environment to maximize his ability to hear and pay attention (such as choosing the best seating placement in the classroom and determining where the best acoustics are), slowing down certain speech sounds when talking to the child so the child can better understand (and gradually speeding these up again as the child improves), and various other exercises to build the child's language skills.

OTHER THERAPIES

Numerous other biomedical treatment options are available. Your practitioner might offer you a variety of treatments that I have not included in this book. You might also read about treatments that are available to you without a prescription that I have not mentioned. I have discussed only the treatments that I am most familiar with—either those that I have tried with my own patients or those that are widely accepted among biomedical physicians. That doesn't mean you should restrict your child to the ones I recommend. Try any treatment that appears safe and has a reasonable chance of being effective. I also advise that you follow the recommendations given to you by your own biomedical practitioner if his or her advice differs from what you've read here. Your provider knows your child much better than I (or this book) ever will.

Here are some of the more advanced treatments a biomedical physician may offer to your child:

Anti-inflammatory medications. As you learned in chapter 4, inflammation is one of the banes of autism. Many of the biomedical treatments are designed to lower inflammation, but there are also various prescription medications that have anti-inflammatory properties that can improve autistic symptoms. I have tried these on a few of my patients but have not yet made it common practice. There are also some natural remedies that your doctor may offer, such as curcumin (Lee Silsby Compounding Pharmacy, see page 355, uses this spice to make their Enhansa product), turmeric (New Chapter makes an herbal blend called Zyflamend; available online), and Moxxor (a fish-and-mussel-oil combo that is a potent anti-inflammatory).

Mitochondrial supplements. As you learned on page 69, many children with autism have defective mitochondrial systems. Many of the biomedical supplements I've recommended will help improve mitochondrial function. On page 298, I list some treatments that may help with the low muscle tone common in mitochondrial dysfunction. Some specific vitamins and natural products may provide an even greater boost for the mitochondria, such as high doses of vitamins B1, B2, B5, and E. Speak with your biomedical practitioner.

Lyme disease treatments. I introduced you to the idea that Lyme infection may play a role in autism on page 109. If you suspect your child may be affected by Lyme, ask your practitioner about testing (I like IGeneX Lab). Treatment involves prolonged courses of various antibiotics guided by an infectious disease specialist or a physician with experience in Lyme disease.

Biofilm treatment. Research by Dr. Anju Usman has shown that yeast and bacteria in a child's intestines can bind together with sugar and protein molecules to form a layer of material that adheres to the wall of the intestines. Natural and prescription treatments may not reach these germs. There is no way to test a child to see if biofilms are present, but anyone with recurrent yeast or bacterial infections, or those who don't respond to aggressive treatment, should consider this possibility. Dr. Usman helped Kirkman Labs develop an enzyme called Biofilm Defense that digests the protein and sugar molecules to break up the biofilm layer and render the germs susceptible to treatment. Taking this enzyme each morning, prior to any other supplements, may allow natural and prescription antibacterial or antifungal treatments to work better. Ask your practitioner about this treatment.

New discoveries are made every year or two that are incorporated into the repertoire of treatments offered by biomedical practitioners. At www.TheAutismBook.com I will post updates anytime I feel there is a new development worth knowing about.

ATTEND A BIOMEDICAL CONFERENCE

Numerous conferences are available in various parts of the country every year, put on by several different autism organizations (the Autism Research Institute, AutismOne, US Autism and Asperger Association, the National Autism Association, and Talk About Curing Autism, to name a few; see Resources, page 356, for websites). These are designed for parents and physicians alike, and lectures are offered for beginners and veterans to learn everything from the basics to advanced and emerging ideas. Go to www.Autism-Conferences.com for a list of such conferences.

13

Treating Associated Medical Problems

When treating children with autism, it's important not to ignore certain medical conditions that may coexist. Some problems can make the symptoms of autism worse, and correcting those problems may lead to some surprising improvements.

CONSTIPATION

It may sound a little far-fetched, but in my opinion there is a definite correlation between constipation and mood and behavior. I see this not only in children with autism but also in neurotypical children. Most kids get grumpy and hyperactive, throw tantrums, and have a poor appetite when constipated. It's not just the pain that creates these behaviors. The colon has its own nervous system that regulates its function. When the colon isn't moving, this nervous system shuts down. Because this nervous system is connected to the central nervous system, brain function can also slow down. This is often apparent in older neurotypical children who may have difficulty concentrating when they are backed up. Ask adults with constipation; they'll tell you they feel a little dull-minded when they can't go. Making sure a child with autism is living with an empty colon is an important part of biomedical intervention.

Symptoms of constipation. Sometimes it's obvious that your child is constipated. He takes forever to go, he has to strain, it hurts, he may go days without going, and you see large logs that look like they should be coming out of an adult. But sometimes it isn't obvious. A special challenge in autism is that the child might not be able to tell you that he is constipated. You may have to do some detective work. Here are some signs that your child may be living with a backed-up colon:

- He doesn't go every day.

- The stool has little balls clumped together (like rabbit poop pellets).

- Behavioral outbursts precede passing a stool.

- He has episodes of unexplained abdominal pain.

- The doctor can feel hard balls of stool in the left lower abdomen.

- He passes small amounts of runny stool several times each day (stool may be leaking around a hard plug of stool).

- He passes very large quantities of stool every few days.

- He places himself in awkward positions, for example, standing crouched over the toilet to go, pushing on his belly while passing a stool, or lying with his abdomen pressed into the arm of a couch or chair.

Getting an X-ray of the belly. If symptoms are obvious, don't bother with an X-ray. Proceed directly to treatment. If the diagnosis is in question, an X-ray can be done. It's useful to know if your child has a tendency to become backed up. This gives you an idea of how aggressive to be with therapy. It also helps determine how vigilant you have to be to make sure the stool doesn't back up again after therapy. If, for example, the X-ray is normal, then you can rest easy and not bother with treatments. But if the X-ray shows that the colon is extremely full, then you know that months of stool-softening and colon-stimulating therapy may be needed to correct the problem permanently.

REPROGRAMMING THE COLON

The colon likes to be empty. Anytime it starts to fill, stretch receptors cause it to contract and push the poop out (that's the sensation we feel when we have to go). If poop stays in the colon and the colon remains stretched, it will lose its elasticity, like a balloon that's been blown up for a while, and remain at that new size (even when empty). In order to contract and push out the poop, the colon will have to stretch even more for the stretch receptors to register. It may take days for enough poop to stimulate the colon. That's why a child won't even feel like going for days. This can become a vicious cycle. The good news is that if you can empty out the colon and keep it emptying often for long enough (it takes a few months), it will regain its elasticity and shrink back down to normal size.

Treating constipation. There are two keys to successful treatment. First the colon needs to be emptied out every day for months in order to regain its elasticity. Then continuous supplements may be needed to keep it that way. I like to try to keep the treatments as natural as possible, using as many of the following supplements as are needed to get things moving. You can add them in one by one (a new one every few days) in the following order until you get your child going comfortably every day:

- *Aloe juice.* Available at most health food stores, this juice looks and tastes like water (well, old hose water, that is). Some brands come flavored with citrus pulp. Kids usually won't drink this straight, but it mixes easily (and undetectably) into other juices. Kids two to five should take about ¼ cup daily. Six- to twelve-year-olds can take ½ cup. George's "Always Active" Aloe is a particularly good brand, available in stores and online at www.WarrenLabsAloe.com.

- *Fiber powder.* Drugstores have a whole selection of various powders made from grains that dissolve completely into liquid. Two that I've used with my patients are Benefiber and Fiber-sure. KHP Natural Fiber (www.KartnerHealth.com) is another good choice, as is Miracle Fiber (www.VitaminShoppe.com). Follow the dosing instructions on the bottle. If a dose isn't specified for a younger child, use half of the six- to twelve-year dose.

- *Magnesium.* If your child is not yet taking the maximum amount of magnesium (see page 221), add another 100 to 200 mg daily. Some B6 and P5P supplements come combined with magnesium, so that can put two needed supplements into one. Some calcium supplements come mixed with magnesium. You can also buy a separate magnesium like H2Go (minty chewable, 200 mg per tablet), Peter Gillham's Natural Calm (liquid, 200 mg per teaspoon), Oxy-Powder (capsule, 700 mg; open and take about ¼), a good-tasting liquid vanilla-flavored calcium/magnesium combo from Integrative Therapeutics (150 mg per teaspoon), or any other type that you can find. All of these are available online.

• *Fruit-Eze.* This jam is made of prunes, raisins, dates, and prune juice. Search online and follow the directions on the label.

• *Smooth Move Senna Tea.* This herbal tea can be taken once a week for a "catch-up" clean-out to make sure your child isn't backing up again. Follow the brewing instructions and give about ½ cup to a child. Do not use every day, as it can cause dependence.

Where to fit this in with the biomedical approach. Some of the biomedical steps that you will be taking may provide enough help with constipation that you won't need to do anything more. The GFCF diet, probiotics, magnesium, and cod liver oil may all help. A good place to add in other treatments for constipation is after you've started the phase one supplements and diet changes but before you treat yeast. If the above treatments don't resolve the problem, talk to your doctor about medications, such as over-the-counter Miralax, to help get the colon jump-started. Severely backed-up children may need a daily suppository or enema for several days to get the colon moving again. A GI specialist can be consulted if such aggressive therapy is needed.

THYROID HORMONE DEFICIENCY

As you read on page 94, the thyroid gland may be affected by whatever factors triggered the autism. This may result in low hormone production, which causes the whole body to slow down: intellectual processing, energy levels, and colon contractions can all decrease. Other symptoms include dry skin and a tendency to feel cold easily. Blood testing is available to assess thyroid function. You can't (and shouldn't) treat your child with thyroid hormones without a doctor's guidance. Here is how I usually treat kids.

Iodine supplements. The body uses iodine to help make thyroid hormone, and supplementing may help with your child's own hormone production. Iodine is added to some multivitamin/ mineral supplements, so your child might already be getting it. If not, and your child's thyroid hormone is low, add about 50 mcg of an iodine supplement (usually derived from sea kelp) once daily.

Thyroid hormone. There are two types of prescription thyroid hormones: synthetic thyroid hormone, used by most mainstream doctors, and natural thyroid hormone, extracted from the thyroid glands of pigs. I prefer the natural type. Two such choices are Armour Thyroid and Nature-Throid. They come in 15 mg tablets (swallowed or crushed into food) and are available at most regular pharmacies. Your doctor will need to guide you on dosing, but I usually start with 15 mg once daily and work up from there according to blood test results and the child's response. Twice-daily dosing can also be used at your doctor's discretion. It's best to be on iodine as well.

Where to fit this in with the biomedical approach. There is no particular time to start thyroid treatments. Your biomedical practitioner can prescribe therapy as soon as a problem is discovered or refer you to your pediatrician or an endocrinologist.

SEIZURES

Seizures are a very complicated medical condition. Any child with seizures should be managed by a neurologist. Antiseizure medications are very complex, and I can't provide you with any guidance. However, I do want to stress the importance of identifying seizures, because ongoing seizures can interfere with autism recovery.

Seizures are usually obvious: rhythmic, uncontrolled twitching of the arms, legs, or face. But sometimes they are subtle and cause only brief staring spells. Any child may zone out from time to time, but you should easily be able to pull his attention back into focus. If your child is staring blankly at nothing on a routine basis and doesn't easily snap out of it, suspect seizures.

An EEG (see page 124) can be ordered by your pediatrician or a neurologist. If seizure activity is found in the brain, an antiseizure medication should be used. Taurine (one of the phase one supplements) has been shown to have some antiseizure properties. This may reduce the child's need for medication but is unlikely to completely eliminate the seizures.

ALLERGIES

I've covered food allergies in detail, but some children also have chronic nasal allergies from pollens in the air or dust or mold spores in the home. Any child with chronic nasal symptoms who doesn't improve with diet changes can be tested for airborne allergies through blood or skin testing (see page 111). As you have already read, allergies can overstimulate the immune system and may contribute to some autistic behaviors, so it's important to try to resolve them. Testing should provide you with a list of substances to avoid. But if some of the allergens are unavoidable, you should try treating the allergies with a daily nondrowsy antihistamine medication. Various over-the-counter options are available, such as loratadine (Claritin) and cetirizine (Zyrtec). I use the prescription med Allegra on occasion for my dust allergies and find it works best for me. You can try an OTC med or talk to your doctor about a prescription. Observe carefully for noticeable improvement in any autistic symptoms, too.

LOW MUSCLE TONE

This is a fairly common condition among children with autism. The occupational therapist will probably be the one to point this out to you and will help correct the low tone. There are a couple of biomedical treatments that may improve muscle strength, tone, and coordination:

Acetyl L-carnitine. This compound is present naturally in the body and plays a role in energy production within the cells. Children with mitochondrial dysfunction (see page 69) may have low carnitine production. Blood levels can be tested, and if it is low, an acetyl L-carnitine supplement can be given (do not use D/L-carnitine). I usually start this supplement early on in the protocol, as soon as I see low levels on the blood test. It is available OTC from various sources. A prescription form known as Carnitor (tablets or liquid) may not work as well because it isn't an acetyl form. The usual dose is about 25 mg per kilogram of body weight taken three times daily (with an upper limit of 1000 mg per dose). A forty-five-pound child weighs about twenty kilograms; he would take about 500 mg three times daily. Follow-up blood levels can be checked whenever other blood tests are routinely being done. This supplement may help in other areas of autism besides just muscle tone, since it may help with overall cellular energy production.

Creatine. This is commonly known as a muscle-building amino acid. It isn't used as routinely in autism as most other supplements are, as it is estimated that it may help only about one in ten kids. Those with low muscle tone are the most likely to benefit. It can be purchased from Kirkman Labs or other similar autism supplement manufacturers. The dosing range is very wide, and it is common practice to keep increasing the dose (as long as no worsening in behavior or autistic symptoms occurs) until improvements in muscle tone and energy are seen. It is recommended to start low, at around 1000 mg twice daily, and work up. Some doctors advise as much as 5000 mg to 10,000 mg twice daily. I have not had experience using this in my own patients. If your child's muscle tone and strength don't improve to normal after a few months on biomedical treatments (including acetyl L-carnitine), talk to your doctor about trying creatine.

Hippotherapy. No, this doesn't involve hippopotamuses (or hippopotami). This is a type of occupational therapy that involves horseback riding. If your child has low muscle tone, hippotherapy can help strengthen the muscles in the central part of the body.

Hyperbaric oxygen therapy. HBOT can improve muscle tone. See page 282.

Gymnastics OT. Some cities have gymnastic centers that offer OT classes to help children with low muscle tone.

FAILURE TO THRIVE

Some children with autism don't gain weight well because of a combination of extreme picky eating and intestinal dysfunction. If your child is on the thin side, follow these tips to increase his caloric intake:

Rice protein powder. Every vitamin store has a variety of protein powder supplements, and rice is probably tolerated best by most children. Mix about 15 grams per day into your child's food or drink. Nutribiotics makes a good product (www.Nutribiotic .com).

MCT (medium chain triglyceride) oil. Like the fish oils, this type of oil provides a good mix of nutritional fats. It is available online. Start with ½ teaspoon twice daily mixed into food. You can increase to 2 teaspoons twice daily. This should be given in addition to fish oils.

High fat/high protein foods. Fish (for example, wild salmon), eggs, nut butters, avocado, seeds, olive oil, legumes, beef, and poultry provide some healthy calories (if your child will eat them).

Food supplements. See the list of supplements on page 184.

If your child isn't gaining weight adequately (as determined by your pediatrician), consult with a nutritionist to assess your child's nutritional status and needs.

INFLAMMATORY BOWEL DISEASE

Some children continue to suffer from abdominal pain and chronic diarrhea despite the biomedical approach. Such children should see a pediatric gastroenterologist to rule out inflammatory bowel disease (IBD), which has come to be known in the world of autism as *autistic colitis*. Pediatric GI doctors are becoming more and more familiar with the association between autism and gut inflammation. Diet changes and yeast treatment often help heal the intestines, but these steps may not be enough. A blood test can be done (I like the IBD Serology 7 panel from www.PrometheusLabs.com) to help the GI specialist decide whether to perform a colonoscopy to visualize and biopsy the colon. Some will also offer a pill cam study, in which the child swallows a capsule with a tiny camera that takes pictures of the small intestines (the area where a colonoscopy can't reach). An upper GI endoscopy can also be considered if gastroesophageal reflux disease or other stomach problems are suspected. There are numerous ways a GI doctor can evaluate the intestinal tract. If IBD or colitis is found, strong anti-inflammatory medications can be taken for several months (or in some cases, years) to heal the gut. This can help the rest of the treatments work better. I don't recommend that children see a GI doctor until they have been on biomedical treatments for a few months to see if that heals their gut.

SLEEP PROBLEMS

Getting a good night's sleep is a common challenge for children with autism. Some have trouble winding down and falling asleep. Others wake up during the night and stay up (very loudly) for hours. The lack of sleep not only disrupts the rest of the family, it isn't healthy for the child's own development. Here are some things you can try:

Melatonin. This hormone is produced by the brain and helps regulate sleep cycles. Production of melatonin is dependent on the methylation cycle, so defective methylation might be why some children with autism don't sleep well. Melatonin is available online from various supplement companies and in most health food stores. Kirkman Labs makes a slow-release formulation that may work well for the middle-of-the-night wakers. Dosing starts at 0.5 mg at bedtime (equivalent to 500 mcg, as some forms are labeled). It is common for older children to need as much as 3 to 5 mg. Some physicians worry that children can become dependent on melatonin. While I have never seen this happen, taking a break from melatonin for about five days at the end of each month might be a worthwhile precaution.

Don't use melatonin simply for convenience, such as to make your child fall asleep quickly (it's common for a child to take about thirty minutes to fall asleep) or to prevent a once-a-night wakening from which your child would easily fall back asleep with a little reassurance from you.

There are some other theoretical benefits to melatonin that have led some families without sleep problems to give it on a daily basis. It is thought to help with constipation, act as an antioxidant, and perhaps help the cells utilize vitamin B6.

5-HTP (tryptophan). This amino acid is used by the body to make serotonin, which is the brain's calming hormone. So, supplementing with tryptophan (in the form of 5-hydroxytryptophan, or 5-HTP) can help produce a calming effect. The body will also convert this serotonin into melatonin. 5-HTP is available online or in stores. Typical doses start at 50 mg at bedtime. Increase to 100 mg if needed.

Magnesium. This mineral can have a sleep-inducing effect, so if your child is taking a separate magnesium supplement or calcium/magnesium supplement, try giving this at bedtime. If your child isn't already taking one, give him about 100 mg at bedtime (see page 294 for suggested brands). Do not use high-dose B6/magnesium at bedtime as this may keep your child awake.

LDN (low-dose naltrexone). Available in capsule or cream (and by prescription from compounding pharmacies; see Resources, page 354), this medication is used in emergency rooms to counteract overdoses of morphine-like drugs. But in that setting, doses of 100 to 200 mg are used. For kids with autism, we only give 3 to 5 mg doses each night at bedtime to prevent middle-of-the-night waking (for children who wake up and want to stay up for hours). It causes drowsiness for about six to ten hours, so if you give it too early in the evening it will wear off in the middle of the night. Apply the cream to your child's skin when you go to bed so the effects will last until morning. It then continues with a slight calming effect that will last through the next day, which can help with hyperactivity. Long-term use for several months or more can also boost the immune system.

Chamomile tea. This old-fashioned remedy works fairly well. Brew a cup every night and make it a story-time drink.

A good night's sleep is important for overall health and neurological function. It is okay for a child to take all of these sleep-inducing and calming supplements if they are needed as long as you build up to them and don't see any negative side effects.

ATTENTION DEFICIT DISORDER

Most children with autism also have ADD. Some children are hyperfocused and do very well in school, but this is more the exception than the rule. Most children with autism have enough hyperactivity to qualify for an ADHD (Attention Deficit Hyperactivity Disorder) diagnosis, too. But for the majority of children with autism, ADD isn't distinguished as an additional or distinct medical problem. There's no need to do any specific testing to see if your child has ADD, too. On the other hand, one of the goals of the biomedical approach is to achieve such a high level of recovery that the child qualifies for a diagnosis of ADD only and not for full autism.

Here are some methods that can be used to help with focus and attention and reduce hyperactivity:

Neurofeedback therapy. This method involves engaging the child in certain games and exercises on a computer screen while monitoring his "brain waves" (more correctly, electrical activity). Several electrodes are placed on the child's scalp, and the electrical activity generated by certain parts of the brain is measured during play. This brain wave information is fed into the computer, and if the child is using the correct parts of his mind (the centers that control focus and attention), the computer responds positively and he will be able to complete the particular exercise on the screen. He does the exercises over and over again in order to reinforce the success. After several months, he should be able to focus better on schoolwork (without being hooked up) and in other areas of his life.

A child needs to be reasonably cooperative to participate successfully in neurofeedback. He should probably be at least six years old and able to sit still and pay attention to a video screen. For more information or to find a provider near you, visit the International Society for Neurofeedback and Research (www.ISNR.org).

Supplements that may improve cognitive abilities and attention. Some of the supplements, such as fish oil, B6, and methyl B12, may improve the thinking power of the brain. Here are several others that may enhance thinking and focus:

- CoQ10 (coenzyme Q10): an antioxidant
- DMAE (dimethylaminoethanol)
- GABA (gamma-aminobutyric acid): a neurotransmitter
- Pycnogenol: a plant extract that improves blood flow and acts as an antioxidant and anti-inflammatory
- Quercetin: a plant extract with similar actions to pycnogenol

You can find these supplements online separately or incorporated into one product. Follow the suggested dosing and watch for any noticeable improvements.

For more information on how to address ADD/ADHD problems with good nutrition, check out *The NDD Book: How Nutrition Deficit Disorder Affects Your Child's Learning, Behavior, and Health, and What You Can Do About It—Without Drugs,* from the Sears Parenting Library.

HYPERACTIVITY

Even though hyperactivity sometimes coexists with ADD, I placed it in a separate category for the purposes of supplementation because it is often a significant and disruptive aspect of autism (not just to others around the child but also to his own participation in life). On page 164 I discussed the various medications used to treat the ADHD aspect of autism. I also want to share with you two supplements that help with sleep that may also be used as calming agents:

5-HTP (tryptophan). This can be used for sleep (see page 302), but I find myself recommending it more often as a natural calming agent for my "bouncing off the walls" patients. The typical dose is 50 to 100 mg twice daily.

LDN (low-dose naltrexone). This cream or capsule used for sleep can also have a calming affect during the day. See page 302 for dosing.

KEEP YOUR CHILD MOVING

Research shows that exercise improves neurological and immunological health. A sedentary lifestyle isn't good for anybody's brain. Encourage outdoor play every day. Participate in organized sports activities on a regular basis. Gymnastics, martial arts, swimming, surfing, horseback riding, and virtually anything else that gets your child moving can help calm the mind and improve behavior.

14

Putting It All Together: Dr. Bob's Ten-Step Program

You have learned so much about what you can do for your child. I have walked you through the process of diagnosis, helped you search for possible causes, shown you how to get started on the right behavioral and developmental therapies, and given you the tools you need to get your child started on the biomedical treatments. I know this is a lot of information to take in. Here is a step-by-step review to help you.

Step 1: Suspect a problem. As soon as you see any signs of autism, get an evaluation by your pediatrician or a developmental specialist. Your child may not be diagnosed with autism unless he demonstrates more and more problems over the coming year. But it's imperative that he be recognized as at risk for autism when he is showing early signs so that intervention can begin.

Step 2: Begin early developmental and behavioral intervention. As soon as a problem is suspected, find an Early Start Center or private therapy program to address your child's specific developmental deficits. This can begin simultaneously with or right after step 1, and you should not wait until a diagnosis of autism is given. Early therapies can include language therapy, occupational therapy, sensory occupational therapy, and ABA.

Step 3: Begin simple biomedical treatments. As you go through step 2, begin the gluten-free, casein-free diet. Start the first-line supplements: digestive enzymes, taurine, cod liver oil, multivitamins/minerals, and probiotics. If you can get immediate access to biomedical testing, delay these steps for a few weeks until testing is done. But it can take months for a family to track down someone to order the right tests and wait for the results. I recommend that you not delay this step too long, especially if your child has gastrointestinal symptoms. This is also a good time to involve yourself with a parent support group such as TACA.

Step 4: Seek a more in-depth evaluation. So far, you are acting preemptively because a problem is suspected. One of two things will now happen. Either your child will respond positively to these early interventions and stop regressing further into autism, or he will continue to regress. It's time for a more in-depth evaluation to determine which direction your child is headed. See a neurologist or other developmental specialist (if you have not yet done so) to look into the possibility that your child has autism and to rule out any neurological disorders.

Step 5: Expand your child's services. Reassess your child's behavioral and developmental services and expand them if necessary. You may have to begin to fight for your child's rights. A state-funded program may or may not be able to provide enough therapy hours. You might need to seek additional private therapy. Guidance from an experienced parent might be useful. A child with autism should be in full-time therapy: six to eight hours a day five days a week, with the majority of the time spent in ABA (or similar behavioral intervention therapy), and twice-weekly sessions of occupational therapy, language therapy, and social skills classes.

Step 6: Address related medical problems with a doctor. Your pediatrician can help your child with constipation, allergies, and yeast treatment, and other medical specialists can assist with challenges like seizures (neurologist), inflammatory bowel disease or failure to thrive (gastroenterologist), thyroid problems (endocrinologist), or any other medical problems specific to your child. If needed, try natural treatments for sleep problems, hyperactivity, and low muscle tone.

Step 7: Clean up your family's diet and lifestyle. If you haven't already done so, it's time to get more serious about going green, from what you eat to what you buy to what you use around the house. Minimize your child's chemical exposures as much as you can. Check out my book *HappyBaby* for more green tips.

Step 8: Maximize supplement doses. Increase your child's doses of B6 and fish oil and add any other biomedical supplements you feel are appropriate. Add on any advanced treatments that you are comfortable with and that don't require a prescription.

Step 9: Seek out a biomedical practitioner. Now it's time for the big guns. You can begin working with a biomedical physician at any time, but I place this step near the end of my list for two reasons. First, many of the biomedical treatments can be implemented on your own or with the help of your pediatrician. Second, there aren't enough biomedical practitioners to go around, so it may take you a while to see one. But when you've done all you can on your own, see a biomedical doctor and explore testing that your regular physician has not done. Begin advanced treatments, such as stronger yeast medication, methylation supplements (especially B12 shots), antiviral medications, chelation if you are comfortable with it, and hyperbaric oxygen therapy (HBOT). Consider dietary options such as the specific carbohydrate diet (SCD) and other restrictions.

Step 10: Consider appropriate medications. If you have been treating your child for a few years in every way possible and he is still in the moderate-to-severe category, seek the advice of a pediatric psychiatrist to explore how psychotropic medications may help. These can decrease autistic symptoms and improve behavior when other treatments haven't been enough.

These steps are only suggested guidelines. Your child's needs and experiences may vary, and you should be ready to adjust your approach accordingly.

15

Five Stories from My Practice

Over the past ten years, I have helped more than five hundred families begin the biomedical approach. I have learned so much from these families, and I want to share with you five stories that illustrate the benefits of biomedical treatments. I hope that you can identify with one or two of these cases and that they motivate you and your family as you continue your journey through autism treatment.

CLASSIC REGRESSIVE AUTISM

Many of the children with autism whom I have seen fit into what I call the classic picture of regressive autism with gastrointestinal problems. I have chosen to share Jeremy's story with you, as it illustrates virtually all of the steps that I typically guide such a child through.

Jeremy's parents brought him to see me when he was two years and four months of age. They shared with me that he had been a completely normal baby in every way for the first year. But that all changed when he was weaned and started on regular milk at thirteen months. He developed runny, mucusy stools several times each day (his normal pattern had been soft stools once daily prior to that). This went on for a couple months, and his pediatrician wrote it off as normal toddler diarrhea. Jeremy's language and all other areas of development were progressing just fine. But at sixteen months he became ill with rotavirus, an intestinal infection, and was hospitalized for dehydration. He recovered without any trouble, but his loose and frequent stools persisted. He had a persistent red diaper rash that looked as if his stools were burning him. He saw a gastroenterologist at eighteen months, and his allergy test results were all normal. However, Jeremy began to show regression in his development. He stopped saying the two words he had learned and his babbling decreased. He started walking on his toes and flapping his hands. Although his parents weren't thinking autism at that time, in hindsight they look back and remember many classic symptoms. Against their doctor's advice, Jeremy's parents put him on the GFCF diet. Just days into the diet, he had a normal bowel movement for the first time in six months. After Jeremy had had a month of normal stools, their doctor convinced them to go off the diet again because he felt they were depriving him of much-needed nutrition. Jeremy's diarrhea instantly returned and he lost some weight. His parents put him strictly on the diet at age two.

Jeremy had a developmental evaluation, was found to have some delays, and began speech therapy. His parents also started him on probiotics, cod liver oil, and a regular multivitamin. By the time I saw Jeremy, his stools had been healthier for months, but he still had loose, foul-smelling stools about a third of the time. Some of his autistic behaviors had decreased, but his parents still felt he had autism. They hadn't yet seen a neurologist, so I referred them to one and recommended they seek additional developmental services (ABA and OT) in the meantime. I also ran the full panel of urine, stool, and blood testing to look for anything that might be related to his symptoms. I also told his parents to start him on a better multivitamin/mineral supplement and to increase his cod liver oil to a more effective dose.

I saw Jeremy six weeks later to go over his test results. Since he was on the GFCF diet, he didn't show much sensitivity to gluten and casein on his tests. But he did have a very high sensitivity to corn, and his parents had taken that out of his diet a few weeks before when I'd e-mailed them about that particular result. They had also stopped soy and various nuts that also tested moderately high. They reported noticing much better eye contact and attention after starting the multivitamin/mineral supplement. He had also started ABA therapy and was receiving more hours of speech therapy, and his language was steadily increasing. His stools were healthy two-thirds of the time, but he would still have days when they were loose, foul, and mucusy. They especially noticed such reactions when he accidentally ate corn (or anything with corn in it).

His tests revealed a very high level of yeast growth and digestive problems in his gut. I was a bit surprised by the yeast, since he had never had any antibiotics. But this gave me something to treat that I knew would help greatly. I added other basic supplements to Jeremy's regimen, including digestive enzymes, calcium, magnesium, taurine, probiotics, and vitamin C. I also put him on a low-yeast diet and colostrum. His parents were reluctant to give him a strong yeast medication, so we started off with a three-month course of nystatin. Once that was going, I put him on transdermal B12 cream (I was still using that back then) and TMG.

Four months later (two months shy of his third birthday), I saw Jeremy again. His parents reported normal stools about 85 percent of the time now, and the few that were loose weren't as foul smelling as they used to be. His tantrums had decreased in frequency and severity to the point that they seemed normal for any young child. His speech, eye contact, compliance, and ability to transition from one task to another were all improving dramatically. They had happened to run out of nystatin two weeks earlier and felt he was a little more "spacey" over the past week. Overall, everything was improving, but he still had some challenges to overcome in his language and social skills. I added glutathione cream, high-dose vitamin A (for two days only), and LDN cream. I restarted nystatin (his parents still didn't want a stronger yeast med).

Jeremy responded well to these measures but lost some ground whenever we took him off nystatin. We finally treated him with two courses of stronger yeast meds, and repeat stool testing showed the yeast had decreased to a very low level. However, behaviorally he would worsen when he was off the meds, and his stools would take a minor turn for the worse. I realized this was a classic picture of the type of child who would do very well with the specific carbohydrate diet. It wasn't easy to persuade his parents to give it a try, but they ultimately did. Jeremy responded very well, and his stools became normal 95 percent of the time. He showed further gains in social skills and language.

There's more to try with Jeremy, such as hyperbaric oxygen therapy and switching to B12 shots, and I look forward to seeing how he responds to these.

PERSISTENCE REALLY PAYS OFF

Every doctor has patients who stick in his mind, and Justin is one such boy. His parents have taught me that I should keep trying everything I can until I find what works best.

I began seeing Justin when he was four and a half years old. His parents shared with me that he had seemed like a normal baby in every way until he was seven months of age, when he underwent surgery to repair a hypospadias (a congenital problem with his penis). Once home from the surgery, he became lethargic and less expressive, began waking frequently at night with prolonged crying episodes (he previously had been sleeping through the night), wouldn't hold his own bottle anymore, and developed extreme oral defensiveness. By twelve months of age many of these problems had gone away, and except for his oral aversion and refusal to hold his own bottle, things had returned mostly to normal. But around thirteen months of age, the few words he had begun to use disappeared and unusual repetitive behaviors began, and by eighteen months, no words had returned. He also developed more signs of sensory processing disorder.

With the exception of the month or two after his surgery, Justin had virtually normal eye contact, smiled, laughed, and sought out interaction with his parents. He had almost no social deficits as a toddler. His problems mainly involved speech, sensory processing, and repetitive behaviors. He was never officially diagnosed with autism, although in hindsight he probably did fit on the spectrum. He received all the same therapies that a toddler/preschooler with autism would: OT, sensory OT, ABA (and some DIR/Floortime), and speech therapy. He did not get sick very often and took antibiotics only a few times. Justin tried some of the biomedical supplements, but he had never tried the full program, including diet changes. His parents felt that all of his behavioral therapies (especially sensory integration OT) were benefiting him greatly, but they were ready to jump right into more biomedical interventions.

When I first saw Justin, his main challenges were frequent hand clapping in response to most visual stimuli, echolalia and video talk interspersed with normal language skills, immature social skills for his age, oral aversions, and occasional spacing out. Because of his severe oral aversions, he required three cans of a milk-based toddler formula every day. He was on the mild to mild-to-moderate end of the autism spectrum.

Blood, urine, and stool tests were normal in most respects but remarkable for a significant overgrowth of clostridium bacteria in his colon (as evidenced on the urine OAT test) and gluten, casein, soy, egg, and nut allergies. Justin started the GFCF diet and I switched him to Neocate Junior formula (casein-free). I started him on a more detailed list of supplements, including a multivitamin/mineral specific to autism, cod liver oil, calcium, magnesium, zinc, vitamin C, carnitine, CoQ10, digestive enzymes, MCT oil, fruit and veggie supplements, B12 shots, TMG, folinic acid, and probiotics, all carefully added one by one over a three-month period. I treated him with fluconazole and metronidazole (for the clostridium and mild yeast) and had him begin colostrum. An X-ray of his abdomen revealed moderate to severe constipation (which wasn't apparent from looking at his stooling pattern), and we treated this with a fiber powder, maximized his magnesium dose, and added aloe juice and Fruit-Eze. I also prescribed DMPS transdermal drops for chelation at the parents' request.

Over the following year Justin steadily improved. His parents reported that the biggest "wows" came after his yeast and clostridium treatment, an increase in his B12 shots from once a week to twice a week, and the GFCF (and soy-free) diet. His behavior became more even, with fewer meltdowns and less rigidity in his demands, and he showed improvement in attention, coordination, language, focus, expressiveness, and overall happiness. His oral and tactile sensitivities diminished and his energy level improved dramatically. The two primary issues that still persisted were hand clapping in response to any exciting stimulus, such as TV or video games, and his conversational language, which was still immature for his current age of five and a half.

I retreated Justin with fluconazole and metronidazole, then followed this up with long-term nystatin to keep yeast away. I added transdermal glutathione to help support his chelation and transdermal low-dose naltrexone and Smooth Move Tea to help with constipation. He also switched over to nasal B12 for convenience.

His parents involved him in a greater variety of physical activities, including karate, gymnastics, and horseback riding, and they felt that this enhanced his coordination and strength.

Over the next few months Justin made even greater strides in his social and language development. His parents attributed a significant jump in his expressive language to the introduction of naltrexone. But two problems that persisted were constipation and hand clapping. Each course of yeast and clostridium meds seemed to help this temporarily, but the problems returned when he went off these strong meds. Various probiotic changes didn't seem to help.

By seven years of age (just over two years after I started to work with him), Justin had improved to the point that he was functioning in virtually every area as a neurotypical six-year-old would. An eight-week course of hyperbaric oxygen therapy created some more language and social gains. But when he took his usual twice-yearly round of yeast and bacterial meds, for the first time in his life he didn't show any response. In fact, his behavior worsened, so I treated him with ketoconazole and vancomycin instead. He showed some very positive gains in behavior. I changed his digestive enzyme to Pancrecarb, and his constipation improved to the point where he didn't need aloe, fiber powder, or Smooth Move Tea anymore in order to have a normal stool every day. We weren't sure if this was due to the change in yeast and bacterial meds, the hyperbaric oxygen, or the digestive enzymes; in hindsight, biofilms, discussed on page 289, may have been a contributor to his persistent bacteria and yeast.

He took a six-month break from DMPS chelation, then restarted it, and his parents felt it still benefited him. He went through a course of Tomatis Auditory Integration Training, and his residual video talk disappeared. He was doing very well in a mainstream classroom at this point and continued to have ABA and/or speech therapy after school almost daily.

Justin is now nine years old, and my most recent meeting with him and his parents was another exercise in "What do we do next?" Although we finally fixed his gut issues, and he has come such a long way in virtually every area, he still has the hand clapping and a few other stims along with some new OCD symptoms. I continue to look for answers: Does he have PANDAS (from strep bacteria)? Are viruses affecting him? Do we give him biofilm treatment? Will IVIG help if he does have PANDAS? What else can we look for?

I see some parents get to the point where they feel they've done all they can do, and they decide not to explore further treatment options. But Justin's parents (fortunately for him) have taught me that it's okay to keep looking for answers to the problems that continue to affect a child. Their persistence and efforts allowed us to find the solution to Justin's constipation. But we aren't done. It takes time, money, and energy to keep going. Our children are worth it.

EARLY INTERVENTION CAN CHANGE A LIFE

Here is a case that clearly illustrates the benefits of identifying problems early on, especially when a toddler fits into the classic picture of regressive autism with gastrointestinal symptoms. Early biomedical intervention can make an enormous difference as I will illustrate by sharing what happened with a little patient named Alex.

Alex was adopted from Japan by a Japanese-American family when he was five months old. There were no known significant health problems during the early months prior to the adoption. Once he was in the States, his parents noticed that his abdomen often appeared bloated. They suspected a milk-based-formula allergy, and switching him to soy formula seemed to help. At nine months of age Alex developed eczema (an allergic skin rash). Other than those minor issues, Alex was healthy, happy, and developing normally in every way for the first twelve and a half months of life.

When Alex turned one, his parents switched him from soy formula to regular cow's milk. He immediately developed abdominal pain, bloating, and diarrhea. Switching over to lactose-free milk (cow's milk but with the milk sugar removed) seemed to help somewhat, but the bloating persisted (due to a milk-protein allergy). A week after turning one, Alex took a course of antibiotics for a respiratory and sinus infection. He also received the usual one-year vaccines during this time period. By twelve and a half months (only two weeks after starting cow's milk and receiving antibiotics), Alex began to quickly regress: he stopped smiling and laughing, lost all eye contact, stopped babbling, and began spinning around and flapping his hands. His parents had "lost" their child. He regressed into almost all of the classic signs of autism.

Fortunately, this family met the parents of a patient of mine who told them about biomedical treatments. I had the privilege of meeting Alex and his parents when he was fourteen months old, only six weeks after his regression had begun. I didn't waste any time. I ordered the usual tests, but I told the parents to start Alex on the GFCF diet as soon as the tests were drawn. With his obvious history of milk allergy, I didn't want to wait for the test results to come back before acting. I also had them begin a multivitamin/mineral, cod liver oil, and probiotics. They began ABA therapy through an Early Start program. We didn't wait for a neurological evaluation or a second opinion.

Three weeks after starting the diet, Alex started babbling, smiling, and waving again. In his parents' own words, "He came back to us." His eczema resolved and his stools became normal again. When I saw Alex four months after his first appointment, he was a different baby, all because these parents acted quickly and decisively. The GFCF diet and three basic supplements made all the difference. But Alex wasn't out of the woods yet. He still had some significant sensory processing problems, obsessive biting (more than expected for a teething baby), and unusual laughing spells. He had already started sensory integration OT and was continuing ABA therapy. Alex's lab tests were surprisingly normal (except for a mild yeast and clostridium infection) and didn't suggest he needed anything but the standard protocol. I started him on digestive enzymes, taurine, fluconazole (for yeast), metronidazole (for clostridium), B12 shots, then DMG with folinic acid and glutathione cream.

Alex refused to take the yeast and clostridium meds, so we had to back off to nystatin (much sweeter tasting). The B12 shots and glutathione helped bring out some language and interaction but made him so hyper that we had to stop them.

By two years of age Alex was doing very well. Because of the diet, supplements, and ABA and OT, he was speaking in sentences and had near normal social interaction. His stools were perfectly healthy, he was growing well, and he was even losing many of his hours of state-funded therapy because his problems had nearly resolved.

I'm not yet done with Alex. I plan to make sure his yeast doesn't come back, I want him to go through some hyperbaric oxygen therapy, and I may give B12 shots and glutathione another try, depending on how he does. Kids like Alex have to be watched closely as they mature into the preschool years to make sure their social development is progressing normally.

What I want you to learn from this case study is the critical importance of acting quickly. I have spoken to hundreds of other parents with the same story as Alex's, but some didn't begin treatments until a diagnosis of autism was made, between ages two and three. Early biomedical intervention can make a lifelong difference.

DON'T KNOCK IT TILL YOU TRY IT

I have had many patients who haven't fit the classic story of regressive autism with gastrointestinal symptoms but who have responded well to biomedical treatments nonetheless. I want to tell you Nicholas's story not only because it illustrates many of the key features of the protocol, but also because it's an example of how well biomedical treatments can work for any child.

Nicholas was born with two eye conditions. One was strabismus, where one eye turns inward toward the nose; the other was nystagmus, where the eye jerks back and forth rapidly. Because of the poor vision associated with these conditions, Nicholas had some mild developmental delays that were assumed to be due to his eye problems. His motor skills were always several months behind, and his social development was slightly delayed. He used several words by eighteen months but didn't progress into short sentences by age two. Nicholas never showed any regression of his skills. After undergoing surgery at age two to correct his vision, he opened up to some degree to the world around him. But over the next year, he didn't blossom socially as much as expected, his language skills remained delayed, and his tantrums became more extreme. At three and a half he was diagnosed with autism and began speech, OT, and ABA therapies.

Fortunately for Nicholas, a few months shy of his fourth birthday, his parents became aware of the biomedical approach and started him on the GFCF diet right away. They saw some great results within just two weeks: His social interaction with peers increased, his tantrums went from two or three per day to only one or two each week, he was much happier and less agitated, and he started playing with toys and taking part in activities he used to ignore. In addition to these immediate changes, his language improved dramatically over the next few months (which could also have been due to his therapies). Despite these gains, he still had a long way to go.

I didn't meet Nicholas until he was four and a half years old, nine months after he'd started the diet. His main problems were decreased social interaction and interest in fun activities, lack of conversational language, stimming on the wheels of toy cars and trains, hyperactivity, and tantrums more severe than expected for his age. Despite a year of behavioral therapies, he was not progressing in these areas as much as he should have been. Nicholas also had more than his fair share of ear infections and antibiotics (about ten courses!). His mother recalls him having more severe tantrums and other behavioral problems during his antibiotic courses. However, he never had diarrhea or constipation. His stools had always seemed healthy.

Testing revealed a number of problems that could be contributing to his autistic symptoms: His zinc level was very low; his thyroid gland wasn't functioning normally; he had evidence of exposure to human herpes virus (HHV 6); he had severe overgrowth of clostridia bacteria in his intestines and a moderate problem with yeast; and he had a few food allergies.

I started Nicholas on the standard supplements and extra zinc with excellent results, except that he became very hyperactive on the multivitamin/mineral, so we set that aside for a while. I prescribed thyroid hormones and iodine. I treated him with fluconazole and metronidazole for his intestinal germs and then started him on B12 nasal spray (Mom didn't want to try shots yet), TMG, and folinic acid. He responded positively to everything we did. Virtually every one of his problems improved with the yeast and bacterial meds, especially his language, and the thyroid hormone improved his energy level and muscle strength. Just one month after he was on this protocol, I received the following e-mail from Nicholas's mom:

Dr. Bob and Susan [my assistant at the time],

I wanted to give you an update on Nicholas since we started with this protocol. I took Nick to speech on Thursday and his therapist (who does not know that we have been doing any of the treatments) said, "Wow his comprehension of complex language has dramatically improved in the last 4 weeks!" We went to Disneyland yesterday for his

5th birthday and in a 7-hour period there was never one behavior…any transitional issues…perfect! Rode all of the rides his siblings did, patiently waited in line (sometimes for 15–30 minutes). Amazing. And just this morning our nanny brought over her little puppy. Nick has been playing with it outside and when his sister woke up he ran up to her and said, "Sophia, come look…there is a puppy in our house." His ability to share perspective and enjoyment is improving as well.

We cannot thank you enough. This is the first birthday in three years I can say I really enjoyed. I have hope and joy in my heart again.

Need a tissue? I do, every time I read this. It is phone calls and e-mails like this that make my job the best job in the world. But I can't take the credit. I'm just providing the treatments that dozens of researchers and physicians in the biomedical world of autism have put together. The thanks go to them.

Nicholas went on to take B12 shots and use glutathione cream. By five and a half he was in a mainstream kindergarten without a shadow or aide and learning at a normal academic level. His only deficit was minor social delays. I moved him on to hyperbaric oxygen therapy, and he continues with yeast and bacterial treatments about twice a year, each time with good results. I have yet to find a multivitamin that doesn't make him hyper. He is now seven years old, and the only thing that is noticeable about Nicholas is a very minor social quirkiness.

Nicholas has taught me that anybody can respond to biomedical interventions. He didn't fit the classic story of regression, and he didn't have GI symptoms. But his response shows how well a child can benefit from even the most basic biomedical treatments and that ongoing diligence in moving through each step can create lasting improvements.

ANY BEHAVIORAL/DEVELOPMENTAL PROBLEM
CAN BENEFIT FROM BIOMEDICAL TREATMENTS

Over the years I have learned that the biomedical approach isn't just for children with autism. It can benefit any child with extreme tantrums, hyperactivity, aggressive behavior, OCD tendencies, learning disabilities, ADD, ADHD, and speech delay (or other types of developmental delay). I could provide you with dozens of such examples, but with one little girl, this lesson really hit home for me.

Samantha was five years old when her parents brought her in to see me because they were worried that she might have ADHD. Her kindergarten teacher had reported that she wouldn't sit still, didn't listen to directions, and wouldn't concentrate on her schoolwork. This is a classic description of a child with ADHD. However, I noticed some subtle behaviors that had me even more concerned. Samantha didn't make a lot of eye contact with me and seemed to be in her own little world. If I engaged her, then she would talk up a storm in a very normal way. But if left alone, she didn't really care about what was going on around her. I certainly agreed with the ADHD diagnosis, but I was worried she might also have delayed social development. I knew that Samantha would never fit the criteria for an autism diagnosis, but I wanted to help her not only with her attention and hyperactivity but also with her social functioning.

Testing revealed some casein and gluten sensitivity and intestinal yeast overgrowth, and with a history of antibiotic overuse, this was no surprise. Interestingly, her parents hadn't come to see me for biomedical treatments. They had been thinking meds. So it took a little effort for me to persuade them to try Samantha on the GFCF diet, basic supplements, and yeast treatments. But they did try them, and two months later, the family was back in my office with a different child. Samantha engaged me in conversation spontaneously. She sat in her chair calmly and cooperated fully with the physical exam. She wasn't fidgety. She didn't bounce around the room. I was pleasantly surprised, but that was nothing compared with how her parents were glowing. And the reports from the teacher were phenomenal. She was truly shocked. (I think she suspected some sort of alien cloning had taken place.)

Samantha stayed on the diet and basic supplements for two years. I never had to move on to methylation treatments or other advanced steps (although I have seen methylation supplements help other children with ADHD). Her parents carefully took her off the diet and gradually stopped the supplements one at a time (except for her fish oil). Today this nine-year-old girl is completely neurotypical and thriving in school and in her social life, without any traces of ADHD.

Treating autism is a challenge. Many children fit the classic profile, and I can work them through the treatments step-by-step without too much variation. However, some kids have unique symptoms, respond differently to treatments, or develop unexpected challenges along the way that necessitate a more individualized approach. It is my hope that these stories will encourage you to begin the diet and standard supplements and then continue to look for more answers, treatments, and approaches that will best fit your child.

Part IV

Preventing Autism

16

Prevention for Your Future Children

With a disorder like autism, in which the precise causes are largely unknown, it's generally frowned upon by the mainstream medical community to discuss prevention. How can we prevent something when we don't know what's causing it? Well, we do know that biological, environmental, nutritional, allergic, and infectious factors contribute to autism. I believe that prevention is possible by minimizing or eliminating as many of these biomedical factors as we can, from preconception through the first several years of life.

Most doctors focus more on early detection as the primary form of prevention. That *is* important, as I've stressed throughout this book. Early intervention, through both therapy and biomedical approaches, can make a tremendous difference. It may help prevent the autism from becoming worse and prevent some long-term behavioral and learning problems. But early detection is *not* prevention; it's simply early detection. This has been an ongoing debate in the area of cancer research. Most research has focused on treatment and early detection, stating that early detection is the best form of prevention. Well, no, it's not. Preventing the disease is the best form of prevention. Early detection can minimize the disease, but it doesn't keep it from happening.

Prevention is very important for any family that has a child with autism. Subsequent children may share the genetic factors that contributed to the first child's autism. Studies have shown that the risk of having another child with autism is 4 percent if the first child with autism is a girl, and 7 percent if the first child is a boy. I will share with you everything I tell such families when they have another baby.

But what about a first child? Most new parents won't think about risk. However, we do know that there is a 1 in 91 likelihood that a first child will develop autism. That's not a small number. While all such families may not need to go as deeply into prevention, they can follow some basic commonsense steps. And they need to be vigilant. Siblings of a child with autism are already watched very closely, and early detection and therapy are almost guaranteed. But this isn't the case for a first child. No one is watching first children beyond simple observation by the family and the pediatrician. These families have to be even more aware of the early signs.

I am going to walk you through various ways you can act preemptively to avoid or minimize the biomedical problems that you've been reading about throughout the latter part of this book. It isn't easy. It takes a lot of work. But it's definitely worth it. These steps are most important for a family that already has a child with autism. If this is your first child, you can decide which steps sound reasonable to you.

AVOID VITAMIN D DEFICIENCY

As you learned on page 120, "hormone D" plays a role in many aspects of health, and we are just now beginning to understand it. Vitamin D deficiency in a mom during pregnancy may result in vitamin D deficiency in the developing fetus and during infancy as well. Most of our population is probably at least mildly deficient, due to our limited outdoor activities and avoidance of sunlight without sunscreen. Here is what you can do to prevent this:

Before pregnancy. Get your vitamin D level up to 65 (normal range is about 50 to 100). Ask your primary care doctor to test your 25-hydroxy vitamin D level (it needs to be specifically that type). If it's low, begin supplementing every day with 1000 IU of vitamin D-3 for every twenty-five pounds that you weigh. So, a 150-pound adult would take about 6000 IU daily. Realize that this is quite a lot higher than the government's RDA, and you should do this only under the guidance of your own physician. Retest your level every month or two until you reach about 65. After that, you can lower your dose to a maintenance of about 1000 IU daily and ensure you get a proper amount of sunlight (see below). Retest about six months later (or during your prenatal lab tests) to see if your level is staying high enough.

During pregnancy. Vitamin supplementation during pregnancy is a touchy subject. Of course, all women should take a prenatal vitamin. Most contain the usual RDA of 400 IU of vitamin D. This amount certainly won't correct a deficiency. It isn't known whether taking higher doses to correct a deficiency during pregnancy is safe. I won't make any specific recommendations to you regarding this. Discuss specific dosing with your health care provider.

After birth. Formula provides the usual RDA of vitamin D. Breast milk does as well, as long as Mom isn't deficient. Since most moms are deficient, it is recommended that a breastfeeding mom give her baby 400 IU of vitamin D every day. You can purchase infant vitamin D drops from any drugstore or health food store. It's okay if a few other vitamins are thrown in as well. Even if a baby doesn't really need these extra vitamins, they won't hurt.

A nursing mom can resume taking extra D for her own health, even if her baby is supplemented.

Sunlight. The sun is our friend. Really. Every person (from newborns to the elderly) needs at least four hours of unprotected sunlight (no sunscreen) every week to maintain normal vitamin D levels throughout their lifetime (this won't correct a deficiency, though). So, be sure you get at least a half hour of sun every day on your bare arms and legs. Protect your face if you want to. Do the same for your baby. Your skin won't burn in half-hour exposures (unless it's during the hottest three hours of the day; 11 a.m. to 2 p.m.). I recommend sunblock only if you and your child are going on an all-day outing.

AVOID MERCURY

This may be a no-brainer, but I'll mention it anyway. Even though "the man" is going to tell you a little bit of mercury is okay, why take the risk if you can avoid it? Here are the main sources of mercury you can control your exposure to:

Mercury in fillings. There is some worry in the world of alternative medicine that the mercury in metal dental fillings may slowly leak into the body. We adults can probably handle this okay, but the brain of a developing baby might not. If you have the opportunity prior to getting pregnant (at least three months prior) to get your metal fillings replaced with a less toxic type by a qualified dentist, do so. Do not do this during pregnancy or while breastfeeding. Some of the mercury may spill into your body during the procedure and get into the baby. There is no reason to stop breastfeeding early just because you have mercury fillings. Very little gets into breast milk. If any of your children require fillings, I recommend composite resin as a first choice, followed by porcelain. Do not get metal fillings.

Mercury in fish. Avoid shark, swordfish, mackerel, and tilefish. Canned tuna also has some mercury.

Mercury in flu shots. The flu can be especially tough on a pregnant woman and her fetus. Some fatalities occur among pregnant women every year. It is therefore recommended that all pregnant women receive a flu shot at the start of flu season (October). A flu shot is also recommended each year for infants six months and older up through age eighteen. If you get a flu shot, make sure you get one without mercury, or at least get one that has only trace amounts of mercury (see page 277). Although the general medical consensus is that the amount of mercury in a flu shot is harmless, it doesn't make sense to take that risk when you have the choice of getting one with little to no mercury. Because flu shots change from year to year, it's hard to keep up with which brands have mercury and which ones don't. I post a new blog on this every October at www.TheVaccineBook.com.

Mercury in RhoGAM? This is a shot that pregnant women with negative blood type have to get to prevent a reaction between their own blood and the fetus's blood. There are three brand names used in the United States: RhoGAM, BayRho, and Win-Rho. Although some of these contained mercury in the past, they no longer do.

GO GREEN

Going green is all the rage, but it's not easy. I do think it's very important to limit the amount of chemicals that you and your family are exposed to, beginning at preconception and beyond. Providing details on this type of lifestyle is beyond the scope of this book. Since this is such a passion for me, I have written a book called *HappyBaby: The Organic Guide to Baby's First 24 Months*. Here are a few basics you should follow:

Eat healthy. Eat as naturally as you can before and during pregnancy and during lactation as well. When you start feeding your child baby foods, stay as organic as possible. The chemicals, pollutants, and pesticides are bad news for a growing brain, even in tiny amounts. Avoid like the plague any food coloring, artificial sweeteners, or preservatives.

Limit chemical exposure. Our knowledge about possible toxic exposures in everyday life has expanded greatly in recent years. We now know about chemicals in plastics, lead in toys from overseas, pollutants in the tap water, and chemicals on new clothes. It seems that every year there's a new report about something to avoid. I believe taking some standard precautions in these areas is important.

Use natural cleaners. So many of our day-to-day household products contain chemicals that aren't good for babies. Soap, lotion, toothpaste, laundry detergent, and cleaning products can all have unnecessary chemicals. There's always a natural alternative.

LIMIT ANTIBIOTICS

Most children need an antibiotic or two during their younger years, but some children get far more than their fair share. Antibiotics are important and useful when prescribed appropriately.

As you read in chapter 4, overuse creates an imbalance in the gut that may raise the risk of autism, or at least make matters worse for a child with autism. Here is how I limit antibiotics among my patients, whether they have autism or not:

Ear infections. The American Academy of Pediatrics no longer recommends antibiotics for mild ear infections or during the first few days of a moderate infection. The Academy does recommend antibiotics if the infection looks severe to the doctor, if the child is acting fairly ill with more than two days of fever, or if a moderate infection persists for several days or worsens at any time. Here is what I do:

- Use Mullein/Garlic ear drops (from Herb Pharm, available online). Warm the bottle in a mug of hot water and drip three drops into the affected ear three times daily until it is better. This works the majority of the time for my patients. You can also start the drops at the beginning of a cold as prevention if your child is prone to ear infections. Turn to antibiotics if things worsen.

- Use ibuprofen for pain relief.

Ear infections hurt, and sometimes it's nice to jump on an antibiotic so your baby doesn't have more than a day of pain. But I believe it's better to try to work through the infection with garlic and ibuprofen for pain relief and avoid antibiotics if you can.

Sinus infections. Again, the AAP recommends not using antibiotics unless the infection is severe and prolonged: fever for five days or more with headache and sinus pain. Antibiotics should not be used just because the snot is green. Here's what I do instead:

- For kids four years and older, use over-the-counter cough and cold meds if needed to minimize symptoms.

- Use steam and nasal saline to help keep the mucus draining out.

Bronchitis. Many parents believe that when a cough turns junky, it's time for antibiotics. Not so. Children can usually get through bronchitis with steam, expectorant cough medicine, and time. Honey is an effective cough suppressant for kids one and older.

Common colds and coughs. If there's no fever, labored breathing, or one of the above complications, let it ride. Antibiotics sometimes help an illness resolve if it's bacterial, but your child's own immune system can often take care of things. Echinacea, vitamin C, and zinc at the start of any illness can help the immune system do its job.

NATURAL SUPPLEMENTS FOR SINUS AND RESPIRATORY HEALTH

Two products that I've come to routinely recommend whenever a child (or adult) needs extra support for the sinus or respiratory tract are Sinupret and Bronchipret. These herbal supplements improve mucus drainage and air flow through the nasal and respiratory passages. Check them out at www.SinupretForKids.com.

Skin infections. These sometimes do need oral antibiotics, but often a prescription topical ointment (to avoid affecting the intestines) is enough to take care of them.

Antibiotics during labor. Many women carry bacteria called group B strep in their vaginal area. This is harmless to the woman, but during a vaginal birth, it can cause the baby to have a severe infection as it enters through his eyes, nose, or mouth. For this reason, all moms are tested near the end of pregnancy, and if they are positive for group B strep, they are given IV antibiotics during labor. This is important, but it can create yeast overgrowth in the mom. Yeast can grow on her nipples and get into the baby via breastfeeding. Or the IV antibiotics can pass through the placenta into the baby and cause yeast overgrowth in the baby's mouth (called *thrush*) or intestines during the first few days of life. This may not create any noticeable problems, but it isn't a good way to start out life. Moms who are given antibiotics during labor (or at any time while breastfeeding) should take probiotics at the same time and for at least a month after.

Use probiotics. Anytime your child does need antibiotics, start him on probiotics right away and continue for the next month. This will help keep the gut germs in balance.

TREATING FEVERS: USE IBUPROFEN INSTEAD OF ACETAMINOPHEN

There is a theory that acetaminophen (the active ingredient in Tylenol) can lower glutathione levels. We do know this happens in cases of acetaminophen overdose, and there is evidence that it may happen with regular doses as well. I believe it is a worthwhile precaution to use ibuprofen (the active ingredient in Motrin and Advil) instead of acetaminophen for treatment of fevers, pain, or in the case of a vaccine reaction (see below).

VACCINES

No discussion of autism is complete without including the topic of vaccines. It would take an entire book to thoroughly cover everything you should know about your child's shots. Allow me to humbly recommend my own book, *The Vaccine Book: Making the Right Decision for Your Child.* Here are a few things to be aware of:

Children with autism. I generally recommend that any child diagnosed with autism not receive any more vaccines. Now, this is a very bold statement, considering that the majority of current research does not support a link between vaccines and autism. However, research has not yet proven there is *no* link, because no study has ever compared the rate of autism in a large group of unvaccinated children with the rate in a large vaccinated group. This type of placebo-controlled study is the gold standard of medical research. Many tens of thousands, if not hundreds of thousands, of parents believe that vaccines may have played a role in their child's condition. As a precaution, I like to leave vaccines out of the equation once a child is suspected of having, or is diagnosed with, autism. Skipping any vaccine does create a risk of catching that particular illness, and parents need to be fully informed about these risks.

Contrary to popular belief, vaccines are not mandatory for school entry in most states. Twenty states allow parents to decline vaccines for personal reasons. In twenty-eight of the remaining thirty states, parents have to claim a religious reason for avoiding vaccines. Most states won't ask parents for proof of membership in an actual religion; the choice simply has to be based on the parents' religious convictions. Two states, West Virginia and Mississippi, don't allow personal or religious exemptions. Parents need a medical waiver from a doctor in these two states.

Younger siblings of children with autism. Your next children might have the same genetic risks that your child with autism has. It's therefore important to limit any factor that may be involved in autism. If vaccines, or the chemicals in them, play a role in autism, then, obviously, limiting vaccines would be smart. However, we don't know that vaccines play a role, and skipping shots poses disease risks. Here are some options to consider:

- *Delayed vaccines.* If you feel okay with the disease risk, you can delay shots until your infant is past the age that regressive autism can occur. Once a child is three years old, regressive autism is almost unheard of. It would be important to avoid group day care and church nurseries during this time in order to limit the disease risk. Extended breastfeeding also helps.

- *Limited vaccines.* If you don't want to leave your baby completely open to vaccine-preventable diseases but you also don't want to overload him with every shot there is, you can follow a schedule that I call *Selective Vaccination*. In *The Vaccine Book* I lay this option out for you in detail. Basically it means vaccinating only for diseases that pose a significant threat to your baby. These include rotavirus, pertussis, and HIB and PC meningitis. These shots don't have to be given all together either. You can spread them out a bit to limit the chemical ingredients as best as you can. You can also give the other shots to your child when he is older and ready for school.

- *No vaccines.* Most parents who believe that vaccines contributed to their child's autism probably will not want to vaccinate their next child or children. I completely understand and respect that decision. I never try to talk such a parent into vaccinating. No matter what mainstream science says, parents should have the right to make this decision for their children.

First babies (no children with autism). If this is your first baby, you've probably already put some thought into vaccination. There are a variety of choices you can make. I suggest that if you do decide to vaccinate, you consider following a schedule that is a little different from the regular schedule. In *The Vaccine Book* I discuss the option of getting the shots spread out over many years in what I call my *Alternative Vaccine Schedule*, which gives no more than two shots at a time (compared with the six vaccines that are recommend at each infant checkup), limits live virus vaccines to one at a time, avoids overlapping vaccines that have similar chemicals, concentrates on the most important shots first, delays some of the less important shots for a year or two, and chooses certain brands that have fewer chemical ingredients. By following this approach, you can ultimately achieve full vaccination but in a way that lowers the possibility of reactions and avoids overloading a baby with many germ and chemical ingredients at once.

Be aware that your baby will be offered his first vaccine (to protect against hepatitis B, a sexually transmitted disease) the very day he is born in the hospital. Many hospitals administer it without the parents' even knowing. Make sure everyone caring for your baby knows you don't want the hepatitis B vaccine (assuming you and your spouse don't have hep B; if you are a carrier for hep B, then vaccinating the baby is very important).

Don't dismiss severe vaccine reactions. Many infants have some fever and fussiness after shots, which is normal and harmless. However, very rarely, some infants react with high fever, extreme fussiness alternating with lethargy, high-pitched screaming, and poor feeding for several days. This type of reaction is due to *encephalitis* (inflammation and swelling of the brain). Most babies seem to recover after a week or two with no lasting effects. However, such a reaction is likely to repeat itself with the next round of shots (babies get the same six shots three times, at two months, four months, and six months). Repeated episodes of encephalitis are not good for any baby's brain. If your baby reacts poorly to some vaccines, make sure your doctor knows about it and consider vaccinating more gradually and carefully in the future. Most doctors make it a priority to complete all vaccines on the prescribed schedule without any interruptions. He or she may advise that you simply continue vaccinating the same way. I prefer to balance that with making sure a baby is tolerating vaccines well.

I believe that there is not enough mainstream scientific evidence that vaccines cause autism in the general population of children. I continue to give vaccines in my office (although I do it differently from most doctors) because there does not seem to be a risk in most children. However, there are cases in which a severe reaction to a round of vaccines seems to have triggered a decline into autism. What we don't yet know is why such rare reactions occur in a few children but not the rest. We also don't know exactly how common these severe reactions are, because no large research study has ever been undertaken to document the rate of severe reactions. And most important, no one has yet compared the rate of autism in a large vaccinated group of children with the rate in an unvaccinated group. Such a comparison would shed some much-needed light on this debate. That research may be coming.

In 2009, the National Vaccine Advisory Committee (a government organization of doctors and researchers) decided to proceed with preliminary studies to determine the type of research that needs to be done, and how to do it, in order to further understand the controversial aspects of vaccines. They are looking into the feasibility of doing a large research study that compares the health of vaccinated and unvaccinated children. They will also examine the rate of autism in the two groups. This research will contain study groups that are large enough to make the findings valid. This is the type of research that has been missing for many years. I hope that within five to ten years we will have some good data that will help us better determine whether or not there is a connection between vaccines and autism. Until then, it's up to parents to review the available research and decide for themselves.

IDENTIFY AND FIX FOOD ALLERGIES EARLY

Most children don't have food allergies. However, most children with autism do, especially to wheat (gluten) and milk (casein) products. I'm not saying that everyone should put their infants on a GFCF diet as a prevention, but any parent whose infant shows signs of food allergies (eczema, chronic nasal or chest congestion, chronic loose stools, or colic) should explore possible food allergies right away. Don't take the wait-and-see approach.

• If breastfeeding, take all sources of casein out of your diet. If symptoms don't improve within two weeks, continue casein-free and go gluten-free as well. If this resolves the allergy symptoms, then continue GFCF (or whichever step you feel helped the most) until you wean your baby. You can reintroduce the foods in your diet every four to six months to see how your baby does.

• If formula feeding with a milk-based formula, try a hypo-allergenic formula with your doctor's permission (Nutramigen, Alimentum, or Neocate, available at drugstores or pharmacies without a prescription). Soy is also an alternative, although it's not an ideal long-term formula. If allergies don't change, talk to your doctor about testing. If the formula change does help, continue with the hypoallergenic formula for an entire year.

• When you start your baby on foods at six months of age, watch for a return of allergy symptoms and continue to avoid any foods you believe the baby reacts to. If you feel your baby responded well to your GFCF diet or to the hypoallergenic formula, I would not start the baby on any gluten or casein foods (or any other foods that a breastfeeding mom had to restrict) until one year of age.

- At age one it will be time to wean your baby off formula. Don't start cow's milk just yet. Use alternative milks instead. You can gradually try some other milder sources of casein, like yogurt and cheese, but watch closely for allergic problems. If your baby tolerates these, you can slowly try cow's milk too. You can gradually introduce gluten foods, but if you see the baby react, keep him gluten-free until age two, then try again. If breastfeeding beyond age one, you don't need to begin any cow's milk until the baby is weaned. You can carefully start other casein foods as well as gluten foods.

- If you see new allergic symptoms in infants nine months and older who have started eating cheese, yogurt, or wheat products, such as bread and crackers, or in one-year-olds who have started drinking cow's milk, take them off these products. Go casein-free for a few weeks and then add in gluten-free steps if the allergic symptoms haven't resolved. If these steps fix the problem, great. Stay with the GF and/or CF diet until your child is two. If the diet doesn't fix the allergies, ask your doctor to do allergy testing.

TAKE CHRONIC LOOSE STOOLS SERIOUSLY

Every parent whose child had chronic runny, mucusy stools throughout infancy or toddlerhood and developed autism wishes they could go back and fix the gut right from the start. In the interest of prevention for your new baby, do everything you can to clear up runny stools. A lot of doctors (myself included before I knew better) simply label runny stools as normal "toddler diarrhea." If a child seems happy and is growing well, they don't worry. A breastfed baby should have yellow stools that are the consistency of a cross between gourmet mustard (seedy) and cottage cheese. Formula-fed babies' stools may vary in color, but they should be soft and mushy (like Play-Doh). Every baby also has the occasional runny stool (a couple times each week at the most). But everyday stools shouldn't be a runny, drippy mess. If they are, make the appropriate GFCF and/or formula changes described under food allergies, above. If these changes don't help, begin probiotics (to treat possible yeast). If this doesn't help, talk with your doctor. One of the specialty stool tests (page 118) can be done to evaluate for yeast and digestive problems. You can also pursue allergy testing. Keeping the gut as healthy as possible is an important part of autism prevention.

SOLVE COLIC AS SOON AS POSSIBLE

Colic is a very controversial condition. The mainstream medical position is that it occurs because a baby's nervous system is immature and can't deal with the overwhelming sensations of life. A baby becomes overstimulated and can't figure out how to relax. Crying is the only way to express this frustration. Fortunately a baby's brain matures and learns to cope better by around four months of age. Mainstream doctors don't believe colicky babies are in any pain. I think that most parents with a colicky baby would disagree; their babies seem to be in a lot of pain—gastrointestinal pain. Doctors also feel that there aren't any medical causes of colic that could be corrected to ease the discomfort. I disagree.

I believe there are two types of colic. One type is exactly what doctors think it is: neurodevelopmental immaturity. The second type occurs because something is irritating the intestinal system, causing pain and fussiness. The first type is diagnosed by excluding all the causes of the second type. I believe both types are treatable, either by eliminating the cause or by using some neurological calming therapies.

The reason I include this discussion in a section on preventing autism is that I believe that untreated and uncorrected colic can be a risk factor for autism. Please realize that I'm not saying all colicky babies are going to develop autism, or even that any of them are. I don't know of any study that has examined this theory. It deserves looking at, however. The reason that I suspect an association is that I believe that colic is a form of sensory processing disorder (or sensory integration disorder), which I discuss on page 49. A colicky baby is extremely bothered by intestinal sensations, often isn't soothed by rocking, may sleep restlessly and wake up frequently, and may not like to be held in certain positions that most babies feel comforted by. Many of the things that should cause warm and fuzzy sensations in a baby don't work for a baby with colic.

Whether or not I am correct may someday be discovered. In the meantime, it's important to try to solve colic, not just for autism prevention, but so the baby can be happy. Here is what I do for babies with colic:

Rule out gastroesophageal reflux disease (GERD). Any colicky baby who is also a spitter-upper should be considered to have GERD until proven otherwise. I don't do any tests on such babies to diagnose the reflux. The best test is to treat it with antacid medication and watch for improvement. Your pediatrician can prescribe either ranitidine (brand name Zantac) or lansoprazole (brand name Prevacid) liquids. Food allergies through the breast milk or formula allergies can cause GERD, so those should be assessed as well.

Manage food allergies. We already touched on this, but food allergies can also present as colic. If formula-feeding, switch to one of the hypoallergenic formulas listed on page 340. Breast-feeding mothers should go on a GFCF (both together) diet. If I had a dime for every patient of mine with colic who improved when Mom went GFCF, I could be driving that Lexus instead of my Honda. This diet is worth at least a three-week trial before you decide it's not helping. If GFCF doesn't help, then eliminating other classic colicky foods, such as soy, corn, chocolate, caffeine, nuts, eggs, gassy vegetables, and iron vitamins (in Mom's prenatals) might end up doing the trick.

The benefits of a GFCF diet for colic really hit home for one mom in my practice last year. She has one child with autism, and when I saw her in the office for her new baby's one-week appointment, Mom was a mess. "It's happening again. This is exactly how it started with my first child!" Her baby was extremely fussy and gassy. I told her to do the GFCF diet (which she already knew about but was reluctant to try). A few weeks later she came in a changed woman (with a changed baby). The colic had completely resolved and the baby was perfectly happy. We'll never know what might have happened if Mom hadn't made those changes, but she's definitely a believer.

Treatments for Mom. I recommend a nursing mom take digestive enzymes (see page 200) to better digest her foods so irritating proteins are less likely to get into her breast milk. I have had some surprising success with this. Even if a mom is on a GFCF diet, this may help with other foods, too. It may also allow Mom to cheat a little on the diet (as long as this doesn't affect the baby). I also have moms take probiotics. These may not directly get into the breast milk, but they will help prevent yeast growth on Mom's nipples, which could then get into baby.

Colic remedies for baby. There are several things besides looking for the cause that you can do for your baby that may make a difference:

• Herbal and medicinal colic remedies like gripe water or simethicone drops can help ease the pain. These don't fix colic, however.

• Probiotics given to baby (buy any infant liquid or powder probiotic and follow the directions; make sure it's milk-free) may help balance out any intestinal yeast or bacteria that are irritating baby's system.

• A naturopathic doctor may have a variety of natural and herbal remedies at his or her disposal that may help colic.

Manipulative therapies for baby. There are five types of therapy that utilize gentle touch and pressure techniques on a baby's head and spine that may calm the nervous system. I have seen these work well enough—and often enough—that I routinely recommend them to my patients. You can search online for a provider near you:

• *Craniosacral therapy.* This is performed by a licensed craniosacral therapist and in my experience is probably the most effective of these types of treatments.

• *Osteopathic manipulation.* This is offered by some doctors of osteopathic medicine. The doctors are trained just like medical doctors but have additional training in natural medicine. They have a DO after their name instead of an MD.

• *Chiropractic therapy.* Don't worry, chiropractors don't "crack the bones" of infants like they do adults'. They use gentle touch and pressure similar to the above two techniques.

• *Sensory integration occupational therapy.* I have had some success with sensory OT techniques helping babies with colic.

- *Acupuncture and acupressure.* These have also been shown to improve colic.

Hold off on vaccines. I like to delay vaccines until colic has resolved. I feel that the brain is under so much stress already, why add to it? This does pose some disease risk, and I make sure the baby stays quarantined. Once a baby is back to his happy self for about a month, then vaccines can begin. See more vaccine information on page 335.

PREVENTION IN YOUNGER SIBLINGS OF A CHILD WITH AUTISM

If you have a child with autism, you will obviously want to do everything you can to prevent autism in your next children. In addition to the above recommendations, here are some specific steps every parent can take with their next baby to lower the risk:

Go GFCF from the start. Don't wait for food allergy symptoms or colic to hit before making changes. Moms should go GFCF right away, even during pregnancy (consult with a nutritionist to ensure your GFCF diet provides everything you need). Continue the diet while breastfeeding until you wean. If using formula, I recommend Neocate brand of hypoallergenic formula. It's the most GFCF of them all. The overall nutritional value isn't as good as breast milk, but it's the best choice for families with autism who aren't breastfeeding. Once your baby starts eating foods, keep his diet GFCF until age two. At that point, if all is well, you can gradually introduce regular foods.

Use injectible antibiotics. I don't recommend this for everyone, just for families with autism. If your baby really needs antibiotics during the first two years of life, ask your doctor about getting a shot of antibiotics in the muscle. This doesn't interfere with intestinal health as much as an oral antibiotic does. Ceftriaxone is the name of the most commonly used form. Once your child is two, an oral antibiotic is probably okay. Definitely use probiotics (even if getting injectibles). You can administer nystatin (see page 239) during a course of oral antibiotics, and continue for about ten days afterward, to prevent yeast growth.

Start supplements. I like to start my sibling patients on some of the biomedical supplements, no matter how the baby is doing. I don't wait for developmental delays to become apparent.

- *Vitamin D.* Formula has enough vitamin D, but if the baby is breastfeeding, I recommend an infant liquid vitamin right from the start to make sure he is getting the 400 IU daily dose.

- *Probiotics.* I recommend starting these at around two months of age. Any infant brand is fine (make sure it's GFCF).

- *Cod liver oil.* Get this going around nine months of age. Give about ¼ teaspoon daily. At eighteen months, you can increase this to half a teaspoon.

- *Multivitamin/mineral.* When the baby reaches age one, I like to add whatever multivitamin/mineral your child with autism is taking. Start with one-quarter of the serving size on the label (this should be about half of the dose you initially started your child with autism on). After three months, increase to half the serving size and continue with that amount indefinitely. Don't use the moderate to high doses of B6. Limit B6 to about 15 mg (or 7.5 mg of P5P). Whatever amount is in the multi alone is probably fine, as long as it's not one of Kirkman Labs' high-dose B6 preparations (those are for children with autism or other developmental/learning delays only).

- *Taurine.* I also like to add about 100 mg of taurine daily into a toddler's food when he turns one.

I don't move on to the more advanced supplements unless the child begins to show some concerns. Once a child turns three, I usually back off from the supplements and see how he does without them.

Begin developmental therapies early if needed. If there is any question about a sibling's development, then speech therapy, OT, ABA, and/or sensory OT (whatever is appropriate) should begin right away. It's best not to wait. Some siblings will have minor delays in development that can easily be overcome.

Afterword

Recovery

Autism treatment is a journey. I have shown you how to get started, but it will take years of hard work to achieve recovery. What I mean by *recovery* is that a child loses the diagnosis of autism, that he improves to such a degree that he no longer fits the criteria.

The consensus among my colleagues is that when biomedical treatments are combined with comprehensive behavioral and developmental therapies, about 5 percent of children with autism will lose their diagnosis, become neurotypical, and not require any ongoing specialized treatment to maintain that recovery.

Another 25 percent will reach this same level of recovery but require ongoing therapy to maintain their functioning. They may have some very subtle "quirks" that are obvious only to a trained eye. With time and maturity, even these residual quirks may resolve. While these odds might seem low to some parents, remember that not too long ago, autism was considered to be a lifelong and untreatable condition. What we offer children today is a wonderful improvement over twenty years ago.

The next 30 percent will show dramatic improvement in many areas but will retain enough autistic deficits to still qualify for a diagnosis of mild autism. Is this considered recovery? That depends on your perspective. Certainly a child who starts off with severe autism and progresses to this level would be considered recovered by his family, therapists, and peers. A child who starts off with very mild autism to begin with but doesn't seem to respond significantly to most treatments might not be considered recovered (yet) by his parents.

Another 20 percent will show modest improvement but remain at a level that would be considered moderate autism, and the remaining 20 percent of children will not seem to respond to treatment at all and will remain in the severely affected category. Dedicated researchers and biomedical practitioners continue to search for new therapies to reach these children and bring them up to a level that would be considered recovery.

In my experience, many children will show dramatic improvement, whether it's primarily from mainstream behavioral therapy, from biomedical treatment, or from both. It is my sincere hope and prayer that you will find healing and recovery during your journey.

Resources

WEBSITES THAT SELL AUTISM SUPPLEMENTS

Throughout this book I have referred to numerous supplements by name. Here are the websites where you can find these products:

www.ArmourThyroid.com. This website provides information on this natural form of thyroid hormone.

www.BioRayNaturalDetox.com. This group makes NDF, a natural chelator.

www.CarlsonLabs.com. Carlson's makes a variety of different cod liver oils for children and adults. I also like their vitamin D drops.

www.CTIscience.com. This is the company that manufactures OSR, an antioxidant and mild chelator.

www.Fruit-eze.com. Their fruit spread is a good treatment for constipation.

www.Herb-Pharm.com. This company makes Mullein/Garlic Ear Drops, echinacea drops, and many other products.

www.Houston-enzymes.com. This group makes a wide selection of digestive enzymes and other supplements.

www.IntegrativeInc.com. This website offers the Learner's Edge line of autism supplements (look under the Children's Health product category), a good-tasting calcium/magnesium liquid from Integrative Therapeutics, and many others products.

www.KartnerHealth.com. This new company has created a line of supplements that cover many of my basic recommendations. Dr. Jerry Kartzinel is one of their advisers.

www.KirkmanLabs.com. This is one of the oldest supplement companies focused on autism treatments. You will find a wide range of multivitamins, minerals, probiotics, fish oils, methylation supplements, and many other products.

www.Klaire.com. This brand's specialty is probiotics and digestive enzymes, with one of the broadest arrays of probiotic types that I have found. They also offer a selection of vitamins. It is better to call their toll-free number when ordering: 888-488-2488.

www.LaneLabs.com. This site sells H2Go, a minty chewable magnesium for constipation.

www.Lauricidin.com. This is a brand of monolaurin that I like to use to fight yeast.

www.LEF.org. Life Extension makes a good brand of TMG powder for methylation treatment.

www.Metagenics.com. This group has a large selection of many products. I especially like their concentrated DHA/EPA liquid.

www.Moxxor.com. This company makes a fish-mussel oil blend.

www.Nature-Throid.com. This company sells a brand of natural thyroid hormone.

www.nbnus.com. This company, NewBeginnings, sells a large selection of vitamins.

www.NordicNaturals.com. This company makes the widest variety of fish oil and cod liver oil that I have found.

www.Nutribiotic.com. This brand is a good source of grapefruit seed extract to treat yeast. They also make a good rice protein powder.

www.Oramune.com. This group makes colostrum and other immune-boosting supplements.

www.Oxypowder.com. This is a magnesium powder for constipation.

www.PeterGillham.com. This site carries magnesium and calcium/magnesium products.

www.PureEssenceLabs.com. This company makes Candex, a natural yeast fighter.

www.ResearchedNutritionals.com. This company makes colostrum with transfer factor and other products.

www.Dr.SearsFamilyEssentials.com. This is my family's website, and it offers fish oils and healthy snacks.

www.SinupretForKids.com. This website offers the natural sinus and lung support supplements Sinupret and Bronchipret.

www.Thorne.com. This site has the immune-boosting supplement myco-immune, along with many other products.

www.WarrenLabsAloe.com. This company makes a particularly good brand of aloe juice used to improve constipation and decrease gut inflammation.

WEBSITES THAT PROVIDE SPECIALTY BLOOD, HAIR, URINE, AND STOOL TESTS FOR AUTISM

The following companies provide many of the specialty urine, blood, and stool tests I refer to in the book. Prices and testing accuracy may vary. On page 126, I provide of list of the specialty tests I generally run at this time, along with the name of the company that I commonly order this test from. I don't know that the companies I run the tests through are necessarily any better or less expensive than other companies. They are simply the ones I have become accustomed to using over the years. My preferences may change, and I will post updates on www.TheAutismBook.com.

- www.DoctorsData.com
- www.FoodAllergy.com (Alletess Labs)
- www.GenovaDiagnostics.com
- www.GreatPlainsLaboratory.com
- www.IGeneX.com
- www.Immuno-Sci-Lab.com
- www.LabBio.net (Laboratoire Philippe Auguste)
- www.Metametrix.com
- www.PrometheusLabs.com

COMPOUNDING PHARMACIES THAT PREPARE SPECIALIZED AUTISM SUPPLEMENTS

Some of the more advanced autism treatments (such as methyl B12, glutathione cream, chelation products, LDN, and compounded antifungal and antibacterial meds) must be obtained from a compounding pharmacy that specializes in products for autism. Here is a list of pharmacies (listed alphabetically in no order of preference) that are routinely used by biomedical physicians. Most will ship anywhere in the United States and some will ship internationally:

- Bedford Pharmacy, Bedford, NH—www.BedfordPharmacy .com
- Coastal Compounding, Savannah, GA—www.Coastal Compounding.com
- College Pharmacy, Colorado Springs, CO—www.College Pharmacy.com
- Fallon Wellness Pharmacy, Latham, NY—www.Fallon Pharmacy.com
- Hopewell Pharmacy, Hopewell, NJ—www.HopewellRx .com
- Lee Silsby Compounding Pharmacy, Cleveland Heights, OH—www.LeeSilsby.com
- Park Pharmacy, Irvine, CA—www.ParkRx.com
- Pine Pharmacy, Williamsville, NY—www.PinePharmacy .com
- Pure Compounding Pharmacy, Naperville, IL—www.Pure Compounding.com
- University Compounding Pharmacy, San Diego, CA—www .UCPRx.com
- Wellness Pharmacy, Birmingham, AL—www.Wellness Health.com

PARENT SUPPORT ORGANIZATIONS

There are many fantastic organizations that support children and parents with general information, local and national treatment providers, research studies, networks of local support groups, fund-raising to provide money to needy families, parent and doctor training seminars on autism treatment, and much more. I encourage you to browse the websites of the following groups and avail yourself of their services and programs:

- www.Autism.org. This is the website for the Autism Collaboration, a group of like-minded organizations that support autism research and education. Many of the following websites (including TACA and the Autism Research Institute) are members.
- www.TACAnow.org (the organization I work with)
- www.AAP.org (the website for the American Academy of Pediatrics)
- www.Act-Today.org (provides grant money to needy families for autism therapy)
- www.AgeOfAutism.com (a daily web newspaper that discusses issues in autism)
- www.Autism360.org (an online tool created by Dr. Sidney Baker that helps parents choose treatments based on their child's specific symptoms)
- www.Autism.com (the website for the Autism Research Institute, the group that regulates and teaches the Defeat Autism Now biomedical approach)
- www.Autism-Conferences.com (provides a list of upcoming biomedical conferences)
- www.AutismOne.org (provides a variety of resources and information)
- www.AutismSpeaks.org (provides information on autism)
- www.Autism-Society.org (offers various resources and informative articles)
- www.CenterForAutism.com (website for CARD, a nationwide provider of ABA and other therapies)
- www.CDC.gov/autism (the Centers for Disease Control and Prevention's website for autism)

- www.Emergenzautismo.org (an Italian website for biomedical treatments in Italy)
- www.FirstSigns.org (has an online video library of symptoms of autism)
- www.FirstWords.FSU.edu (has an online video library of symptoms of autism)
- www.GenerationRescue.org (Jenny McCarthy's organization)
- www.Mindd.org (a foundation dedicated to providing resources and information)
- www.NationalAutismAssociation.org (raises public awareness, advocates for affected families, and provides resources)
- www.SafeMinds.org (dedicated to researching mercury)
- www.SARnet.org (The Schafer Autism Report, a periodic publication of the latest autism research and treatment)
- www.SPDfoundation.net (information on sensory processing disorder)
- www.TheAutismTrust.com (a British group that provides education and treatment for autism)
- www.TreatingAutism.co.uk (a guide to biomedical treatments in Europe)
- www.UnlockingAutism.org (raises awareness and provides information for families)
- www.VitaminDCouncil.org (information on correcting Vitamin D deficiency)

RESEARCH ORGANIZATIONS

Numerous university medical centers and research institutes are heavily involved in autism research. The Autism Research Institute is the primary source of biomedical treatment information that I rely upon. I would like to highlight two mainstream scientific groups dedicated to understanding autism, searching for causes, and studying effective treatments. You will find the information on their websites and in research articles and books useful for gaining a better understanding of autism.

• The Autism Research Foundation and Autism Research Consortium. Headed by Dr. Margaret Bauman, this Boston-based group is at the forefront of collaborative autism research. They have a Current Trends in Autism Conference every fall. Their book, *Neurobiology of Autism*, provides an excellent overview of current research on autism. Visit www.LADDERS.org for more information.

• The MIND Institute at University of California, Davis. This group is heavily involved in researching autism causes and treatments. Check out the Medical Investigation of Neurodevelopmental Disorders Institute at www.ucdmc.ucdavis.edu/mindinstitute.

RECOMMENDED READING

There is so much information on autism, it can seem overwhelming. I have included everything I believe you should know about how to begin traditional and biomedical treatments for your child, but you may want to study specific areas further. Here is a list of books that I refer to within the text, as well as some other books that you may find interesting:

Autism: Caring for Children with Autism Spectrum Disorders (A Resource Toolkit for Clinicians), from the American Academy of Pediatrics. I learned a lot from this informative guide for pediatricians.

Autism: Current Theories and Evidence, edited by Andrew W. Zimmerman, MD. A collection of the most up-to-date research articles on the causes of autism, with references to over a thousand research studies.

Autism: Effective Biomedical Treatments, by Jon Pangborn,

PhD, and Sidney MacDonald Baker, MD. The definitive guide to the Defeat Autism Now biomedical approach. There is also a 2007 supplement that provides some updated information.

Breaking the Vicious Cycle: Intestinal Health Through Diet, by Elaine Gottschall. The book that first described the specific carbohydrate diet.

The Child with Special Needs: Encouraging Intellectual and Emotional Growth, by Stanley Greenspan, MD, and Serena Wieder, PhD. These pioneers of behavioral treatments for autism provide guidance on how to help your special-needs child grow to his or her full potential.

Children with Starving Brains: A Medical Treatment Guide for Autism Spectrum Disorders, by Jaquelyn McCandless, MD. A comprehensive guide to biomedical treatments.

The Complete IEP Guide: How to Advocate for Your Special Ed Child, by Lawrence Siegel. Guides parents through the confusing world of public school special education.

Families with Autism Journey Guide: A Starting Point for Parents Facing Autism, by Lisa Ackerman from TACA. Explores every aspect of getting started with a child with autism.

Books by Temple Grandin. This accomplished PhD in animal science is a dedicated animal rights advocate and has made great strides in educating the world about humane livestock handling techniques and facilities. She also has autism, and three of her books provide an insider's look at growing up with autism:

- *Developing Talents: Careers for Individuals with Asperger Syndrome and High-functioning Autism,* with Kate Duffy
- *Thinking in Pictures: My Life with Autism*
- *The Way I See It: A Personal Look at Autism and Asperger's*

HappyBaby: The Organic Guide to Baby's First 24 Months, by Robert W. Sears, MD, and the Founders of HappyBaby. This is a complete guide to raising a "green" family free of chemicals and toxins.

Healing the New Childhood Epidemics: Autism, ADHD, Asthma, and Allergies, by Kenneth Bock, MD, and Cameron Stauth. A biomedical guide to treating these four disorders.

Healing and Preventing Autism: A Complete Guide, by Jenny McCarthy and Jerry Kartzinel, MD. Dr. Kartzinel helped train me in the biomedical protocol.

The Late Talker: What to Do If Your Child Isn't Talking Yet, by Marilyn Agin, MD, Lisa F. Geng, and Malcolm J. Nicholl. This neurodevelopmental specialist provides invaluable guidance on how to address a delayed child's language needs.

The NDD Book: How Nutritional Deficit Disorder Affects Your Child's Learning, Behavior, and Health, and What You Can Do About It—Without Drugs, by William Sears, MD. A guide to the importance of good nutrition, from the Sears Parenting Library.

The Neurobiology of Autism (The Johns Hopkins Series in Psychiatry and Neuroscience), by Margaret L. Bauman, MD, and Thomas L. Kemper, MD. A collection of articles discussing various aspects of autism research and therapy.

Special Diets for Special Kids and *Special Diets for Special Kids Two,* by Lisa Lewis. The definitive guide to the gluten-free/casein-free diet.

The Vaccine Book: Making the Right Decision for Your Child, by Robert W. Sears, MD, FAAP. My own complete guide to understanding vaccines, from the Sears Parenting Library.

STUDIES DISCUSSING POSSIBLE CAUSES AND CONTRIBUTORS TO AUTISM

The following studies don't constitute proof of any one cause of autism. They demonstrate that there are many factors involved in autism and provide insight into what researchers are working on.

Increasing Prevalence of Autism

Centers for Disease Control and Prevention. Prevalence of autism spectrum disorders—autism and developmental disabilities monitoring network, United States, 2006. *MMWR Surveill Summ.* 2009 Dec 18;58(SS-10):1–20.

Kogan, M, et al. Prevalence of parent-reported diagnosis of autism spectrum disorder among children in the US, 2007. *Pediatrics.* 2009 Oct 5; published online.

Hertz-Picciotto I, et al. The rise in autism and the role of age at diagnosis. *Epidemiology.* 2009 Jan;20(1):84–90.

Chakrabarti S, et al. Pervasive developmental disorders in preschool children: confirmation of high prevalence. *Am J Psychiatry.* 2005 Jun;162(6):1133–41.

Genetic Factors

Kinney DK, et al. Environmental risk factors for autism: do they help cause de novo genetic mutations that contribute to the disorder? *Med Hypotheses.* 2009 Aug 21; published online ahead of print date.

Bourgeron T, et al. Autism: more evidence of a genetic cause. *Bull Acad Natl Med.* 2009 Feb;193(2):299–304.

Pickler L, et al. Genetic evaluation of the child with an autism spectrum disorder. *Pediatric Annals.* 2009 Jan;38(1):26–29.

Weiss LA, et al. (Autism Consortium). Association between microdeletion and microduplication at 16p11.2 and autism. *N Engl J Med.* 2008 Feb;358(7):667–75.

Autism Genome Project Consortium. Mapping autism risk loci using genetic linkage and chromosomal rearrangements. *Nat Genet.* 2007;39:319–28.

Campbell DB, et al. A genetic variant that disrupts MET transcription is associated with autism. *Proc Nat Acad Sci USA.* 2006 Nov 7;103(45):16834–39.

D'Amelio M, et al. Paraoxonase gene variants are associated

with autism in North America, but not in Italy: possible regional specificity in gene-environment interactions. *Molec Psych.* 2005 Nov;10(11):1006–16.

Jiang YH, et al. A mixed epigenetic/genetic model for oligogenic inheritance of autism with a limited role for UBE3A. *Am J Med Genetics A.* 2004 Nov 15;131(1):1–10.

Muhle R, et al. The genetics of autism. *Pediatrics.* 2004 May;113(5):e472–e486.

Spence SJ. The genetics of autism. *Semin Pediatr Neurol.* 2004 Sep;11(3):196–204.

Beyer KS, et al. Mutation analysis of the coding sequence of the MECP2 gene in infantile autism. *Human Genetics.* 2002 Oct;111(4–5):305–9.

International Molecular Genetic Study of Autism Consortium. A genomewide screen for autism: strong evidence for linkage to chromosomes 2q, 7q, and 16p. *Am J Hum Genet.* 2001 Sep;69(3):570–81.

Risch N, et al. A genomic screen of autism: Evidence for a multilocus etiology. *Am J Hum Genet.* 1999 Aug;65(2):493–507.

Prenatal and Birth Complications

Kolevzon A, et al. Prenatal and perinatal risk factors for autism: a review and integration of findings. *Arch Pediatr Adolesc Med.* 2007;161:326–33.

Juul-Dam N, et al. Prenatal, perinatal, and neonatal factors in autism, pervasive developmental disorder—not otherwise specified, and the general population. *Pediatrics.* 2001 Apr;107(4):e63.

Heavy Metals

Yorbik O, et al. Chromium, cadmium, and lead levels in urine of children with autism and typically developing controls. *Biol*

Trace Elem Res. 2009 Aug 18; published online ahead of print date.

Martin BJ. Biomarkers of environmental toxicity and susceptibility in autism. *J Neurol Sci.* 2009 May 15;280(1–2):127–28.

Geier DA, et al. A prospective study of prenatal mercury exposure from maternal dental amalgams and autism severity. *Acta Neurobiol Exp.* 2009;69(2):189–97.

Palmer RF, et al. Proximity to point sources of environmental mercury release as a predictor of autism prevalence. *Health Place.* 2009 Mar;15(1):18–24.

Geier DA, A comprehensive review of mercury provoked autism. *Indian J Med Res.* 2008 Oct;128(4):383–411.

Austin DW, et al. An investigation of porphyrinuria in Australian children with autism. *J Toxicol Environ Health A.* 2008 Jan;71(20):1349–51.

Aschner M. Blood levels of mercury are related to diagnosis of autism: a reanalysis of an important data set. *J Child Neurol.* 2008 Apr;23(4):463.

Adams JB, et al. Mercury, lead, and zinc in baby teeth of children with autism versus controls. *J Toxicol Environ Health A.* 2007 Jun;70(12):1046–51.

Roberts EM, et al. Maternal residence near agricultural pesticide applications and autism spectrum disorders among children in the California Central Valley. *Environ Health Perspect.* 2007 Oct;115(10):1482–89.

Grandjean P, et al. Developmental neurotoxicity of industrial chemicals. *Lancet.* 2006 Dec 16;368(9553):2167–78.

Kern JK, et al. Evidence of toxicity, oxidative stress, and neuronal insult in autism. *J Toxicol Environ Heath B Crit Rev.* 2006 Nov–Dec;9(6):485–99.

Nataf R, et al. Porphyrinuria in childhood autistic disorder: implications for environmental toxicity. *Toxicol Appl Pharmacol.* 2006 Jul 15;214(2):99–108.

Windham GC, et al. Autism spectrum disorders in relation to

distribution of hazardous air pollutants in the San Francisco Bay Area. *Environ Health Perspect.* 2006 Sep;114(9):1438–44.

Lanphear BP, et al. Low-level environmental lead exposure and children's intellectual function: an international pooled analysis. *Environ Health Perspect.* 2005 Jul;113(7):894–99.

James SJ, et al. Thimerosal neurotoxicity is associated with glutathione depletion: protection with glutathione precursors. *Neurotoxicology.* 2005 Jan;26(1):1–8.

Waly M, et al. Activation of methionine synthase by insulin-like growth factor-1 and dopamine: a target for neurodevelopmental toxins and thimerosal. *Mol Psychiatry.* 2004 Apr;9(4):358–70.

Holmes AS, et al. Reduced levels of mercury in first baby haircuts of autistic children. *In J Toxicol.* 2003 Jul–Aug;22(4):277–85.

Baskin DS, et al. Thimerosal induces DNA breaks, caspase-3 activation, membrane damage, and cell death in cultured human neurons and fibroblasts. *Toxicol Sci.* 2003 Aug;74(2):361–68.

Makani S, et al. Biochemical and molecular basis of thimerosal-induced apoptosis in T cells: a major role of mitochondrial pathway. *Genes Immun.* 2002 Aug;3(5):270–78.

Müller M, et al. Inhibition of the human erythrocytic glutathione-S-transferase T1 (GST T1) by thimerosal. *Int J Hyg Environ Health.* 2001 Jul;203(5–6):479–81.

Environmental Working Group. Body burden: the pollution in newborns. 2005 Jul 14. www.EWG.org.

Neurochemical Imbalances

Blaylock RL. A possible central mechanism in autism spectrum disorders, parts 1, 2, and 3. *Altern Ther Health Med.* 2008 Nov–Dec;14(6):46–53 and 2009 Jan–Feb;15(1):60–67 and 2009 Mar–Apr;15(2):56–60.

Hoshino Y, et al. Blood serotonin and free tryptophan

concentration in autistic children. *Neuropsychobiology.* 1984; 11(1):22–27.

Hoshino Y, et al. Plasma free tryptophan concentration in autistic children. *Brain Dev.* 1986;8(4):424–27.

Chugani DC. Serotonin in autism and pediatric epilepsies. *Ment Retard Dev Disabil Res Rev.* 2004 May;10(2):112–16.

Inflammation, Autoimmunity, and Immune Dysfunction

Atladóttir HO, et al. Association of family history of auto-immune diseases and autism spectrum disorders. *Pediatrics.* 2009 Aug;124(2):687–94. Dr. Bob notes: The autoimmune dis-eases found to increase the risk of autism were celiac disease, rheumatoid arthritis, and type 1 diabetes.

Mostafa GA, et al. Frequency of CD4+CD25high regula-tory T cells in peripheral blood of Egyptian children with autism. *J Child Neurol.* 2009 Aug 27; published online ahead of print date. (This study demonstrates an autoimmune connection to autism.)

Saresella M, et al. An autistic endophenotype results in complex immune dysfunction in healthy siblings of autistic children. *Biol Psychiatry.* 2009 Aug 21; published online ahead of print date.

Theoharides TC, et al. Autism: an emerging 'neuroimmune disorder' in search of therapy. *Expert Opin Pharmacother.* 2009 Sep;10(13):2127–43.

Singh VK. Phenotypic expression of autoimmune autistic dis-order (AAD): a major subset of autism. *Ann Clin Psychiatry.* 2009 Jul–Sep;21(3):148–61.

Pardo CA, et al. Immunity, neuroglia, and neuroinflammation in autism. *Int Rev Psychiatry.* 2005 Dec;17(6):485–95.

Vargas DL, et al. Neuroglial activation and neuroinflam-mation in the brain of patients with autism. *Ann Neurol.* 2005 Jan;57(1):67–81.

Sweeten TL, et al. Increased prevalence of familial autoimmunity in probands with pervasive developmental disorders. *Pediatrics.* 2003 Nov;112(5):e420.

Vojdani A, et al. Infections, toxic chemicals and dietary peptides binding to lymphocyte receptors and tissue enzymes are major instigators of autoimmunity in autism. *Int J Immunopathol Pharmacol.* 2003 Sep–Dec;16(3):189–99.

Jyonouchi H, et al. Proinflammatory and regulatory cytokine production associated with innate and adaptive immune responses in children with autism spectrum disorders and developmental regression. *J Neuroimmunol.* 2001 Nov 1;120(1–2):170–79.

Comi AM, et al. Familial clustering of autoimmune disorders and evaluation of medical risk factors in autism. *J Child Neurol.* 1999 Jun;14(6):388–94.

PANDAS

Chmelik E, et al. Varied presentation of PANDAS: a case series. *Clin Pediatr* (Phila). 2004 May;43(4):379–82.

Snider LA, et al. PANDAS: current status and directions for research. *Mol Psychiatry.* 2004 Oct;9(10):900–907.

March JS. Pediatric autoimmune neuropsychiatric disorders associated with streptococcal infection (PANDAS): implications for clinical practice. *Arch Pediatr Adolesc Med.* 2004 Sep;158(9):927–29.

Warren RP, et al. Deficiency of suppressor-inducer (CD4+CD45RA+) T cells in autism. *Immunol Invest.* 1990 Jun;19(3):245–51.

Gupta S, et al. Th1- and Th2-like cytokines in CD4+ and CD8+ T cells in autism. *J Neuroimmunol.* 1998 May 1;85(1):106–9.

Methylation and Oxidative Stress

James SJ, et al. Metabolic endophenotype and related genotypes are associated with oxidative stress in children with autism. *Am J Med Genet B Neuropsychiatr Genet.* 2006 Dec 5;141B(8):947–56.

Yao Y, et al. Altered vascular phenotype in autism: correlation with oxidative stress. *Arch Neurol.* 2006 Aug;63(8):1161–64.

Chauhan A, et al. Oxidative stress in autism. *Pathophysiology.* 2006 Aug;13(3):171–81.

Kern JK, et al. Evidence of toxicity, oxidative stress, and neuronal insult in autism. *J Toxicol Environ Heath B Crit Rev.* 2006 Nov–Dec;9(6):485–99.

Zoroglu SS, et al. Increased oxidative stress and altered activities of erythrocyte free radical scavenging enzymes in autism. *Eur Arch Psychiatry Clin Neurosci.* 2004 Jun;254(3):143–47.

Chauhan A, et al. Oxidative stress in autism: increased lipid peroxidation and reduced serum levels of ceruloplasmin and transferrin—the antioxidant proteins. *Life Sci.* 2004 Oct 8;75(21):2539–49.

James SJ, et al. Metabolic biomarkers of increased oxidative stress and impaired methylation capacity in children with autism. *Am J Clin Nutr.* 2004 Dec;80(6):1611–17.

Stadtman ER, et al. Oxidation of methionine residues of proteins: biological consequences. *Antioxid Redox Signal.* 2003 Oct;5(5):577–82.

Miller AL. The methionine-homocysteine cycle and its effects on cognitive diseases. *Altern Med Rev.* 2003 Feb;8(1):7–19.

Vitvitsky V, et al. Redox regulation of homocysteine-dependent glutathione synthesis. *Redox Rep.* 2003 Feb;8(1):57–63.

James SJ, et al. Evaluation of S-adenosylhomocysteine and DNA hypomethylation: potential epigenetic mechanisms for homocysteine-related pathology. *Journal of Nutrition.* 2002;132:2361S–66S.

Alberti A, et al. Sulphation deficit in 'low-functioning' autistic children: a pilot study. *Biol Psychiatry.* 1999 Aug 1;46(3):420–24.

Bains JS, et al. Neurodegenerative disorders in humans: the

role of glutathione in oxidative stress–mediated neuronal death. *Brain Res Rev.* 1997 Dec;25(3):335–58.

Banerjee RV, et al. Cobalamin-dependent methionine synthase. *FASEB J.* 1990 Mar;4(5):1450–59.

Stubbs G, et al. Adenosine deaminase activity decreased in autism. *J Am Acad Child Psychiatry.* 1982 Jan;21(1):71–74.

Mitochondrial Dysfunction and Autism

Shoffner J, et al. Fever plus mitochondrial disease could be risk factors for autistic regression. *J Child Neurol.* 2009 Sep 22; published online ahead of print date.

Pastural E, et al. Novel plasma phospholipids biomarkers of autism: mitochondrial dysfunction as a putative causative mechanism. *Prostaglandins Leukot Essent Fatty Acids.* 2009 Oct;81(4):253–64.

James SJ. Cellular and mitochondrial glutathione redox imbalance in lymphoblastoid cells derived from children with autism. *FASEB J.* 2009;23:2374–83.

Weissman JR, et al. Mitochondrial disease in autism spectrum disorder patients: a cohort analysis. *PLoS One.* 2008;3(11):e3815.

Gargus J, et al. Mitochondrial energy-deficient endophenotype in autism. *Am J Biochem Biotechnol.* 2008;4(2):198–207.

Holtzman D. Autistic spectrum disorders and mitochondrial encephalopathies. *Acta Paediatr.* 2008 Jul;97(7):859–60.

Oliveira G, et al. Mitochondrial dysfunction in autism spectrum disorders: a population-based study. *Dev Med Child Neurol.* 2005;47(3):185–89.

Mostafa GA, et al. Polyunsaturated fatty acids, carnitine, and lactate as biological markers of brain energy in autistic children. *Int J Ch Neuropsychiatry.* 2005;2(2):179–88.

Filipek P, et al. Relative carnitine deficiency in autism. *J Autism Dev Disord.* 2004 Dec;34(6):615–23.

Filipek P, et al. Mitochondrial dysfunction in autistic patients with 15q inverted duplication. *Ann Neurol.* 2003 Jun;53(6):801–4.

Fillano J, et al. Mitochondrial dysfunction in patients with hypotonia, epilepsy, autism, and developmental delay: HEADD syndrome. *J Child Neurol.* 2002 Jun;17(6):435–39.

Chugani D, et al. Evidence of altered energy metabolism in autistic children. *Prog Neuropsychopharmacol Biol Psychiatry.* 1999 May;23(4):635–41.

Lombard J. Autism: a mitochondrial disorder? *Med Hypotheses.* 1998;50:497–50.

Jain A, et al. Glutathione deficiency leads to mitochondrial damage in brain. *Proc Natl Acad Sci USA.* 1991 Mar 1;88:1913–17.

Gastrointestinal Disease

Rhoads JM, et al. Altered fecal microflora and increased fecal calprotectin in infants with colic. *J Pediatr.* 2009 Jul 23; published online ahead of print date.

Campbell DB, et al. Distinct genetic risk based on association of MET in families with co-occuring autism and gastrointestinal conditions. *Pediatrics.* 2009 Mar;123(3):1018–24.

Valicenti-McDermott MD, et al. Gastrointestinal symptoms in children with an autism spectrum disorder and language regression. *Pediatr Neurol.* 2008 Dec;39(6):392–98.

Ashwood P, et al. Spontaneous mucosal lymphocyte cytokine profiles in children with autism and gastrointestinal symptoms: mucosal immune activation and reduced counter regulatory interleukin-10. *J Clin Immunol.* 2004 Nov;24(6):664–74.

Torrente F, et al. Focal-enhanced gastritis in regressive autism with features distinct from Crohn's and Helicobacter pylori gastritis. *Am J Gastroenterol.* 2004 Apr;99(4):598–605.

Ashwood P, et al. Intestinal lymphocyte populations in

children with regressive autism: evidence for extensive mucosal immunopathology. *J Clin Immunol.* 2003 Nov;23(6):504–17.

Uhlmann V, et al. Potential viral pathogenic mechanism for new variant inflammatory bowel disease. *J Clin Pathology: Mol Pathol.* 2002;55:84–90.

Horvath K, et al. Autistic disorder and gastrointestinal disease. *Curr Opin Pediatr.* 2002 Oct;14(5):583–87.

Cade R, et al. Autism and schizophrenia: intestinal disorders. *Nutr Neuroscience.* 2000;3:57–72.

Wakefield AJ, et al. Enterocolitis in children with developmental disorders. *Am J Gastroenterology.* 2000;95(9):2285–95.

Wood JD. Neuropathy in the brain-in-the-gut. *Eur J Gastroenterol Hepatol.* 2000 Jun;12(6):597–600.

Torrente F, et al. Small intestinal enteropathy with epithelial IgG and complement deposition in children with regressive autism. *Molecular Psychiatry.* 2000;7:375–82.

Horvath K, et al. Gastrointestinal abnormalities in children with autistic disorder. *J Pediatr.* 1999;135(5):559–63.

D'Eufemia P, et al. Abnormal intestinal permeability in children with autism. *Acta Paediatr.* 1996;85(9):1076–79.

Imbalances of Intestinal Bacteria

Ambrose NS, et al. The influence of single dose intravenous antibiotics on faecal flora and emergence of Clostridium difficile. *J Antimicrob Chemother.* 1985 Mar;15(3):319–26.

Bonnemaison E, et al. Comparison of fecal flora following administration of two antibiotic protocols for suspected maternofetal infection. *Biol Neonate.* 2003;84(4):304–10.

Samonis G, et al. Prospective study of the impact of broad-spectrum antibiotics on the yeast flora of the human gut. *Eur J Clin Microbiol Infect Dis.* 1994 Aug;13(8):665–67.

Song Y, et al. Real-time PCR quantitation of clostridia

in feces of autistic children. *Appl Environ Microbiol.* 2004 Nov;70(11):6459–65.

Gregg CR. Enteric bacterial flora and bacterial overgrowth syndrome. *Semin Gastrointest Dis.* 2002 Oct;13(4):200–209.

Gluten Sensitivity and Neurological or Autoimmune Problems

Chin RL, et al. Peripheral neuropathy and celiac disease. *Curr Treat Options Neurol.* 2005 Jan;7(1):43–48.

Chin RL, et al. Celiac neuropathy. *Neurology.* 2003 May 27;60(10):1581–85.

Abele M, et al. Prevalence of antigliadin antibodies in ataxia patients. *Neurology.* 2003 May 27;60(10):1674–75.

Pengiran Tengah CD, et al. Multiple sclerosis and occult gluten sensitivity. *Neurology.* 2004 Jun 22;62(12):2326–27.

Hadjivassiliou M, et al. Headache and CNS white matter abnormalities associated with gluten sensitivity. *Neurology.* 2001 Feb 13;56(3):385–88.

Gluten and Casein Effects Specifically in Autism

Jyonouchi H. Food allergy and autism spectrum disorders: is there a link? *Current Allergy and Asthma Reports* 2009;9(3):194–201.

Jyonouchi H, et al. Dysregulated innate immune responses in young children with autism spectrum disorders: their relationship to gastrointestinal symptoms and dietary intervention. *Neuropsychobiology.* 2005;51(2):77–85.

Jyonouchi H, et al. Evaluation of an association between gastrointestinal symptoms and cytokine production against common dietary proteins in children with autism spectrum disorders. *Journal of Pediatrics* 2005 May;146(5):605–10.

Aytac U, et al. CD26/dipeptidyl peptidase IV: a regulator of immune function and a potential molecular target for therapy. *Curr Drug Targets—Immune Endocr Metabol Disord.* 2004 Mar;4(1):11–18.

Vojdani A, et al. Heat shock protein and gliadin peptide promote development of peptidase antibodies in children with autism and patients with autoimmune disease. *Clin Diagn Lab Immunol.* 2004 May;11(3):515–24.

Vojdani A, et al. Immune response to dietary proteins, gliadin and cerebellar peptides in children with autism. *Nutri Neurosci.* 2004 Jun;7(3):151–61.

Fan H, et al. Dipeptidyl-peptidase IV/CD26 in T cell activation, cytokine secretion and immunoglobulin production. *Adv Exp Med Biol.* 2003; 524:165–74.

Reichelt KL, et al. Can the pathophysiology of autism be explained by the nature of the discovered urine peptides? *Nutr Neurosci.* 2003 Feb;6(1):19–28.

Okada Y, et al. Endomorphins and related opioid peptides. *Vitam Horm.* 2002;65:257–79.

Schade RP, et al. Cell-surface expression of CD25, CD26, and CD30 by allergen-specific T cells is intrinsically different in cow's milk allergy. *Allergy Clin Immunology.* 2002;109(2):357–62.

Jyonouchi H, et al. Innate immunity associated with inflammatory responses and cytokine production against common dietary proteins in patient with autism spectrum disorder. *Neuropsychobiology.* 2002;46(2):76–84.

Mentlein R. Dipeptidyl-peptidase IV (CD26)—role in the inactivation of regulatory peptides. *Regul Pept.* 1999 Nov 30;85(1):9–24.

Fleischer B, et al. Molecular associations required for signaling via dipeptidyl peptidase IV (CD26). *Adv Exp Med Biol.* 1997;421:117–25.

Tučková L, et al. Molecular mimicry as a possible cause of autoimmune reactions in celiac disease? Antibodies to gliadin cross-react with epitopes on enterocytes. *Clin Immunol Immunopathol.* 1995 Feb;74(2):170–76.

Reichelt KL, et al. Nature and consequences of hyperpeptiduria and bovine casomorphins found in autistic syndromes. *Dev Brain Dysfunct.* 1994;7:71–85.

Shattock P, et al. Role of neuropeptides in autism and their relationships with classical neurotransmitters. *Brain Dysfunct.* 1990;3:328–45.

Iyngkaran N, et al. Causative effect of cow's milk protein and soy protein on progressive small bowel mucosal damage. *J Gastroenterol Hepatol.* 1989 Mar–Apr;4(2):127–36.

Reichelt KL, et al. Biologically active peptide-containing fractions in schizophrenia and childhood autism. *Adv Biochem Psychopharmacol.* 1981;28:627–43.

Viral Infections

Nicolson GL, et al. Evidence for mycoplasma ssp., chlamydia pneumoniae, and human herpes virus-6 coinfections in the blood of patients with autistic spectrum disorders. *J Neurosci Res.* 2007;85(5):1143–48.

Libbey JE, et al. Autistic disorder and viral infections. *J Neurovirol.* 2005 Feb;11(1):1–10.

Sweeten TL, et al. Brief report: autistic disorder in three children with cytomegalovirus infection. *J Autism Dev Disord.* 2004 Oct;34(5):583–86.

Singh VK, et al. Elevated levels of measles antibodies in children with autism. *Pediatric Neurology.* 2003;28(4):292–94.

Singh VK, et al. Abnormal measles-mumps-rubella antibodies and CNS autoimmunity in children with autism. *J Biomed Sci.* 2002 Jul–Aug;9(4):359–64.

Ghaziuddin M, et al. Autistic symptoms following herpes encephalitis. *Eur Child Adolesc Psychiatry.* 2002 Jun;11(3):142–46.

Hornig M, et al. Infectious and immune factors in the pathogenesis of neurodevelopmental disorders: epidemiology, hypothesis, and animal models. *Ment Retard Dev Disabil Res Rev.* 2001 Aug 31;7(3):200–210.

Caruso JM, et al. Persistent preceding focal neurologic deficits in children with chronic Epstein-Barr virus encephalitis. *J Child Neurol.* 2000 Dec;15(12):791–96.

Kawashima H, et al. Detection and sequencing of measles virus from peripheral mononuclear cells from patients with inflammatory bowel disease and autism. *Digestive Disease and Sciences.* 2000 Apr;45(4):723–29.

Hornig M, et al. An infection-based model of neurodevelopmental damage. *Proc Natl Acad Sci USA.* 1999 Oct 12;96(21):12102–7.

Singh VK, et al. Serological association of measles virus and human herpesvirus-6 with brain autoantibodies in autism. *Clin Immunol Immunopathol.* 1998 Oct;89(1):105–8.

Wakefield AJ, et al. Illeal-lymphoid-nodular hyperplasia, non-specific colitis, and pervasive developmental disorder in children. *Lancet.* 1998 Feb;351:637–41.

Katayama Y, et al. Detection of measles in RNA from autopsied human specimens. *J Clin Microbiol.* 1998;36(1):299–301.

Ivarsson SA, et al. Autism as one of several disabilities in two children with congenital cytomegalovirus infection. *Neuropediatrics.* 1990 May;21(2):102–3.

STUDIES IN SUPPORT OF BIOMEDICAL TREATMENTS FOR AUTISM

Many of the articles listed above support numerous aspects of the biomedical causes of autism. However, when it comes to actually proving these theories in the treatment realm, large-scale published research is lacking. Here are some studies that have demonstrated benefits to biomedical treatments. Most of these apply directly to autism. Some treatments have been studied in other disorders but may be applied to autism.

Probiotics

Gill HS, et al. Probiotics and human health: a clinical perspective. *Postgrad Med J.* 2004 Sep;80(947):516–26.

Miraglia del Giudice M, et al. The role of probiotics in the clinical management of food allergy and atopic dermatitis. *J Clin Gastroenterol.* 2004 Jul;38(6 Suppl):S84–85.

Tanaka K, et al. Role of intestinal bacterial flora in oral tolerance induction. *Histol Histopathol.* 2004 Jul;19(3):907–14.

Finegold SM, et al. Gastrointestinal microflora studies in late-onset autism. *Clin Infect Dis.* 2002 Sep 1;35(Suppl 1):S6–S16.

Czerucka D, et al. Experimental effects of Saccharomyces boulardii on diarrheal pathogens. *Microbes Infect.* 2002 Jun;4(7):733–39.

Periti P, et al. Preclinical and clinical pharmacology of biotherapeutic agents: Saccharomyces boulardii. *J Chemother.* 2001 Oct;13(5):473–93.

Majamaa H, et al. Probiotics: a novel approach in the management of food allergy. *J Allergy Clin Immunol.* 1997;99(2):179–85.

Salminen S, et al. Clinical uses of probiotics for stabilizing the gut mucosal barrier: successful strains and future challenges. *Antonie van Leeuwenhoek* (Kluwer). 1996 Oct;70(2–4):347–58.

Langhendries JB, et al. Effect of a fermented infant formula containing viable bifidobacteria on the fecal flora composition and pH of healthy full-term infants. *J Pediatric Gastroenter Nutr.* 1995;21(2):177–81.

Berg R, et al. Inhibition of Candida albicans translocation from the gastrointestinal tract of mice by oral administration of Saccharomyces boulardii. *J Infect Dis.* 1993 Nov;168(5):1314–18.

Chelation (Heavy Metal Detoxification)

Lonsdale D, et al. Treatment of autism spectrum children with thiamine tetrahydrofurfuryl disulfide: a pilot study. *Neuro Endocinol Lett.* 2002 Aug;23(4):303–8.

Treating Intestinal Bacteria

Servin A. Antagonistic activities of lactobacilli and bifidobacteria against microbial pathogens. *FEMS Microbiol Rev.* 2004 Oct;28(4):405–40.

Hart AL, et al. The role of the gut flora in health and disease, and its modification as therapy. *Aliment Pharmacol Ther.* 2002 Aug;16(8):1383–93.

Sandler RH, et al. Short-term benefit from oral vancomycin treatment of regressive-onset autism. *J Child Neurol.* 2000 Jul;15(7):429–35.

Sandler RH, et al. Relief of psychiatric symptoms in a patient with Crohn's disease after metronidazole therapy. *Clin Infect Dis.* 2000 Jan;30(1):213–14.

Gluten-free/Casein-free Diet

Hsu CL, et al. The effects of a gluten and casein-free diet in children with autism: a case report. *Chang Gung Med J.* 2009 Jul–Aug;32(4):459–65.

Elder J. The gluten-free, casein-free diet in autism: an overview with clinical implications. *Nutr Clin Pract.* 2008 Dec–2009 Jan;23(6):583–88.

Knivsberg AM, et al. A randomised, controlled study of dietary intervention in autistic syndromes. *Nutr Neurosci.* 2002 Sep;5(4):251–61.

Knivsberg AM, et al. Reports on dietary intervention in autistic disorders. *Nutr Neurosci.* 2001;4(1):25–37.

Pellecchia MT, et al. Cerebellar ataxia associated with sub-clinical celiac disease responding to gluten-free diet. *Neurology.* 1999 Oct 22;53(7):1606–8.

Reichelt KL, et al. Gluten, milk proteins and autism: dietary intervention effects on behavior and peptide secretion. *J Appl Nutrition.* 1990;42(1):1–11.

Specific Biomedical Vitamins and Nutrients

Rossignol D. Novel and emerging treatments for autism spectrum disorders: a systematic review. *Annals Clin Psych.* 2009; published ahead of print date.

Meiri G, et al. Omega 3 fatty acid treatment in autism. *J Child Adolesc Psychopharmacol.* 2009 Aug;19(4):449–51.

Desjardins S, et al. Treatment of a serious autistic disorder in a child with Naltrexone in an oral suspension form. *Encephale.* 2009 Apr;35(2):168–72.

Morris CR, et al. Syndrome of allergy, apraxia, and malabsorption: characterization of a neurodevelopmental phenotype that responds to omega 3 and vitamin E supplementation. *Altern Ther Health Med.* 2009 Jul–Aug;15(4):34–43.

Johnson M, et al. Omega-3/omega-6 fatty acids for attention deficit hyperactivity disorder: a randomized placebo-controlled trial in children and adolescents. *J Atten Disord.* 2009 Mar;12(5):394–401.

James SJ, et al. Efficacy of methylcobalamin and folinic acid treatment on glutathione redox status in children with autism. *Am J Clin Nutr.* 2009 Jan;89(1):425–30.

Mequid NA, et al. Role of polyunsaturated fatty acids in the management of Egyptian children with autism. *Clin Biochem.* 2008 Sep;41(13):1044–48.

Torrioli MG, et al. A double-blind, parallel, multicenter comparison of L-acetylcarnitine with placebo on the attention deficit hyperactivity disorder in fragile X syndrome boys. *Am J Med Genet A.* 2008 Apr 1;146(7):803–12.

Amminger GP, et al. Omega-3 fatty acids supplementation in children with autism: a double-blind randomized, placebo-controlled pilot study. *Biol Psychiatry.* 2007 Feb 15;61(4):551–53.

Garstang J, et al. Randomized controlled trial of melatonin for children with autistic spectrum disorders and sleep problems. *Child Care Health Dev.* 2006;32(5):585–89.

Mousain-Bosc M, et al. Improvement of neurobehavioral disorders in children supplemented with magnesium-vitamin B6. II. Pervasive developmental disorder–autism. *Magnes Res.* 2006 Mar;19(1):53–62.

Dvořáková M, et al. The effect of polyphenolic extract from pine bark, Pycnogenol, on the level of glutathione in children suffering from attention deficit hyperactivity disorder (ADHD). *Redox Rep.* 2006 Aug;11(4):163–72.

Trebatická J, et al. Treatment of ADHD with French maritime pine bark extract, Pycnogenol. *Eur Child Adolesc Psychiatry.* 2006;15(6):329–35.

Richardson AJ, et al. The Oxford-Durham study: a randomized, controlled trial of dietary supplementation with fatty acids in children with developmental coordination disorder. *Pediatrics.* 2005 May;115(5):1360–66.

Adams J, et al. Pilot study of a moderate dose multivitamin/mineral supplement for children with autistic spectrum disorder. *J Alt Comp Med.* 2004 Dec;10(6):1033–39.

Bilici M, et al. Double-blind, placebo-controlled study of zinc sulfate in the treatment of attention deficit hyperactivity disorder. *Prog Neuro-Psychopharmacol Biol Psychiatry.* 2004 Jan;28(1):181–90.

Kuriyama S, et al. Pyridoxine (vitamin B6) treatment in a subgroup of children with pervasive developmental disorders. *Dev Med Child Neurol.* 2002;44(4):283–86.

Van Oudheusden LJ, et al. Efficacy of carnitine in the treatment of children with attention-deficit hyperactivity disorder. *Prostaglandins Leukot Essent Fatty Acids.* 2002 Jul 1;67(1):33–38.

Ellaway C, et al. Medium-term open-label trial of L-carnitine in Rett syndrome. *Brain and Develop.* 2001;23:S85–89.

Bolman W, et al. A double-blind, placebo-controlled, crossover pilot trial of low dose dimethylglycine in patients with autistic disorder. *J Autism Dev Disord.* 1999 Jun;29(3):191–94.

Rimland B. What is the right 'dosage' for vitamin B6, DMG and other nutrients useful in autism? *Autism Research Review International.* 1997;11(4):3.

Dolske MC, et al. A preliminary trial of ascorbic acid (vitamin C) as supplemental therapy for autism. *Prog Neuro-Psychopharmacol Biol Psychiatry.* 1993;17(5):765–74.

Mårtensson J, et al. Glutathione is required for intestinal function. *Proc Nat Acad Sci USA.* 1990 Mar;87(5):1715–19.

Beutler E. Nutritional and metabolic aspects of glutathione. *Ann Rev of Nutrition.* 1989 Jul;9:287–302.

Barthelemy C, et al. Biological and clinical effects of oral magnesium and associated magnesium-vitamin B6 administration on certain disorders observed in infantile autism. *Therapie.* 1980 Sep–Oct;35(5):627–32.

Lelord G, et al. Clinical and biological effects of high doses of vitamin B6 and magnesium on autistic children. *Acta Vitaminol Enzymol.* 1982;4(1–2):27–44.

Martineau J, et al. Vitamin B6, magnesium and combined B6-Mg: therapeutic effects in childhood autism. *Biol Psychiatry.* 1985 May;20(5):467–78.

Airaksinen EM, et al. Effects of taurine on epileptic patients. *Prog Clin Biol Res.* 1980;39:157–66.

Rimland B, et al. The effect of high doses of vitamin B6 on autistic children: a double-blind crossover study. *Am J Psychiatry.* 1978 Apr;135(4):472–75.

Miscellaneous Studies of Interest

Zhang GQ, et al. Effects of auditory integrative training of autistic children. *Beijing Da Xue Xue Bao.* 2009 Aug 18;41(4):426–31 (article in Chinese).

Reichow B, et al. Social skills interventions for individuals with autism: evaluation for evidence-based practices within a best evidence synthesis framework. *J Autism Dev Disord.* 2009 Aug 5; published online ahead of print date.

Brunelle F, et al. Autism and brain imaging. *Bull Acad Natl Med.* 2009 Feb;193(2):287–97.

Van Dyke EM. Autistic disorder: early interventions can improve outcomes. *JAAPA.* 2009 Jul;22(7):18–19.

Rossignol DA, et al. Hyperbaric treatment for children with autism: a multicenter, randomized, double-blind, controlled trial. *BMC Pediatr.* 2009 Mar 13;9:21.

Myers, SM. Management of autism spectrum disorders in primary care. *Pediatric Annals.* 2009 Jan;38(1):42–49.

Foxx RM. Applied behavioral analysis treatment of autism: the state of the art. *Child Adolesc Psychiatr Clin N Am.* 2008 Oct;17(4):821–34.

Chungpaibulpatana J, et al. Hyperbaric oxygen therapy in Thai autistic children. *J Med Assoc Thai.* 2008 Aug;91(8):1232–38.

Acknowledgments

Thank you to Lisa Ackerman, the founder and director of Talk About Curing Autism (TACA) and mother of Jeff, for her valuable input into this work, her friendship, and her endless hours of dedication and sacrifice for countless families across America who are searching for help and answers. I would also like to thank my dear friend Dr. Jerry Kartzinel, a pediatrican, biomedical practitioner, and author of *Healing and Preventing Autism,* for taking me under his wing ten years ago to open my eyes to the world of autism treatment, for trying to teach me everything he knows, and for offering his insights into this work. Thank you to Dr. Doreen Granpeesheh, psychologist and founder of the Center for Autism and Related Disorders (CARD), for her input as well. Thank you to Dr. Liz Mumper from the Rimland Center for her teaching and guidance. Thanks to Dr. Marilyn Agin, neurodevelopmental pediatrician and author of *The Late Talker,* for her valuable input into this book. To Dr. Sidney Baker and everyone at the Autism Research Institute, thank you for taking the reins on this journey to discover more causes and treatments.

Index